VOICES OF RONDO

VOICES OF RONDO

Oral Histories of Saint Paul's Historic Black Community

AS TOLD TO

Kateleen Jill Hope Cavett

OF

HAND in HAND Productions

FOREWORD BY

Dr. David Vassar Taylor

SYREN BOOK COMPANY
Minneapolis

Most Syren Books are available at special quantity discounts for bulk purchases for sales promotions, premiums, fund-raising, and educational needs. For details, write

    Syren Book Company
    Special Sales Department
    5120 Cedar Lake Road
    Minneapolis, MN 55416

Published by
Syren Book Company
5120 Cedar Lake Road
Minneapolis, MN 55416

Printed in the United States of America on acid-free paper

ISBN-13: 978-0-929636-48-1
ISBN-10: 0-929636-48-1

LCCN 2005927227

Cover design by Katannah Day
Book design by Rachel Holscher

To order additional copies of this book see the form at the back of this book or go to www.itascabooks.com

CONTENTS

A DEFINITION OF ORAL HISTORY

Oral history is the spoken word in print.

Oral histories are personal memories shared from the perspective of the narrator. By means of recorded interviews, oral history documents collect spoken memories and personal commentaries of historical significance. These interviews are transcribed verbatim and minimally edited for readability. The greatest appreciation is gained when one can read an oral history aloud.

Oral histories are not edited to meet traditional writing standards; they are edited only for clarity and accessibility. The hope of oral history is to capture the flavor of the storyteller's speech and convey his or her feelings through the tenor and tempo of speech patterns.

An oral history is far more than a family tree with names of ancestors and their birth and death dates. Oral history is recorded personal memory, and that is its value. What it offers complements other forms of historical text, and does not always require historical collaboration. Oral history recognizes that memories often become polished as they sift through time, taking on new meanings and potentially reshaping the events they relate.

Memories shared in an oral histories create a picture of the narrator's life: the culture, food, eccentricities, opinions, thoughts, idiosyncrasies, joys, sorrows, passions—the rich substance that gives color and texture to this individual life.

KATE CAVETT
oral historian

HAND in HAND Productions

FOREWORD

David Vassar Taylor, Ph.D.

One of the earliest pictures in my life history scrapbook was taken in front of 1016 Rondo Avenue. It may have been the summer of 1948, for I appear to have been about three years of age. My family lived in an upstairs apartment above the McFarland family in a block of substantial homes. In subsequent years my family would move back and forth between Oatmeal Hill[1] and Cornmeal Valley[2] on streets on either side of Rondo—St. Anthony, Central, Carroll, and Dayton Avenues. This was my neighborhood. It did not have a name; it just *was*.

Several of my mother's sisters, Grandpa Vassar, cousins, and other relatives all lived within walking distance and visited often. My world was defined by the church to which we belonged, the schools I attended, the community centers that provided recreation and entertainment, and proprietary stores from which we purchased (or stole) sweets. There was an order to life that was defined by certain values. As children we were admonished to adhere to principles like the Golden Rule (Do unto others . . .) and the Ten Commandments (Thou shall not . . .), even though our parents selectively exempted themselves from some of these provisions. It was a secure world where everyone knew his or her place and everyone had a place. It was not until much later that I understood and appreciated socioeconomic class differences as they played out in such a small, compact community.

The name "Rondo community" is of more contemporary origin arising out of an attempt to recapture the sense of community lost during the Model Cities Program days. Model Cities was a national program in the 1960s designed to encourage restoration of America's inner cities through a program of urban renewal and economic revitalization. In the name of progress, whole urban neighborhoods of blighted housing and declining businesses were eradicated and replaced with new concepts of urban de-sign, space utilization, and reconstituted neighborhoods.

In Saint Paul "our neighborhood" became known as Summit-University—an area enclosed by University Avenue on the north, Lexington on the west, Summit Avenue on the south, and Summit and John Ireland Boulevard on the east. The program area contained the largest percentage of Black resi-dents in the city. Rondo Avenue, renamed Concordia Avenue upon com-pletion of Interstate 94 and now a service road, runs from east to west. The name "Rondo Neighborhood" became the rally cry of former and present residents of the area who attempted to create a more positive image of the community by sponsoring activities to raise the consciousness of our resi-dents to the unique history of this area of the city. The first "I Remember Rondo Day Celebration" was held in the Reverend Denzil A. Carty Park[3] Later annual celebrations included parades, craft booths, food, and enter-tainment. The celebration has been compared to a large family reunion with former residents living as far away as California and Texas returning to re-connect with their earlier lives.

Nostalgia surrounding "our neighborhood" has been partially responsible for the annual "Rondo Day" celebration success. People experience commu-nity life from different perspectives. Each perspective is valid and can be au-thenticated. The history of this community, in part, rests upon the stories of individuals' experiences. These perspectives have been captured in such liter-ary works as *The Days of Rondo* by Evelyn Fairbanks, *Son of Rondo* by James Griffin, *A Choice of Weapons* by Gordon Parks, *Standing Tall* by Roy Wilkins, and many other sources. Earl Spangler (1963), *The Negro in Minnesota,* and David Taylor (2002), *African Americans in Minnesota,* provided more com-prehensive reviews of the historical development of the Black community in Saint Paul. The Minnesota Historical Society possesses a rich collection of oral interviews taken from former and present Black residents of Duluth, Fergus Falls, Alexandria, Lutsen, Stillwater, and the Twin Cities.

The use of oral histories has been critical to understanding community history. Although we live in a society rich in documents that establish our official identities (census data, government records, health records, etc.), these records do not and cannot speak to the quality of our lives, our hopes, or our dreams and common experiences. The story of a community lies be-neath the surface of everyday life, where personal experiences are shaped by common experience, culture, language, religion, and shared belief systems. Each individual experiences and interprets these aspects of life in different ways. By sitting down and exploring these questions in person on an individual basis we begin to better understand the essential nature of human communities.

Oral histories are also reflective of socioeconomic class structures. Although in most African American communities racism and discrimination were and are pervasive influences (and great levelers), even in the smallest of communities we find socioeconomic class differences. Thus, remembrances of things past are influenced by family resources, perceived social class status, and aspirations. In the past century skin color directly or indirectly influenced the perception of social class standing.

A rich source for oral history lies in the life experiences of our most senior citizens. Theirs is a collective memory of things past and present. They have experienced forces that have both altered and changed the physical nature of their communities as well as the social, cultural, and economic realities of their times—both local and national. They remember the "when" and are grounded in the "now." By exploring their individual and collective experiences we come to better appreciate human adaptability in the presence of change, the will to persevere in the face of hardships, and the faith and enduring values that not only served as a moral compass for them but also instruct the next generation of youth and community leaders.

Voices of Rondo is a rich collection of edited interviews taken from persons who lived, worked, or played in the Rondo neighborhood ranging in age from 100 years to their mid-50s. For the most part these individuals are second- or third-generation African Americans whose grandparents settled in Saint Paul at the end of the nineteenth and the beginning of the twentieth centuries. The grandparents came in search of employment opportunities and to raise families. Although Minnesota appeared to be more liberal with respect to race relations, the lives of these pioneers still were compromised by persistent racism, discrimination, and the compromising of fundamental rights. Therefore, it is not surprising to note that in almost every interview there are references to the often debilitating effects of racism on personal aspirations and community vitality.

Faced with discrimination, the community developed organizations and activities designed to educate, provide recreational outlets for children and adults, and to attend to their spiritual needs. Small African American business flourished, trained professionals attended to health needs, and the Black press kept the community in contact with national movements. These pioneers recognized the importance of honest work, family, home ownership, and education. The lives of the interviewees reflect those basic values, and, more often than not, their children went on to earn advanced degrees.

The text of *Voices of Rondo* has been enriched with pictures that capture the interviewees in their youth, middle, and golden years. Many photographs depict youth activities, adult social clubs, homes and businesses, work sites and relatives. They provide a brief glimpse into a world from the perspective of ordinary people who lived in it. Absent from these pictures are images of overwhelming impoverishment. These are images of strong, proud people.

It is our hope that this effort to capture the essence of Rondo community history will empower others to explore their past.

◆ NOTES

1 Oatmeal Hill was a term referring to Rondo west of Dale Street toward Lexington, sometimes known as Upper Rondo. More affluent residents tended to move into this area, giving the impression that residents had a higher social standing. This middle-class neighborhood consisted of predominantly single-family homes.

2. Cornmeal Valley, also known as Lower Rondo or Deep Rondo, was east of Dale Street. This was a lower-middle-class residential neighborhood with predominantly single-family homes. From the 1930s, this part of the community struggled with growing poverty.

3. Carty Park is located between Iglehart, St. Albans, Carroll, and Grotto. Father Denzil Carty (1904–1975) was born in the British West Indies, educated in New York City, and served Episcopal churches in that city until he came to Saint Paul in 1950 to serve as rector of St. Philip's Episcopal Church. He was an outstanding leader and activist for civil and human rights.

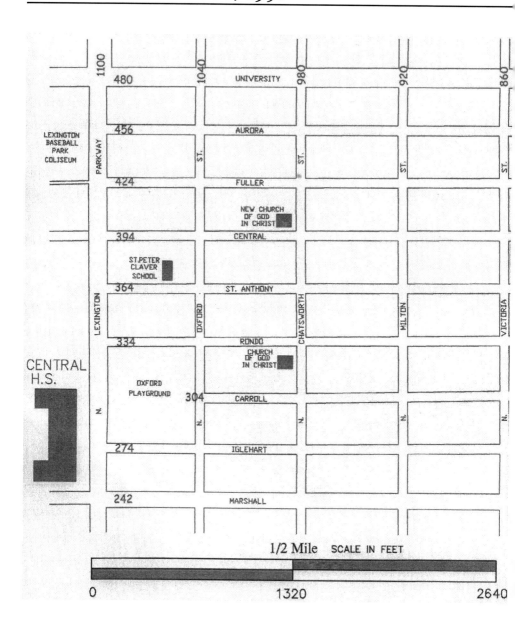

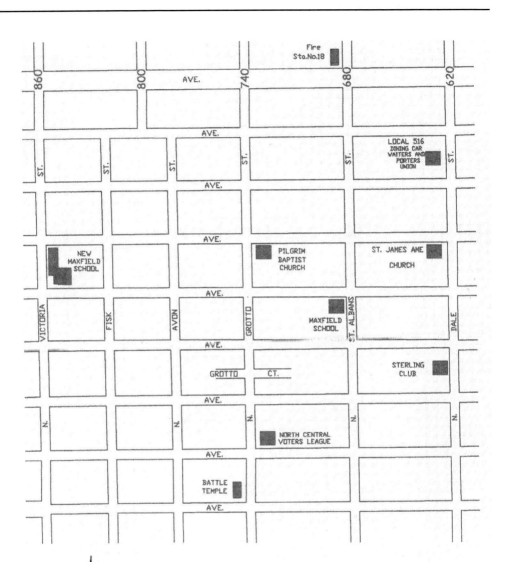

NORTH and WEST side of streets———ODD street numbers
SOUTH and EAST side of streets———EVEN street numbers

North

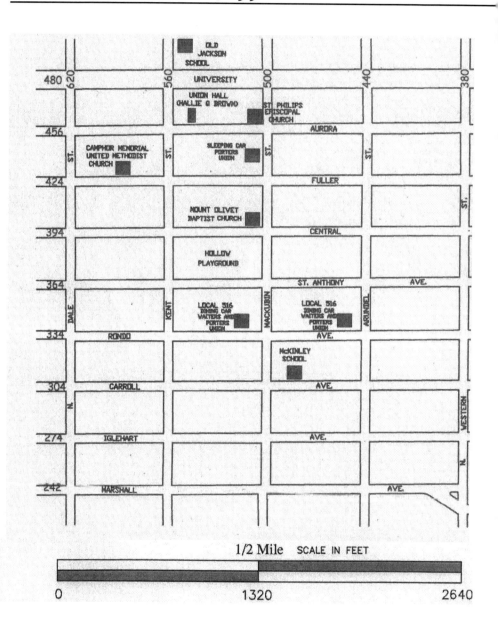

1/2 Mile SCALE IN FEET

0   1320   2640

NORTH and WEST side of streets----ODD street numbers
SOUTH and EAST side of streets----EVEN street numbers

North

As the Black poet J. Saunders Redding (1906–1988) said:

The relationship between a people and their history is the same as the relationship between a child and its mother; history is a clock that people use to tell their time of day; it is a compass that people use to locate themselves on the map of human geography; history not only tells a people where they are and what they are—history also informs us what we still must be and what we still must do.

MARY CHAMBERS
BRADLEY HAMILTON

Welcome Hall had music on Saturdays.

MY FULL NAME IS MARY CHAMBERS BRADLEY HAMILTON,[1] and I was born in 1903. My grandfather[2] lived in the state of New York, in Troy, and the woman he married lived in New York City. I don't know how they met, but my grandmother[3] was a millionaire. She married this Black man and her people wiped their hands on her, didn't want to have anything to do with her. She and her husband came to Saint Paul, Minnesota. My great-grandparents cried, "Don't come to Saint Paul, Minnesota, 'cause the wolves will eat you!" But they came here anyway and they made good money. My grandmother always had plenty of money. She and her husband were cooks. That would be in the 1870s. My grandmother was Jane, and her maiden name was McGuiness, Jane McGuiness, and she married a Jackson, Jane McGuiness Jackson. My grandfather was William Francis Jackson. My grandfather sold the first chicken sandwich in the city of Saint Paul, and when he died they had an article in the *Dispatch*[4] about him. He dropped dead walking home, heart trouble.

My mother[5] was born in 1885. Her brother[6] was born in 1881 and the other one[7] in 1883. All three children were born in Saint Paul. My uncles went to Cretin High School.[8] It was built for White children only. My grandmother being White, Irish and German, and real light and pale, started her first son in Cretin High School and the teachers didn't know he was Black. They thought he was White. The other brother went to Cretin, and they thought he was White because the children all took after the mother.

But my mother, Phoebe Elizabeth Jackson, the only girl, took more after her father, so St. Agnes School wouldn't take my mother because she had curly hair, more like the Blacks. A lot of Blacks were turned away from St. Agnes High School. My mother was real light, but she had curly hair. She showed her Colored blood. I think she went to the Cathedral School[9] for a while, but she went to the Jefferson School.[10]

My father[11] was much older than my mother, but they met somewhere in Saint Paul. My father, he was an asphalt man. He was a tamper. Years ago they didn't have rollers. They had this long stick with a big iron at the bottom and when the men would pour the asphalt on the street my father would walk behind them and tamper it down and make it smooth.

He was working on top of a building and he was falling and he grabbed hold of the roof and strained himself. He had what they called suspension of the kidneys or something, and he didn't live very long. He had seven little girls and I was the oldest, and he died and left us. My mother was only thirty-two years old, and my father was in his fifties when he died in 1914.

I always wanted to be a nun, but my father died. I just stayed with my mother to help her with other sisters. I must have been about twelve years old, twelve and a half, and my sisters were all younger. I liked being home with my mother and I liked helping with my sisters. I would like going out in the woodshed and chopping wood so my mother could make a fire to cook breakfast. I went to the store for my mother. We lived at 266 Rice Street and my mother would send me. She said, "Here's a nickel. Go buy five cents worth of potatoes." And I'd point, and I'd say, "Five cents worth of that."

Mary at ten years old with her sisters

And then on my way home I would stop in the blacksmith's shop and watch the smithy shoe the horse and the horse would back up to him and he would pick up the horse's foot and put the shoe on him. He'd shape the shoe on the big anvil and nail the shoe in to the horse's foot. I'd watch him do that a couple of times.

At funerals they had what was called hacks. A hack is a buggy pulled by a horse, and it seated about four or five people. I rode in a hack to my father's funeral. He was buried from an undertaking parlor called Welcome Hall.[12] I rode in the hack to my grandmother's funeral, and to my sister Frances's funeral we rode in hacks.

Mary at seventeen with friend
Dodson Graham, September 20, 1920

Welcome Hall had music on Saturdays, only on Saturdays. During the weekdays they had a lady that would teach sewing and English. I would go there because I knew her real well, and I wanted her to have a class. She was an awfully nice lady and she was a member of the University of Minnesota. She was very smart. She was—I forgot how many graduation classes she had. She was Black and her name was Laura Jeffreys. I took sewing from her and from Alberta Coram, another lady from the University. She would come and visit my mother and I'd take sewing. I took up drawing and different things, you know, that we didn't have in the regular school.

I went to the Neill School.[13] Only my sister and I and one other girl were Blacks there. I graduated from grade school in 1915, I think it was.

We'd go to dances. My mother would say, "Go to the dance, but you must be home by 12:00. If you're not home by 12:00 , you can't go back." So I made it my business. I was home by 12:00 . We'd walk. It was called Union Hall. That's where the Colored could go and dance and have plays.

A man two doors up from where I lived called Mr. Tibbs, he had kind of a large home. In his front room he made it like a dance hall where the Blacks teens could go and dance and have a little fun every Saturday night. I liked to dance, so they always had me there. It was records he had, but it wasn't too long, just a few hours. He had a lovely daughter.

And then I went to Mechanics[14] for about three years and then I married and that was it. I married Charles Bradley in 1921. He didn't live too far from me after I moved in the Rondo district, and he went to Mechanics. I was married about seven years, not too long. I had five children and stayed home and cleaned the house and watched the children, and sewed, went to church. We enjoyed going to church. Charles Francis[15] was the oldest boy, born in 1921. My girls are Mary Louise[16] and Lorraine Phyllis.[17] The next one was Richard Ferdinand[18] and Vernon Randolph.[19]

My boys were altar boys, and I would go to early mass with them. They also went to St. Adalbert's Elementary School and I would go to St. Adalbert's Church, a Polish school and church, with the children. The Sisters would have me come to help with their Polish. The children won the medal for speaking the best Polish. Then the three oldest went to Mechanic Arts. And the younger two, I think it was Marshall Senior High.[20]

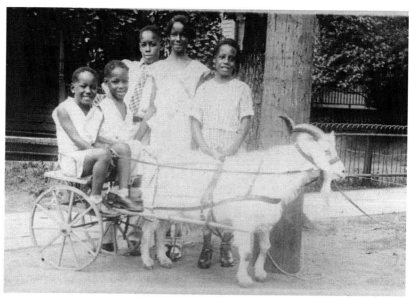

Vernon, Richard, Charles, Mary Louise ("Cookie"), and Lorraine
408 St. Anthony Avenue in 1934

MARY CHAMBERS BRADLEY HAMILTON is proud of raising her five children by herself. To date she has five children, thirty grandchildren, dozens of great-grandchildren, and a handful of great-great-grandchildren. Everyone marvels at how she taught them all how to work hard and do the right thing. Her family stays connected to her and has had family reunions for her 99th, 100th, and 101st birthdays at her church—St. Peter Claver—and celebrated with picnics at Como Park. Mary's life has been balanced between work and family, and she is known for always wanting to help people, and for knitting items and bringing them to shut-ins, even after she was 100 years old.

◆ NOTES

1. Mary Chambers Bradley Hamilton was born August 12, 1903.

2. Grandfather William Francis Jackson passed in 1900.

3. Grandmother Jane McGuiness Jackson was born April 1857 and passed in 1914.

4. *Pioneer Press Dispatch* newspaper: In 1849 the weekly *Pioneer* began, becoming a daily paper in 1854. In 1861 the *Saint Paul Daily Press* appeared. In 1868 the Saint Paul Dispatch appeared. The *Pioneer* and the *Press* merged in 1875 to become the *Pioneer Press*. In 1909 the *Pioneer Press* and *Dispatch* merged. The *Pioneer Press* was published as a morning newspaper and the *Dispatch* as an evening paper. In 1985 the name became only the *Pioneer Press*.

5. Mother Phoebe Jackson Chambers was born October 4, 1885, and passed November 23, 1956.

6. Uncle William Francis Jackson Jr. was born August 18, 1881. His date of passing is unknown.

7. Simon Peter Jackson was born in 1883. His date of passing is unknown.

8. Cretin High School is located at 550 South Albert Street at Randolph and Hamline. This all-boys Catholic school was established as an elementary school in the 1850s, adding a high school in 1871. Later the grade school was discontinued. In 1987 Cretin merged with Derham Hall, an all-girls Catholic school that was established in 1905.

9. Cathedral School was located at 238 Kellogg Boulevard and Mulberry Street. The school closed in the 1950s. The school building became the Monsignor Hayden Center/Catholic Archdiocese Education Center.

10. The first Jefferson School was built in 1858 on Pleasant Avenue and burned in 1866. The second Jefferson School was built in 1870 at Pleasant and Sherman. An addition was built in 1887. This building was demolished in 1932. The site is now the location of United Hospital.

11. Father William Chambers was born December 25, 1861, and passed in 1914.

12. Welcome Hall Community Center was located at 321 St. Anthony and Farrington. It was founded in 1916 next to Zion Presbyterian Church, a Black mission congregation, by several White Presbyterian congregations under the leadership of Rev. and Mrs. George Camp. The center offered recreation activities, Bible classes, a girls club, and the first day-care facility in the Black community.

13. Neill School, located at the northeast corner of Laurel and Farrington, was originally built in 1870. This building was demolished and replaced with a larger building in 1884. The property was sold to the City of Saint Paul for public elderly housing known as the Neill Apartments in 1962.

14. Mechanic Arts High School was located between Central, Robert, and Aurora from 1911 to 1976. It was sold to the state and then torn down in 1978.

15. Charles Francis Bradley was born May 27, 1922, and passed October 22, 1987.

16. Mary Louise Bradley Breedlove was born August 23, 1923, and passed January 1989.

17. Lorraine Phyllis Bradley Hopwood was born in June 1925.

18. Richard Ferdinand Bradley Sr. was born February 9, 1927, and passed October 17, 2004.

19. Vernon Randolph Bradley Sr. was born November 20, 1928.

20. Marshall School was built in 1925 at Grotto, Holly, Ashland, and St. Albans. It was Marshall Junior High from 1926 to 1937. In 1937, tenth grade was added; in 1938, eleventh grade; and in 1939, twelfth grade was added, with graduating classes from 1940 to 1953. It returned to junior high only in 1954. Webster Elementary School was built on the same site in 1926. The two buildings were connected in 1975 and become Webster Magnet Elementary School.

RICHARD MORRIS MANN

It was a gathering place and the people were just like a large family.

MY NAME IS RICHARD MORRIS MANN.[1] My first job was for my grandfather, Turner Starks,[2] who came up from Mississippi. His parents were slaves. He came up here by boat and worked for a White doctor as a valet. He never went to a barber college or anything like that. He used to cut the doctor's hair and the boys in the family's hair and that's where he got his knowledge of cutting hair. Finally he got disassociated with the doctor and got a job working on the river unloading boats. He started saving money. He was very conservative, and he raised his family. My mother and two sisters and two brothers were born right near the Schmidt's Brewery, Palace Avenue. He bought a house out there on Palace Avenue. He was the first Black out there.

He became a successful barber in the Twin Cities. It had nothing to do with the Rondo area or the Black community, because his shop was on Grand and Macalester, out by Macalester College and he catered to White clientele, like most of the Black barbershops—there were four to my knowledge in Saint Paul, besides my grandfather's. They catered to Whites and the politicians and the doctors and musicians and so forth. And if a Black person would come in, well, they would turn them down, their own people. Either that or take them in the back room and cut their hair, because they thought it would be a detriment to their White business.

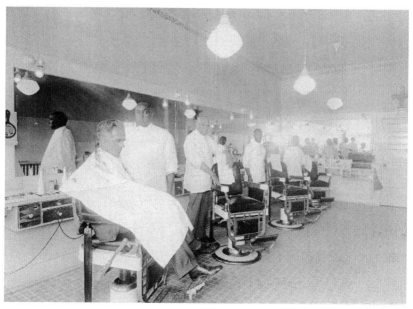

Turner J. Starks's Barbershop at 1656 Grand Avenue. Grandfather in the rear of picture

When my father died and I was ten years old, I went to work in my grandfather's barbershop shining shoes and cleanup, and that was a means of helping my mother in income, and my grandfather would always give me a little extra money. His business was strictly the rich in the Summit area and the Grand-Macalester area. When I say the rich, the Bohns, the Fligimans, the Sands were all wealthy people. The majority of them had Black chauffeurs and maids and Black gardeners and that type of thing, and that's the Summit area, I would say, from Cleveland to the downtown area. The Black chauffeurs used to bring the children to my grandfather's barbershop. He catered to women and children.

His shop was spotless. He would not allow smoking, so we had quite a business. He also started a second business. He built a building on St. Clair, 2028 St. Clair, which is still in existence. He had problems building that building during the 1930s, because of the fact that he was Black and at one time the Ku Klux Klan was active around the Twin Cities here. I'm not biting my tongue at all about that. I'm sure that that is knowledge to people back in that time, that the Ku Klux Klan was active in the Twin Cities. And during the time he was building his building at 2028 St. Clair, he had a Black contractor who was putting in the basement. Twice at night during the construction a person would go down and tear down some of the construction that had been started. This was finally resolved because my grandfather had contact with some of these politicians in the downtown courthouse and the police department. They made sure the building completed. So at one time he owned two barbershops.

After high school I always had menial jobs, like I worked in a car garage polishing cars. I had a shoeshine job. Then I got a job in Minneapolis at a clothing store, called Godnick's Clothing Store[3] and that was during the time that I was going to high school, or it might have been right after that. But anyway, I got a job as a porter cleaning up Godnick's Clothing Store in Minneapolis. And Mr. Godnick found out that I was pretty well known in the community and he offered me a proposition that any Blacks that I would bring in there, he would give me a five percent commission if they bought any clothing. At that time you could buy a suit for $35, a tailor-made suit, for $35, $40.

And I remember very distinctly knowing Gordon Parks.[4] Gordon Parks was quite a dapper person. He liked nice clothes and things, and I was responsible for selling him some of his nicer clothes that he bought through Godnick's. I also remember Lester Young,[5] who was a professional musician, who was located in and out of Minneapolis at that time. I had known him through activities in some of the nightclubs and things, and I talked him into coming and buying a suit and the Godnick's store advertised in the *Minneapolis Spokesman*.[6] Had my picture in the paper. I was making salary-wise something like $15 a week. With my five percent commission I made from selling clothes I was able to make $25, $30 a week, which at that time made me pretty independent and everybody thought I was always rich 'cause I liked to spend money.

As a porter I kept the place clean. They had several display windows, and whenever the window decorators would come in to change the windows, the mannequins, et cetera, I washed the windows, carpet, and cleaned. You also had a tailor, ready-made tailoring department, which was on the second floor, and I had to keep that up. But Godnick's main business concentrating on businessmen was tailor-made clothes, and I think I had one or two Black persons that I sold to. One of them was a businessman in Minneapolis that I sold tailor-made suits to.

I would bring my friends in to buy clothes. I would make suggestions to them, but when it came to the finalizing of the sales, the salesman would write up the sale and make the final decisions. The salesmen were all White. I didn't feel that I was capable of being a salesman at the level a salesman had to be in order to sell. I was so happy to get the five percent commission with my regular $15 a week salary that it never dawned on me whether or not I would ever become a salesman. That was the farthest thing from my mind, to concentrate on being a clothing salesman.

During the time that I was employed in the clothing store, there were no Black salesman to my knowledge in any other clothing stores. And at one time, there were several prominent clothing stores in the Twin Cities. One of them, which is still in existence if I'm not mistaken, was Hubert White's.[7] Juster Bros., Rothchild's[8] were prominent for men's clothiers, but there was no Black salesmen and I'm sure it was a case of the pattern of not employing Blacks in a certain area or a certain level, especially of salesmanship.

Employment of Blacks from the Rondo neighborhood was often limited. There were several Blacks in the packinghouse. In fact, at one time to my knowledge, we had five or six Black meat inspectors in Saint Paul, and that was a top job as far as employment goes. There was a paint manufacturing company that employed some Blacks, so that salary was comparable to the Whites because of the risk of working in a paint factory. The post office, meat inspectors, railroads, and hotels were the means of livelihood during that era.

Not a lot in the community had college degrees. I mean, you find the meat inspectors naturally had to have a degree. Most of them went down to Iowa. I think they have a veterinary program at University of Iowa. They were professional and they had to have a degree and they made the money. Post office, civil service, naturally there couldn't be any discrimination there. If you passed the civil service you were entitled to the same salary as anybody else. The only problem in the area was promotions. During the time I was in the postal system, we had a director of personnel who was LeRoy Lasenbury, and that was one of the top jobs as far as a Black was concerned in the Saint Paul Post Office.

The majority of the hotels had waiters, Black waiters, in them. And the clubs, the prominent clubs, the Athletic Club,[9] they employed Blacks. Saint

Paul First National Bank[10] had Black elevator operators, which was a pretty good average wage.

The means of livelihood was mainly the railroads and the hotels. And that was during the era of the 1940s to the '60s. This is about the same time that they decided to build a freeway right through the middle of the Rondo area, and there were a lot of homes that were purchased for the construction of the freeway, which helped people relocate. In some instances it was a hardship on people to have to move out of the area. In my opinion, today when you look back, the freeway is an asset. At that time, I didn't think too much of it, not only because of the relocation, because of the hardships of relocating. The businesses were affected, relocated to a degree, by the freeway. Most of them were small pa and ma businesses. It was a hardship for relocation, especially for the businesses as well as the families. In some instances it was advantageous for some people because they did better themselves as far as housing. But the majority of people, because of their low income and securing mortgages, they had a hard time relocating.

In 1948 and '49, with my stepbrother Claude Mason, and Howard Brown, I was associated with a nightclub out on Rice Street and Larpenteur. It was called Treasure Inn.[11] This was very, very popular with folks from Rondo. We furnished live Black music from local musicians. Percy Hughes,[12] who had a five-piece band. The current Prince's dad, whose name was at that time Prince Rogers. That's why his son Prince today has taken his name from his dad. He was also a musician and belonging to Percy Hughes's band. They played music usually on Fridays and Saturdays, and we had matinee dances on Sunday afternoon. We catered mainly to a lot of college kids. We had a clientele from the University of Minnesota, Hamline University, all the colleges.

At that time, we were able to sell setups because we were out of the City of Saint Paul. Actually, were under the jurisdiction of Roseville. The dividing line was Larpenteur Avenue and we were just north of it. And we had a tragedy there—our business fell off, we sold out, and left the area.

Melvin Carter, with suspenders playing trumpet, Dave Faison playing bass,
and Buddy Davis playing piano at Treasure Inn

Two years prior to the building of the freeway my partner, Ed Salter, and I rented a beer tavern from a lady who had owned the building. We ran the 3-2 beer tavern there called The Chatsworth Inn at 979 Chatsworth for about two years. This was during the Korean War,[13] and our business was real profitable for a while because at that time, a lot of the people, a lot of our customers were employed in the different facilities during the war and we were quite successful for about a year and a half.

The Chatsworth was definitely a beer parlor. We served only beer, and foodwise we did not have a restaurant license per se, but we sold hot dogs and bratwurst and potato chips and that type of thing, along with beer. We also had recreational games like skeet ball or bowling ball and that type of machine. We had about three different types of machines where people could play for a dime or a quarter. And they were quite profitable because they created competition.

Mann with partner Ed Salter by Chatsworth Inn

And we were very fortunate in the location we were in. We had a clientele of not only families, but about sixty percent of our business was afternoon women—ladies that were homemakers that were not employed during the war and the different war situations. We had quite a few people come from Minneapolis because of the camaraderie and the area. Our clientele were people that were socially acquainted in the community, and the majority of them were friends.

Mann at pinball game

It was a gathering place and the people were just like a large family. We were well known. We never had any problems there. Because of the location there was never any ruckus outside of the few disputes that were controlled. But the two and a half years or three years we were there, we never once had to call the police because of a dispute or misunderstanding.

The job market changed because of the ending of the war. Most of the war plants had two or three shifts. They worked around the clock and we were able to profit from the different shifts. People would work all night long, and sometimes they'd stop in for a beer on their way home. And then in the afternoon we'd get the shift for people going home for dinner, after

dinner. And then we had the late-night shift, which were not always employees of the different plants, ammunition plants,[14] et cetera. They were
local as well. But when the war wound down, why naturally we were not
supported by the people that we had been supported by the war, because of
the economic situation.

Actually, there was a time that unemployment started to escalate and
there was a change in the area and in our business, and all business. During
these times people did not have the money to drink beer that they had during the war. The economics in the community began to gradually change.
So in 1953 I sold out my interest in the tavern to my partner practically for
nothing.

I made an application at the post office and passed the post office test
and went to work in the post office. I sold out my interest in the tavern to
concentrate full time at the post office, which was necessary because of my
family life.[15] I worked in the post office for thirty years, from 1953 until '83.
When I first took the examination I was a mail handler and I didn't like that
because it was manual labor and I thought I was more capable. So I took the
test as a clerk, which I passed with no problem. And during my thirty years,
with the exception of one year as a mail handler, I was a window clerk. And
during the years of 1970 and '71, I was an EEO counselor of the Saint Paul
Post Office and, like I say, I retired in '83. Having accumulated one year of
sick leave, I was able to retire for thirty years benefits with only have served
twenty-nine years in the post office.

One of the things that helped me in business was being a member of the
Sterling Club, which I have been a member of since 1949. At this time I am a
Life Time Member, having become an honorary member three years ago. The
Sterling Club was founded as a social, charitable, and civic organization. The
Sterling Club encourages its members and club to cooperate with other orga-
nizations and provide beneficial activities and programs for the community.

Another purpose of the club is to provide leadership in the community.
The club was chartered as a nonprofit cooperative organization. In order to
be a member of the Sterling Club, originally was males only, age of fifty-five
and older, and this is the reason we obtained our nonprofit organization,
because it was organized as a nonprofit organization for senior members,
and we're incorporated under the State of Minnesota.

Membership classifications include regular members, incorporated members, life members, and honorary members, of which I am now a life member. We have our regular meetings on the second Friday evening of each month, and the board, which consists of nine members, meets on the first Friday of each month.

When the Sterling Club first started, their meetings were in the old Hallie Q. Brown Community Center,[16] which didn't last too long. Originally there was a membership of nine members who got together and put a few dollars together and bought some property on Dale and Rondo. They built a five-room structure that was designed by the late Clarence Wigington,[17] who also designed several other buildings in Saint Paul, including the Harriet Island Pavilion, several schools, Highland Golf Course Club House, and the Highland Water Tower on South Snelling Avenue.

Mr. Wigington designed the Sterling Club as a bungalow living quarters for tax purposes, in order that we would not be classified as a commercial building. It had four rooms on the top floor, including a kitchen and a bath. The lower level, which was the basement at that time, was never finished until later years. In fact, the furnace was installed on a cement slab in the basement.

The Sterling Club was not created for professional people alone. It just so happened that it was an asset to professional people to belong to a community organization like the Sterling Club. The Sterling Club also caused professional people to have closer contact with the Afro-American people in the vicinity. Also, it was prestigious to belong to the Sterling Club, because of the membership's background and because of the original creators and members who were the majority of social, prominent Black people in the Twin Cities.

At that time we first established up on Dale Street it was popular for the breweries to obtain liquor licenses for individual organizations, and the Schmidt's Brewery[18] obtained a license for us to dispense beer. We could sell, dispense beer, tap beer or bottle, within the facility, nothing for off-sale. The only license that we had to have from the city was a restaurant license, and that permitted us to serve food and soft drinks, 'cause we were covered by the beer license from the Schmidt's Brewery.

In the late 1940s, prior to the new facility, an auxiliary was formed for the wives of the members of the Sterling Club, which as I mentioned before was strictly male. The auxiliary was an asset to the club because they helped us raise moneys for the operation of the facility. They paid dues within their own organization and they were an asset to the club. Always have been, and there's a great respect for the auxiliary of the Sterling Club as well as the members. If a member is deceased their wife can still be a part of the auxiliary. However, the women are not allowed to have keys or the pass cards to get into the club. They have to have their spouse or someone associated with the club in order to gain entrance into the club.

To me the Sterling Club has been a social asset. As I was in business myself a couple of times, it has been an advantage to my being recognized and knowing people of the community, socializing with people in different professions, and actually the camaraderie is one of the main things in the Sterling Club as far as I am concerned.

I am proud of the fact that I have accomplished what I have and raised a family, and I love my family. And I am proud to the fact that I've endured the hardships that a lot of Blacks and most Blacks have had to go through in this century, especially in the Twin Cities, which is liberal in comparison with a lot of other cities I've lived in during my life. And my belief is that the City of Saint Paul, the Twin Cities, is a good place to live in regardless of the problems we've had in the past, and I appreciate the fact that I was able to endure.

◆ ◆ ◆

RICHARD MORRIS MANN was married to his first wife, Anne, for twenty years before she passed. He has been married to Mildred H. Mann for about forty years. Mr. Mann retired from the post office in 1983, and continues to be an active member of St. Philip's Episcopal Church, Hallie Q. Brown Retired Men's Club, and TSTC Club. Jimmy Griffin was one of his lifelong friends. On his ninetieth birthday his children created the Richard Morris Mann Scholarship for Arlington High School students. He is the proud father and grandfather of Richard (self-employed) and his wife, Peggy, and their children Julia (music conservatory student) and Laura (Hamline University student); Stephan (deputy director of the Census Bureau of Kansas City) and his wife, Terrell, and their son Stephan Jr.; and Margo Mann Lanier (assistant principal in Saint Paul) and her husband, Virtis, and daughter, Anne Elizabeth. Dick continues to enjoy golfing with the Senior Highland Nine.

◆ NOTES

1. Richard Morris Mann was born March 8, 1914.

2. Turner J. Starks was born in Starkville, Mississippi, in 1858 and passed in Saint Paul in 1949.

3. Godnick and Fassbinder was located at 400 Nicollet Avenue in downtown Minneapolis. Louis S. and Stanley A. Godnick were the owners.

4. Gordon Parks (born 1912) was the youngest of fifteen children. His mother died when he was young, and he went to live with a sister in Saint Paul. Unwelcome by his brother-in-law, he soon found himself living on his own and struggling to attend school and support himself. He was self-taught in many areas, including photography and filmmaking, and became a nationally recognized photographer for *Life, Vogue,* and *Glamour* magazines. He won many firsts for a Black photojournalist. He was the first Black to direct a major Hollywood film, *The Learning Tree,* which he wrote and produced. He also gained recognition as a writer, poet, and composer.

5. Willis Lester Young (1909–1959) was a nationally recognized jazz saxophonist who played with Blue Devils, King Oliver, Count Basie, Fletcher Henderson, Teddy Wilson, and Billie Holiday, who allegedly gave him his nickname "Pres" or "Prez."

6. The *Minneapolis Spokesman* was founded in 1934 by Cecil E. Newman and is the longest-lived Black newspaper in Minnesota. The *Saint Paul Recorder* later began publication under Newman. The newspaper remains under the same family ownership and is now known as the *Minnesota Spokesman-Recorder.*

7. Hubert W. White's slogan is "Fine Apparel for Men since 1916." They were located in the old Radisson Hotel on Seventh Street between Hennepin and Nicollet. When the hotel was moved they moved into the IDS Building in Minneapolis.

8. Maurice L. Rothchild & Co. was located at 315–329 Nicollet Avenue at Fourth Street in Minneapolis.

9. The Saint Paul Athletic Club was located downtown at 340 Cedar Street. It closed in the early 1990s.

10. First National Bank was located in downtown Saint Paul between Minnesota Street, Robert Street, Fourth Street, and Fifth Street.

11. Treasure Inn was located at 1685 Rice Street at Larpenteur near McCarron Lake. This establishment was known as a welcoming place for Black and White patrons where they could hear great music.

12. Percy Hughes broke the "color line" for Black bands in Minnesota as a pioneer jazz "big band" leader after World War II. He continues as an active musician and band leader in the Twin Cities.

13. The Korean War was fought in Korea between 1950 and 1953.

14. Twin Cities Army Ammunition Plant of the Federal Cartridge Corporation covered a four-square-mile area in New Brighton. In 1942, it began production of four billion rounds of ammunition for war efforts. It was placed on inactive and standby status from 1950 to 1965, and again began production of ammunition during the Vietnam War. The facility was placed on shutdown status in 1971. In 2002, some land was transferred to Ramsey County Parks. The Ordinance Plant, as it was known, hired Blacks at all levels according to their skills, education, and training. At one point it employed twenty percent of the state's adult Black population.

15. Children are Richard John Mann, born 1945; Stephan Turner Mann, born 1948; and Margo Grace Mann Lainer, born 1950.

16. Hallie Q. Brown Community Center, Inc., was opened in the Union Hall at Aurora and Kent Streets in 1929 as a community center specifically to serve the Black community when the Black YWCA closed in 1928. Hallie Q., as it is affectionately known, has served all ages through child care, youth and senior clubs, athletics, music, and social events. In 1972, Hallie relocated in the Martin Luther King Building at 270 Kent Street at Iglehart in Saint Paul. The center's namesake was an educator who pioneered the movement of Black women's clubs in the late 1800s.

17. Clarence Wesley "Cap" Wigington (1883–1967) was born in Kansas City and raised in Omaha. He moved to Saint Paul in 1913, and for thirty-four years was a municipal architect for the City of Saint Paul, designing numerous Minnesota historical landmarks, including the Roy Wilkins Auditorium, the pavilion on Harriet Island (now called the Clarence W. Wigington Pavilion), and the Highland Water Tower.

18. Jacob Schmidt Brewing Co. was located at 882 West Seventh Street. Beer was first made on this land in 1855 by German settlers. Cave Brewery was at this location in the 1800s. They sold to Saint Paul Brewing in 1897, who sold to Schmidt in 1900. By 1936, Jacob Schmidt Brewing Co. was the seventh-largest brewing company in the United States. The facility was sold several times in the later 1900s, until Minnesota Brewing closed the doors in 2002.

WILLIE LEE FRELIX

My name is not George.

MY NAME IS WILLIE LEE FRELIX.[1] My wife[2] and I were living in Mississippi, going to different places to find work. She come to Minnesota on a visit with her auntie, and while she was here she put in applications for jobs. Later her auntie called her and told her there was a job. We had two kids at that time. She took them and she took off. I had a broken foot on a job and was walking on two crutches 'cause I had a cast on my foot up to my knee. So after I got it off, I came to Minnesota. When I got to Minnesota, she was working at night out in New Brighton at the Arsenal.[3] I was just company for a while with her aunt and uncle.

I found work for the Great Northern[4] Commissary where I was stocking the food on the dining cars before they would leave to go out on a run. That was down in the Great Northern shop yards.[5] It was somewhere on Mississippi Street before any freeway. I worked there maybe four or five months. But I didn't work for the Great Northern every day. I always tried to keep two jobs. I started working for Pullman Company[6] cleaning cars.

It was so hard 'cause I was getting sixty cents an hour back South. When I come here I was only making forty-three cents an hour. That was a cut down from what I was doing back in the South. It was hard to live on that

Willie Frelix, c. early 1940s

kind of money. My wife was making eighty-three cents an hour, and I was only making about half as much.

Plus, at night I would go and work as a bus boy at the Saint Paul Hotel[7] every time that they would call me. At that time I was living at Mackubin and Larpenteur. Most of the time after work at the hotel, I'd be walking home all the way from downtown, 'cause I didn't mind walking and you got off after one in the morning after the streetcars didn't run. Most of the time I'd take the shortcut through the Elmhurst Cemetery.[8] I remember one night I was coming through there and the snowdrifts were so high. I run and I was gonna try to jump over it, but I jumped in the middle of it and I couldn't get out. I had to take my hands and scratch my way out, so I could get out of that snowdrift. When I finally got out, I turned around and walked all the way around. At that time we had bad snow. Snowdrifts would be six, seven foot high sometimes in different places.

Everybody was telling me, "You take snow like you was raised up around here." But I was raised up tough. I started taking care of myself when I was about ten, eleven years old, and I knowed how to survive. Anytime you were raised up back in Mississippi, you could take anything. So the snow, the bad weather, nothin' didn't bother me when I got here. After I started working for the Pullman Company, I had it a little better, especially all during war[9] days.

When I started to work for Pullman Company cleaning cars, I was getting $113 a month. That just wasn't no money at all. But after I started to run on the railroad I made pretty good tips that kind of helped out quite a bit. I learned everything there was about being a Pullman Porter[10] while I was cleaning cars. In the first place, I started reading more. I got all the diagrams. Everything concerned in being a Pullman Porter, I got it and I studied it, so when I took the test, I passed it just like that. But they didn't call me to be a porter until I threatened to quit. 'Cause the boss—I was so good at everything that I did, he didn't want me to quit. So I told him if I didn't get called that I was gonna do something else. So the head boss of the yard, he had a brother working for the boss of the porters. So they finally called me, and after then he told me I was the best one he ever had.

But working for the Pullman Company was a slave-driving outfit. They drove the men.

I had an uncle that worked for Pullman. He started in 1925 and he told me how it was. They were only getting very little money, like $25 a month. And they had to keep up with everything there was on that car. They come up with a towel or anything short, they would take it out of their $25. Now a lot of people would get off the train, they'd take a towel with them or something like that, and then that porter, he'd have to pay for that towel.

No matter how good you was, they was always looking for something to try to fire you for or to do you something bad. When they got a good man, they should treat him nice instead of always trying to dig up some dirt on you. As long as I worked, there were very few bosses that was nice. All the bosses in the office, they were just as rotten as dirt to you. They didn't ever want to speak to you right. They always had some kind of slander or something.

I remember one morning I pulled in Seattle, Washington, and the train stopped, so I get down with my stepping box[11] and put it on the ground and the train moved up about a couple of car-lengths so I grabbed my box and jumped back up in the door. And when it stopped, it stopped right in front of the boss. You always had a boss out there. They called him a platform man. He met all the trains when they come in. And when that train stopped he was standing there. I said, "I know he gonna start something." So after I unloaded all my passengers, I got my box put back up, here he comes. He said, "You are really something. You come in here hanging on the side of the train with your stepping box in your hand. You know better than that." You know what I did? I jumped all over him. When I'm right, don't nobody tell me that I'm wrong. I told him, "You listen. My word is just as good as yours. Now you seen what happened. I seen you standing down there in the first place. The train stopped. I thought it was where it was gonna be. That's all I had time to do is to get my box and step back up in there. Now, you just remember this. Write whatever you wanna write. You just remember my word is just as good as yours." He wrote down everything that I said.

Now in the olden days they would have called me in, but at this time we had a union.[12] If they called me in, they'd have to pay me. They would always wait when I was getting paid to ask me about it. So the next time

I was going down, the boss come down to the train. I told him exactly what happened. But that just was the way they were, just a slave-drivin' bunch that Pullman Company. It was just terrible. And all the railroad jobs I understand for Black folks it was the same way. But working for the Pullman Company was quite educational. I got to go all over the country. I run on practically every railroad there was in the United States and Canada.

I had papers to report for the military, but I got turned down at Fort Snelling. I couldn't ever pass a urine test and that's what kept me out of the service. So I served by hauling soldiers during World War II. It was quite educational for me. It was just a pleasure really to have a job like that. You run into a lot of people that was nice, and you run into a lot of people that wasn't so nice. But actually, most of the time it was just a pleasure to be a porter.

I wanted to be a Pullman Porter because I wanted to go all over the country. The waiters, they only run on one railroad, like from here to Seattle or Chicago or someplace like that. But being a porter, the Pullman cars would transfer to different railroads and went a lot further. I could get to see all of Canada and Mexico and the United States. So I seen it all.

I had the most fun trips during war days. We went as far as you could go by land, we went up to—oh, boy, I can't think of the name. It was about 1,000 miles north of Winnipeg. We went up there in August. When I left here, it was real hot and by the time we got there it was about 3:00 in the morning and it was still light outside. It just had got just kind of gloomy looking. It was in August and oh, it was cold. But I got a kick out of that just got gloomy looking for maybe an hour and then it was right back daylight again. That was a lot of fun.

As a porter I took care of one car. We had to keep the car clean all the time. Actually, you wasn't nothing but an inside hobo. Only thing about it, you was inside all the time. At night after 10:00 you would have two cars until 2:00. I would go to bed at 2:00 and get up at 6:00. You'd get four hours sleep a night. Then the porter from the other car would cover my car until I got up at 6:00. So at night you had two cars to watch. You had a connection between two cars. If somebody rang in the other car, they rang the bell in your car and you go look on your meter. It wasn't your car, you had to go to the next car and answer that call. And if you had somebody to put off during the night, you would have to do that. At 6:00 you'd get up, shine shoes or do whatever. You had to shine all the shoes on the train. You'd either do it before or else after 6:00.

You were always assigned to a bed. You were assigned to an upper berth in the back of the car. That's where you slept your four hours every night. Unless if something happened and you didn't get no rest, they'd have to sign your book for no rest. Your boss would or the conductor on the train would sign it. There was some nights you wasn't able to get in a rest.

A nine-room sleeper car, that was a car that had all rooms in it. But they had some cars, they call them a sixteen section car. That had thirty-two beds in it. Now you just imagine, during war days you got thirty-two beds in a car. There was times you got from here to Seattle—you'd be worked to death. 'Cause during war days, them beds, all of them was filled up all the time. And every time somebody would get off during the night there was somebody waiting for that bed. You had to remake it. In other words, you pretty much walked all the way from Seattle on a nonstop. We were on our feet, walking back and forth between cars and taking care of passengers during the whole trip to Seattle. During war days you made pretty good money in tips. At the time I liked that thirty-two bed. You would pretty much get twenty-five cents, a quarter, every time you made up that bed and sometimes you would get more. So it was pretty nice.

When I began I made about forty or forty-three cents an hour. I started out at $113 a month. We had a union when I first started. The pay wasn't no good, but you made a lot of money in tips when I first started and that's what I loved. The soldiers would tip you real good. Sometimes when I'd get back home, I'd have $60, $70, or $100 when I got back home, according to how long I was gone. And if I got on a passenger train, made a round trip to Seattle, you'd be gone about a week. Well, you made good tips from the passengers then. Everybody would tip you. Maybe one person from here to Seattle would give you $5.

Seventeen years later I was getting $350 a month and that was hard to live on, 'cause you wasn't making any tips at that time. All the tips was cut off. I would run from here to Seattle at that time on the club car. You didn't make any tips. The company started advocating, "We have raised their salary. You don't have to tip the porter." Now the company did that. You couldn't live on no $350. You were just starving to death.

Yeah. Some of the passengers was real nice and some of them wasn't. I remember one time that I was running from here to Vancouver, B.C., and they had a washout of a bridge. We set in on place for better than forty-eight

Willie with wife Verna and sons Clifford, Harold, and Bill on a picnic
with other railroad families at Battle Creek Park, c. 1947

hours. So we run out of everything. The cars were getting to run out of food, we run out of linen, couldn't make down the beds every night. After we all run out of linen, we tell the passengers, "I can't change your bed. You'll have to sleep on the same linen, but anything else that I can help you out with I'm at your service."

One time I was on a nine-room car and the conductor come and told me that this passenger said he asked for some towels and I was so sarcastic to him. I said, "Let's go talk to this gentleman right now." So I got the conductor and we went to his room, knocked on the door, and I said, "Mister, why did you want to tell that conductor that? I was just as nice to you as I could ever be. You only asked me for some more towels, and I went and got those towels for you and did everything I could and you know that. Now, why did you want to tell this conductor that I was so sarcastic to you?" He ate his words right in front of the conductor. Now why he wanted to tell that conductor that? I told the conductor, "I think what he was trying to do when he gets to Vancouver, he wasn't gonna give me no tip." That's the only thing that I could see. But when he got there he gave me $4.50. But that's just the way I was.

I had another gentleman one day. Everybody on the train had this old way of calling the porters George. They had a way of calling you, "Hey

George, so-and-so." George this and George that. At each end of the car you had a place to put your name so everybody would know your name. So I asked a gentleman one day, I says, "How would you like for somebody just come up and call you George? How would you like for somebody to walk up to you and just give you a name?" He said, "I wouldn't like it." I said, "What a nerve you got. You gonna walk up and just give me a name, and you're gonna tell me that you wouldn't like for somebody to do you like that." So I got him real good about that. I don't know why some of the men allowed themselves to be called George, but I always set people straight and we got along just great. But there was really some mean ones.

And I know there was nobody working for the Pullman Company no greater than I was. I was number one. I had a perfect record when I started, and I had a perfect record when I stopped after seventeen years. I got to be a conductor. I got to be a bartender. I got to be everything there was about the railroad. I could sell tickets. I did everything. When I finally stopped, I was running from here to Seattle, running a bar car where they sold whiskey and everything. I learned it all while I was working for Pullman Company.

After the wars, in the 1950s the railroads took over most of the club cars. I know in 1957 when they abolished the Pullman car and the railroads put their own club car in that space. And right after that they just abolished all the Pullmans and put their own sleeping cars on. After the war, I was mostly on the extra board, then got laid off. So I went down the next day and got a job at Minneapolis Moline. I continued to work hard all my life till I retired.

Being a porter was really an upgrade job for a Black man at that time. It had its ups and it had its downs, but I really loved that job.

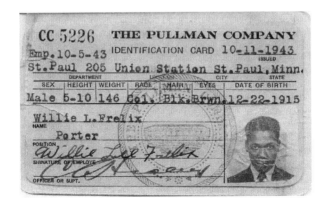

WILLIE LEE FRELIX is the proud father of Clifford, Harold, William, Marion, Charles, Johnny, and Stanley. He was with the Pullman Company from 1942 to 1957, Steinberg Construction from 1958 to 1969, Total Asphalt from 1970 to 1979, and worked as a guard for Business Security Guard from 1985 to 1995, when he retired. He has always had extra part-time jobs to support his family's needs. Willie's family always came first, and though he has had a challenging life, he always worked hard to support and has enjoyed his children.

◆ NOTES

1. Willie Lee Frelix was born December 22, 1915.

2. Wife Verna Mae Smith Frelix was born May 6, 1920, and passed January 24, 1987. She was the mother of Clifford, William, and Harold Frelix.

3. Twin Cities Army Ammunition Plant of the Federal Cartridge Corporation covered a four-square-mile area in New Brighton. In 1942, it began production of four billion rounds of ammunition for war efforts. It was placed on inactive and standby status from 1950 to 1965, and again began production of ammunition during the Vietnam War. The facility was placed on shutdown status in 1971. In 2002, some land was transferred to Ramsey County Parks. The Ordinance Plant, as it was known, hired Blacks at all levels according to their skills, education, and training. At one point it employed twenty percent of the state's adult Black population.

4. The Great Northern Railroad's home offices were located at 175 Fourth Street at the northeast corner of Jackson Street in Saint Paul. Saint Paul's early empire builder J. J. Hill built the Great Northern. In 1980, he acquired the Northern Pacific line and legally merged theses two lines and others to create the Burlington Northern.

5. The Great Northern yard was located at Mississippi Street on the northwest corner at East Minnehaha.

6. The Pullman Company was founded by George Pullman right after the Civil War and provided a standard for luxurious travel. Beginning in 1867, the earliest staff were the genteel servants of the plantation South. The early porter worked receiving passengers, carrying their luggage and making up their

rooms, serving beverages and food, keeping the guests happy, and making themselves available at all hours of the day or night. In Saint Paul, the Pullman Company was located at 214 Fourth Street.

7. The Saint Paul Hotel opened in 1910 and is located in downtown Saint Paul at 363 St. Peter Street between Fourth Street, Fifth Street, and Market Street. The entrance to the hotel currently is at 350 Market Street.

8. Elmhurst Cemetery is located at 1510 North Dale Street.

9. World War II was fought between the Allied powers (England, the Soviet Union, the United States) and the Axis powers (Germany, Italy, Japan) from 1939 to 1945. The United States entered the war in 1941 following the bombing of Pearl Harbor by the Japanese.

10. Pullman Porters worked for the Pullman Company and carried baggage only for Pullman sleeping car passengers. The Pullman sleeping cars would be transferred between railroads and traveled all over the country.

11. A stepping box was a wooden box to help passengers step between the high train car and the platform.

12. The Brotherhood of Sleeping Car Porters union was founded under the direction of A. Philip Randolph. By 1925, the generation of freeborn Black employees were not as accepting of the poor treatment and low wages as their slave-born predecessors had been. Randolph had many challenges and lack of support from the White union. Against all odds and with the support of many brothers, this Black-controlled union came into existence. In 1978 the Black union merged with the larger union, the Brotherhood of Railway and Airline Clerks.

BENJAMIN LOUIS
ALEXANDER SENIOR

We proved we could fly.

I'M BEN ALEXANDER.[1] In 1939 I was going to Langston University in Oklahoma and I met a young lady, Jewel Mann,[2] from Minneapolis. We conversed and so forth and got to know each other and started going with each other. To help pay for school, in the summertime I'd run on the road[3] as a waiter from Chicago to Minneapolis and I'd get a chance to come up and see her. That was back in 1939.

We got married and in 1942 I joined up with the Army Air Corps. I was fortunate enough to be a Tuskegee Airman.[4] At Tuskegee[5] you had to learn how to fly the machines. A lot of the boys never seen the inside of an airplane before. But they went down there and they grasped it, which the big wheels of the Air Corps said, "Those Black boys can't fly. They're too scared." But we proved to them that we could fly just like that White boy. And if I got shot, my blood's the same as that White boy's was. Our training officers were a few Whites in there, but most of them were Black. Sometimes, the White officers were disrespectful. "Boy, you can't do this." Or, "Boy, what are you doing?" Or, "What the hell's wrong with you?" We caught hell. The Black officers always said, "Don't give up. Just go ahead and take it and do your job." This training lasted for four months.

There were twenty-five, thirty in my class. I imagine there was around

Ben Alexander second from right

1,500 flyers from all the classes. That wasn't the ground officers and the mechanics. Our crews were Black, too. It was strictly Black, strictly Black.

After our training we moved from base to base. They didn't know what to do with us. They tried to disband the Black unit because they didn't know what to do with us. You know, they didn't want us to fight and they didn't want us to keep drawing pay.

In the end they sent some of us to Africa. I didn't get overseas myself, but some of my buddies did. Those of us stateside didn't have much to do but fly and keep hours up. Just fly from one base to the other. I was located at [Air National Guard Base] Selfridge Field, and [Air Force Base] Eglin Field in Florida and Michigan. I was a lieutenant. Whites would sometimes salute you, and sometime they wouldn't. White officers were always saluted.

It didn't happen to me, but some of the fellas related that they were in Georgia there and the MPs didn't believe that there was any Black flyers down there. They had to call for the commanding officer to come get them out of jail. Hearing that, it felt bad. You know, we were in the service and then we're humiliated like that. Same way with coming back from overseas.

Ben Alexander at Tuskegee

I didn't see it, but I heard. They'd have two lines. They said the Colored on this side and the Whites come down on this side. They were all fighting for the same thing, democracy. Supposed to be democracy. I'm very bitter at times. That's just the way America is. It's just the way America is. Boys went over there and fought like everybody else, but still they wasn't good enough to get any recognition till the last few years. Now they're just recognizing the Tuskegee Airmen. I mustered out in 1946 at Patterson Field in Ohio.

After the war[6] we stopped in Chicago, Illinois, my hometown. I ran a streetcar there for five years, what they called the Green Hornet in Chicago there. We stayed there for five years. Then they lost the streetcars to buses. And I was in pre-med when I was in college and so my wife said, "Well, why don't you go to mortuary science and get your license and we'll move up to Saint Paul, Minnesota?" Which I did. I moved back to Minnesota in 1950, went to the University of Minnesota, got my degree and license, and opened up the Alexander Hyde Park Chapel.[7] We were in business for forty-seven years.

I heard about the Sterling Club[8] when I moved over here back in the 1950s. They tried to get me to join and I said, "No, I don't want to be there with the old men." But I ended up with them! I'm an ex-president of the Sterling Club. I've been in the Sterling Club for over fifty years.

In the club we have a plaque that says, "The Sterling Club, Incorporated, Saint Paul, Minnesota, Founded November 1918, Incorporated, August 28, 1919." And it lists the original founding members, who are W. E. Alexander, Richard H. Anderson, Bismark C. Archer, Walter R. Dywer, Orrington D. Hall, O. E. Howard, Joseph E. Johnson, Frederick B. McCracken, Howard F. McIntyre, Dwight T. Reed, William Taney, Hammond Turner, and W. Wiginton.

You know, we're the only Black club owned and operated by Blacks either side of the Mississippi River. A lot of clubs,[9] like the Credjafawn, Forty

Club, all have been in existence as long as we have, but they still meet at homes. They don't have a clubhouse. We used to go with the Forty Club or the Credjafawn where you'd have picnics in the fall of the year together. The three of us would have picnics, but they don't do that anymore.

We needed our clubs because we couldn't go down to the restaurants or hotels downtown. If there was places that would serve you, they'd serve you and break the glass in front of you. And we'd have them break maybe two dozen glasses. They would pour you a drink, you would drink it, push it back, and let them break it. They would break the glass in front of you as an insult. Their actions indicated they would not serve a White person from a glass used by a Black person. And some of them would say, "You look like an Indian." And they had a law they couldn't serve Indians. So I'd walk in, "You're Indian, so I can't serve you." It was embarrassing and humiliating It really was. Yep, it really was.

To join the Sterling Club you have to be recommended by a member. You just can't walk off the street and say, "I wanna be a member." You've got to be recommended by an outstanding member. Then you're voted upon. We've always had dues. They've been $15, 20, 25, 35. It's $35 a man now. We got around sixty active members. We've got chartered members, like I am, that's been in twenty-five years or more.

The history as it was told to me was that the men would have their events at different homes because they would want to go downtown to have their little events or dances. The hotels would say, "We don't rent to Blacks." Or, "We're booked up. We don't have any room." So the men said, "Well, we'll get us a place of our own." So they met at their homes and they got Cap Wigington[10] to draw up the plans. Originally the plans were to have a storefront down-

stairs and the Sterling Club upstairs so they'd get a little rental
property from downstairs. The
city said, "No, you have to build
a house." Now they couldn't build
a big enough house because they
didn't have that much money
to accommodate 150, 200 people. That was the Sterling Club at
315 North Dale Street.

The original Sterling Club, 315 Dale Street

The club was formed by mostly postal workers or railroad men. Initially that was the makeup of the Sterling Club men. Now they've got engineers from 3M. They've got members from all walks of life now. We're not stuck up, but you know, we want to keep our image up as much as possible.

Once a year we have the annual dance. We still have those. We use to have our dances right at the clubhouse, right at 315 North Dale Street. They'd pack them in there, but they'd have their little fun. I like being a member here for the friendship, camaraderie, being around storytellers.

◆ ◆ ◆

BENJAMIN LOUIS ALEXANDER SR. was born in 1918 in Evanston, Illinois. He and his wife, Jewell, were proud of their sons Benjamin Jr. ("Skip"), Douglas, and Rodney, and grandsons Douglas Jr. and Kyle. A proud World War II Tuskegee Airman, Mr. Alexander received the American Theater Ribbon, a Good Conduct Medal, a WWII Victory Medal, and in 2004 the Hallie Q. Brown Man of the Year award. He was president and dedicated member of the Sterling Club, an active member of St. Philip's Church, member of Kappa Alpha Psi, and other community organizations. Having graduated from the University of Minnesota as a mortician, he and Jewell had one of five Black-owned funeral homes in the Twin Cities. Ben was an avid golf enthusiast.

◆ NOTES

1. Benjamin Louis Alexander Senior was born February 11, 1918, and passed February 3, 2005.

2. Wife Jewell Patricia Mann Alexander was born July 31, 1918, and passed September 3, 1998.

3. "Running on the Road" refers to serving travelers on trains as a waiter or porter.

4. Tuskegee Airmen were the 1,000 Black American fighter pilots of the 99th Pursuit Squadron, later incorporated into the 332nd Fighter Group, who fought during World War II in the U.S. Army Air Corps. Their training took place at Tuskegee Army Air Field, Tuskegee, Alabama. A total of 445 Tuskegee Airmen went overseas as combat pilots in the European Theater of Operations, North

Africa, and the Mediterranean. None of the bombers they escorted were lost to enemy fighters. They destroyed 251 enemy aircraft and won more than 850 medals, but sixty-six Tuskegee Airmen were killed in action. Their legacy was the eventual desegregation of the U.S. Air Force and the recognition that Black pilots were equal to White pilots. The Tuskegee Airmen have gained much respect and admiration.

5. Tuskegee Normal and Industrial Institute was founded in 1881 by Booker T. Washington in Tuskegee, Alabama. In 1937 the name was changed to Tuskegee Institute and in 1985 changed again to Tuskegee University. It is one of ninety historical Black colleges and universities. The Tuskegee Archives, devoted to Black history, was established in 1904. The famous Tuskegee Airmen trained at the Institute.

6. World War II was fought between the Allied powers (England, the Soviet Union, the United States) and the Axis powers (Germany, Italy, Japan) from 1939 to 1945. The United States entered the war in 1941 following the bombing of Pearl Harbor by the Japanese.

7. Alexander Hyde Park Chapel was first located at 513 North Dale Street in 1956. The new funeral home was built at 400 North Oxford Street.

8. The Sterling Club was founded in 1918 and incorporated in 1919. It was located at 315 North Dale Street at Rondo. In 1958 it built a new home at 300 North St. Albans at Carroll. This private club was formed to give prestigious Black men, who were not allowed in White facilities, a place to meet and network.

9. Social clubs were formed out of necessity since recreation and entertainment facilities for Black people were limited in the 1920s and '30s. None of the better restaurants served them, nor did the major hotels rent rooms to them. By 1935 there were two dozen clubs of various kinds in the Twin Cities. By the 1940s the hotels began to rent party rooms to these social clubs.

10. Clarence Wesley "Cap" Wigington (1883–1967) was born in Kansas City and raised in Omaha. He moved to Saint Paul in 1913 and for thirty-four years was a municipal architect for the City of Saint Paul, designing numerous Minnesota historical landmarks, including the Roy Wilkins Auditorium, the Harriet Island Pavilion (now called the Clarence W. Wigington Pavilion), and the Highland Water Tower.

GLADYS CLEMONS MILLER

Some people came to the store every day.

I AM GLADYS CLEMONS MILLER.[1] My husband, Jesse Miller, I always called him Miller,[2] was born in Mississippi and he went to college at Tennessee State in Memphis. He graduated with a B average. So he had an education and everything. He had a teaching certificate where he could teach school. They told him, "No, we don't have any Black teachers here in Saint Paul," so he didn't get the teaching job. So he ran on the road[3] for a while, as a waiter.

When we got married, he was working for the place that made refrigerators and washing machines. He was working for Seegers.[4] He asked for an office job at Seeger's. They said, "Oh, we've come a long way, but we don't have any colored people in the office." So he quit. They wouldn't let him work in the office. So that was pretty rough! And then he waited tables a lot in the hotels, and first one place and another to try to help himself.

I worked at the Arsenal[5] during World War II.[6] I was a machine operator. And then during the Korean outbreak, I worked again as a machine operator. At that time they had what they called a token few. They hired Blacks, three or four, on machinery, but the rest of them were matrons and janitors.

And that's when Miller went out there to see about getting hired, and they told him, "You take a job as a janitor and watch the bulletin board, and if anything comes up, then we will see what we can do about it." And he said, "No, I'm not hungry. If I was hungry and I couldn't take care of my wife, then I would scrub floors, but I worked too hard to graduate from college to take a job as a janitor."

And as luck would have it, I was on a machine. I was already there. I worked in building 104. And the man that was over the whole arsenal, his name was Charlie Horn. He would come by my machine. He'd always stop and talk with me. I was on the end machine and we just talked. Just "How do you like working here? What do you think about the plant?" and "What were you doing before?" Those were the kind of things we talked about.

Jesse Miller

So after the person at personnel told him, "You can work as a janitor," I got on the telephone and called Charlie Horn. I said, "I don't think you know who I am. I know you don't. You don't know my name," I said, "but I'm the Colored girl that works on the end machine in building 104 and you always stop and talk with me." And he said, "Oh, okay." And he was over the whole arsenal. And he says, "Yeah, I remember." And I told him what was going on. He says, "Give me your telephone number and I'll get back with you." So he called me back the next day and he says, "You tell him to go to building 105 and he starts in the office." So that's what happened there. So me knowing somebody kind of helped and he got work out there.

My brothers had opened a grocery store,[7] and then he and I took it over and worked in the grocery store at 499 Rondo and Mackubin. And we worked at that until the freeway came through.

It was a complete grocery store because we had meat and everything. We didn't know anything about butchering, so they had a man come in and train my brothers how to cut the meats and stuff like that. So they all even had me cutting pork chops and neck bones, and steak and everything else—bacon, hamburger, and stuff like that. I was right in there working with them as far as that goes.

But I really hadn't planned to go in there. I wanted to be a barber. So I was saving and that's how I had money to put into the store. I was saving my money to go to barber school. I had $500 or $600 saved to go, so I wouldn't

Lincoln Food Market

have to quit. So consequently, I didn't get to be a barber. So that's what happened there.

The store name when we bought it was Lincoln Market, and we just kept it as Lincoln Market the whole time. We didn't change the name. My two brothers and I bought the store together, and we ended up buying that whole little property. We had the grocery store and next door there was a beauty shop[8] in that building and two apartments up over that, and we had a vacant lot there and a house at 350 Mackubin. We bought that whole parcel there. After a while my husband and I ran the store. We lived at the three- story home at 350 Mackubin.

I had a chance to meet more people. We didn't run the streets. We didn't know anybody much. We were just a kind of close little clan, like. We opened the store and I had a chance to meet a lot of people that I wouldn't have known otherwise, and most of them were really, really nice. All except, we did let out credit and that wasn't too good. Some people never paid ever and some still owe today, but most the people that came in were nice. So I enjoyed working in the store.

We opened at 8:00 A.M. Sometimes people would be waiting for us to open at eight and that was a funny thing to me because we, our family, didn't go to the store every day. Some people came to the store every day. Some from the same family would come two or three times. I said, "What's wrong with these people?" And then it dawned on me, "This is your livelihood. Let them come in ten times if they want to." But it was really kind of strange to me that they would come to get a package of bacon and a dozen eggs. "Oh, we forgot the bread," and they would come back and so that was really kind of fun and I enjoyed it. I really did.

We were open 8:00 to 8:00. And my brothers would come in when I opened up and they would come in at 2:00 and work for two or three hours. Another one would come in about 4:30 and stay until closing time, so all three of us took turns at working at the store. We all worked and kept our other jobs.

My brothers were working at the bank, First National Bank,[9] as elevator men.[10] The two that opened in the beginning was Marcellus Clemons and Thomas Clemons. They worked at the bank until they retired. They did help out in the store. If we needed help, they would all pitch in and come and give us a break on it like that. So Julius retired from the bank. They were elevator operators. They didn't have the automatic like they have now. Sometimes they would change off as starters and stuff like that.

I didn't have another job because it had gotten pretty hard for me trying to help take care of my mother and father in between. It was really hard. They didn't have nursing homes, of course. I don't think I would have put them in there because they weren't bedridden, but they were getting pretty old. I'm down on the end of the family. It was a large family and by the time it got to me, my parents were pretty old. As a matter of fact, my mother was about forty-six years old when my youngest sister was born. So I stayed home and helped them until they passed, and I worked pretty hard.

A milkman would check every day or two to see what we needed and everything. We very rarely ran out of anything. And my brothers would go to the wholesale house and pick up the canned goods and stuff like that. In the summertime, my brothers or husband would go down to the market, buy fresh vegetables and stuff like that. But otherwise everything was delivered to us.

Gladys Clemons Miller in 1950 at age thirty-two

Children had to bring notes from their parents, with their signature on it, if they were to charge. That's how we did that, even if the parents would call. Some didn't have phones at that time and some did, but we didn't let them do much charging without a note from their parents.

I lived near Dale and I had some other friends that lived out on the other end. They would call me and say, "When the streetcar goes by your house call me and let me know because I don't wanna have to stand on the corner very long." And so they'd call me and ask me what time it had gotten to the place. It was a very, very nice neighborhood to have a business. We could go off, leave our doors open, and the last one to come in at night would lock the door. We never missed anything there, and we were right in a busy section, Dale and Rondo. That's the kind of neighborhood it was. People were really friendly. We had no complaints, none.

◆ ◆ ◆

GLADYS CLEMONS MILLER is proud of her loving Clemons family, her relationship with her son, Richard Lewis Miller, and her marriage. Her father was a minister and she cared for her mother after her father passed. She worked hard as a nurse's aide, as a matron at an emporium, and in sales at Dayton's. She is still active as the oldest member of her church—Gospel Temple, and her son, Richard, is now a preacher in Denver, Colorado. Mrs. Miller had been married to Jesse Miller for forty-seven years when he passed. She wishes every woman could have a husband like him. Every time he went to the market for fresh fruits and vegetables he would bring her back flowers, and he grew a garden of more than 300 rose bushes in their yard for her. Gladys is always seeking to share love and kindness with others.

◆ **NOTES**

1. Gladys Versie Clemons was born April 19, 1917.

2. Jesse W. Miller was born August 15, 1920, and passed February 11, 1997.

3. "Running on the road" refers to serving travelers on trains as a waiter or porter.

4. Seeger's was located at 850 Arcade at Wall Street on the East Side of Saint Paul.

5. Twin Cities Army Ammunition Plant of the Federal Cartridge Corporation covered a four-square-mile area in New Brighton. In 1942, it began production of four billion rounds of ammunition for war efforts. It was placed on inactive and standby status from 1950 to 1965, and again began production of ammunition during the Vietnam War. The facility was placed on shutdown status in 1971. In 2002, some land was transferred to Ramsey County Parks. The Ordinance Plant, as it was known, hired Blacks at all levels according to their skills, education, and training. At one point it employed twenty percent of the state's adult Black population.

6. World War II was fought between the Allied powers (England, the Soviet Union, the United States) and the Axis powers (Germany, Italy, Japan) from 1939 to 1945. The United States entered the war in 1941 following the bombing of Pearl Harbor by the Japanese.

7. Lincoln Food Market, at 499 Rondo at Mackubin, was owned by Ethel Gottesmans and family, and later owned by brothers Thomas and Marcellus Clemons, their sister Gladys Miller, and her husband, Jesse Miller. The men learned to cut meat, so they sold fresh meat, dairy, and dry goods—"a full service grocery."

8. Mrs. Eulah Clemons's Beauty Shop was located at 497 Rondo.

9. First National Bank was located in downtown Saint Paul between Minnesota Street, Robert Street, Fourth Street, and Fifth Street.

10. An elevator man manually operated the elevator. The male starter would direct which elevator was to be used next.

ANISAH HANIFAH DAWAN

Grew up in the Rondo neighborhood as
Elizabeth Payne Combs

Those years were hard, but I have good memories.

I'M ANISAH HANIFAH DAWAN[1] and I've lived in Saint Paul since 1922. I was
born in North Dakota. I was transferred to a home[2] for orphan children because my mother had died. That was in Owatonna, Minnesota.[3] And I remember being in an orphanage or hospital where there were cribs in the
room, and there was another little boy. He was a Black boy. He had a big,
red truck in his crib, and I think that's when I fell in love with the color red,
because I wanted that so bad. And there were two White nurses, and they
were laughing and making fun of me. They called me a little pickaninny.[4] I
remember it so plain, and I wondered why we were there. But anyway, the
next thing I remember is being on Rondo, at 250 Rondo in a flat. We were
upstairs and the lady's name was Mrs. Holiday. She was showing me off to
my adopted mother.[5] And I was brought here to be adopted by a family that
lived on Carroll, 403 Carroll—Martha and Albert Payne. He was a railroad
man. I believe it was Northern Railroad that he worked for. He was a waiter.
I was in a crib down there on Rondo, because I remember the little dog
would jump up and look at me, and I'd look at him. And people were standing around looking at me like, "Here she is."

So that was the day that Mama brought me home to 403 Carroll. I
must've been two or three, something like that, because I can remember

it so plain. We lived between Western and Arundel. It was an integrated neighborhood, and all the children would play together. There were Italians, Irish, and Polish.

Catholics lived next door to us on one side. There was another family, a Black family, who lived on the right side of us, and their last name was Green. The mother was Anna Green, and the son was Douglas Green. She seemed to be sickly all the time, because when we would play outside on the lawn, we'd be making a lot of noise, and she would get someone to tell us to cut it down a little.

Then I remember different businesses and things on Rondo. There was a restaurant, Potts,[6] at Farrington and Rondo. On the lower east corner there was something like a Salvation Army or secondhand store across the street from him, across the street from the restaurant. And I think there was a store[7] across from the restaurant on the north side. I can't remember the name of those people. I think they were Jewish, though.

There was a store on the corner of Mackubin and Rondo. That was the Miller Store.[8] Gladys and Jesse Miller. Chief Finney's mother had a beauty parlor.[9] I used to get my hair done there. That was Arundel and Rondo. And across the street from her was a barbecue place, Ed Warren's Restaurant.[10] They had the best barbecue. Let's see now, going way back, there was Rondo Police Station[11] at Western and Rondo. It was closed, and we used to go there and look through the keyhole. When I was younger, maybe five probably, it was working, but when I got to be around ten it wasn't there. It was there, but it wasn't working. Later Neal's Funeral Home[12] between Mackubin and Kent.

There was a big playground there, between Virginia and St. Anthony, and Rondo and Western. They had swings there. And we crossed the playground to go to the Welcome Hall.[13] It was like a community center. It was right next door to the Zion Presbyterian Church[14] that I went to. Reverend George W. Camp, his family lived on St. Anthony and he was the minister of the Presbyterian church there. We used to have music down at the Welcome Hall, but it would be somebody playing the piano or something like that. Miss Camp would say, "Now, children, you have to dance because you're going home at eight or ten o'clock." Whatever it was. And she'd make us dance. Oh, dear, it was fun. They had a lot of projects over there.

We could leave our doors open. We could go around town, go anywhere, go shopping and come home, and nothing would be moved. Can you imagine that? I got two locks on that door now. But it was just beautiful. I think now how well we got along in the neighborhood. All the kids played together, all would roller-skate together in the street, and parents would be mingling and talking. And the kids would be out there having a ball. It was just wonderful, all these different families, different hues of people. We all got along.

The kids all played together out in the street. Jews, Italians, Blacks, Swedes.

The boys mostly played ball. There were some twins that lived up the street, and they were the whitest White people I'd ever seen. They were just pale. They were blond. But they were cute. Oh, my gosh! And there was a real pretty—I don't know what nationality she was, but she was a brunette, and she would always come over and we would play because Mama had fixed up the back shed. It was like a little playhouse for us, and I had my dolls out there and everything. She'd come over and play in my backyard, too.

We were all friendly. We got along. I mean, there wasn't nothing to it. They weren't prejudiced, that's for sure. And we weren't prejudiced, so we all got along good. Everybody just looked out for the kids, and it didn't make any difference what color they were. Their mothers would look out for me. I don't remember all the kids' names, but I could remember their faces, and we used to have so much fun.

My dad, he brought me a little car, a little roadster—and, oh, was I popular! The kids would ride on it. I was looking at some old pictures. They used to come around and photograph kids, you know. I was in my car and they

took a photograph of me in my little car. When I would take it out on the sidewalk, all the kids would get on that could get on. Mama didn't like that too much because they can't be all on the car.

Then the Depression[15] came and Daddy lost his job. He had a brother out in Seattle and his mother lived out there, too. The next thing I know, he was packing up to go out there, maybe to a better life or whatever. And that was one day that I cried so hard, because he was trying to explain to me that he was going. I didn't understand what was going on, but I knew that Daddy was leaving.

My mom didn't have to work until then. My grandmother came here to live for a while, and then things got rough and she had to go to Seattle, and I didn't understand what was going on. When the Depression came, I remember we had a six-room house with hardwood floors, a furnace, a stove. I'll never forget that. A gas stove. It was really nice. Our furniture was all leather, and we had an old console radio, and Mama had a piano because she liked to play. And our house was really nice. In fact, I would say that we lived like middle-class people.

My father[16] was making good money, and he'd always come home and teach me how to count with silver dollars and all that stuff. I think he only went through the fourth grade. But he got hired onto the train. You know, if you could do the work, there was no problem. And he would go up to Seattle and Winnipeg. He stayed out there, and he only came back to visit us. In fact, when he passed, we didn't even have money to go out there to the funeral and that hurt pretty bad. I must've been about seventeen. The Depression lasted a long time.

My mama took in wash. I don't know how she knew these people, but their name was Love. Well, Mom had to wash the clothes. We were pretty broke. We lived in that house one winter. I don't think we made it through the winter, but Mama would get bricks from the basement or out in the backyard. She'd put them on the gas stove to heat them up, so we wouldn't freeze. She'd wrap them up in blankets and put them up in bed, during the Depression. We had been buying our home, but we lost it. We were homeless, you might say.

Since we couldn't pay for our house at 403 Carroll, we rented it out to some poorer White people. They had gotten off the farm. They couldn't make it out there, and they sent their boys to the CCC Camp,[17] whatever that was. We rented the house out for $9 a month! And they would come over to pay it in pennies! I mean, it must've been a pretty hard Depression. And because I was adopted, or because I was dependent, the welfare started giving us surplus food.

Some neighbor that lived on Fuller, her name was Miss Arvilla

McGregor. I never will forget her. She used to visit. They'd visit, back and forth. Well, she died, and I remember when Mr. McGregor let us live at his house. We moved. Mama pulled me in a sled, took me over to McGregor's house at 494 Fuller. Boy, that was the first time I'd ever seen a stove. And it was a big thing! It was way up like that, and it was silver, and it had isinglass or something all around, like it was plastic. But it wasn't plastic. It was the prettiest thing I'd ever seen.

Mr. McGregor was a Redcap,[18] worked on the depot.[19] I remember they used to give tips down there, and we ate off of the tips. He had had two sons, but they died when they were young. And his wife died, so he started renting the upstairs out. We had the upstairs.

Later the WPA[20] had come in, and my mom was working for the WPA. That was when I was nineteen. And I remember ironing and starching their uniforms. They were green. She was a matron for the WPA at their offices, because she didn't know how to sew. She cleaned toilets. We could've moved back to our house, if we'd have had $200, but we didn't have it.

The Mount Olivet Baptist Church[21] was right there on the corner of Central by McGregor's home. That's where I met my husband when I was about sixteen. We had to court for two years, because I wasn't old enough to be going around.

I went to Mechanic Arts High School.[22] And when I was sixteen, I went down to the Public Safety Building,[23] in the basement. They had a tailor shop down there, and I worked for this lady tailoring. I can't remember her name, but I worked for $2 a week. Forty hours. Walked to work and walked back. And you talk about proud! I'm thinking, "I'm makin' money!" Two dollars a week! Oh my goodness! So that was about 1935. I did that in the summertime. Yeah, I bought my fall shoes. I never will forget. A pair of black suedes. I used to work in the summer, but I thought, "Oh boy, this is my first job," and I used to go down and get chow mein somewhere down on Robert Street or something.[24] The young women that worked there, they'd bring their skirts and I'd press them.

I was going to the Hallie Q. Brown[25] like it was my second home, which it was, at Aurora and Kent. I was in a girls' group. We would be selling cookies and different things like that. Whenever money we made, we wanted to have a dance. So we did. I can't remember now what our music was, but it was good, because we danced! We were all teenagers, and Lola Finney used to come in and teach us about cosmetology. She was working out of that business. She had to go to Chicago and get some studying. She was really good. We would have carnivals. After the carnival, we'd have a party with the money we made. All the young men had to wear white coats, and I made my dress, because I was always tall and store-bought dresses were too short for me. So Mom started buying material, and she brought material home and patterns. She said, "You're on your own."

I'd stay up all night and made a formal. You could get material for about ten cents a yard. Five yards would do it. We made formals all the time because we had parties from our club. And I started sewing by hand. Yeah! I made my first formal. Oh, it was pretty—purple flowers on a white background. It was flared out. And then a jacket, too. It was pretty.

Those years were hard, but I have very good memories. At Hallie they taught you how to get along with people in the workplace and everywhere else. You had to be prepared, and many of my successes have come from that early training.

◆ ◆ ◆

ANISHA HANIFAH DAWAN, adopted into the Rondo community as Elizabeth Payne, is very proud of her nieces and nephews and proud to be a Muslim woman. In 1994 she made a two-week Hajj to Mecca in Saudi Arabia. The Koran, the Islamic holy book, instructs every Muslim to make this journey. Sister Anisha shares that this experience enhanced her beliefs in her faith and humankind. She was married to Cliff for forty-seven years before his death in 1985. She worked at Ramadan Meat and Seafood and the Urban League. Sister Anisha has volunteered at United Hospital in the gift shop and continues to volunteer with the NAACP.

◆ NOTES

1. Elizabeth Payne/Anisah Hanifah Dawan was born December 23, 1920.

2. The Minnesota State School for Dependent and Neglected Children, located in Owatonna, Minnesota, from 1886 to 1946. It served as the temporary home for thousands of children of all ages.

3. Owatonna is a town seventy miles south of Saint Paul.

4. A racial slur used in reference to Black children.

5. Mother Martha Payne McGregor.

6. Pott's Restaurant was located at 314–316 Rondo.

7. Drucker's Grocery Store was located at 313–315 Rondo.

8. Lincoln Food Market, at 499 Rondo at Mackubin, was owned by Gladys and Jesse Miller and Gladys's brothers, Thomas and Julius Clemons.

9. Finney's Hair Salon, owned by Lola Finney, was located at 437 Rondo. Mrs. Finney's son Bill served as Saint Paul police chief from 1992 to 2004.

10. Ed Warren's Restaurant was located at 483 Rondo.

11. Rondo Avenue Police Station was located at 334 Rondo. It opened in 1888 when all four city police substations opened. They all closed in 1934, when the headquarters building opened at 100 East Eleventh Street downtown.

12. Squire Neal Funeral Parlor was located at 525 Rondo after MaGavoch Funeral Home closed.

13. Welcome Hall Community Center was located at 321 St. Anthony at Farrington. It was founded in 1916 next to Zion Presbyterian Church, a Black mission congregation, by several White Presbyterian congregations and under the leadership of Rev. and Mrs. George Camp. The center offered recreational activities, Bible classes, a girls club, and the first day-care facility in the Black community.

14. Zion Presbyterian Church was located at St. Anthony and Farrington as a Black mission congregation sponsored by several White Presbyterian congregations.

15. The Great Depression began in late 1929 with the stock market crash and ended in 1941 with America's involvement in World War II.

16. Father Albert Payne.

17. Civilian Conservation Corps camps were created in 1933 to provide work for young men who could not find work during the Depression. The goal of this New Deal–era program was to solve two serious problems, unemployment and natural resource degradation.

18. Redcap Porters worked at the Saint Paul Union Depot. The uniform included a red cap, so as to be easily identified by passengers. Redcaps' salaries were minimal, and they supported their families mostly through tips. Responsibilities included carrying baggage for travelers, mopping floors, polishing brass, parking cars, and cleaning offices.

19. Saint Paul Union Depot is located at 214 East Fourth Street on the southeast side of downtown.

20. WPA: The Works Progress (later Work Projects) Administration was a relief measure established in 1935. The WPA provided work through programs in highway construction, building construction, slum clearance, reforestation, rural rehabilitation, the Federal Writers' Project, the Federal Arts Project, and the Federal Theatre Project. Its average employment was 2,300,000. The WPA employed more than 8,500,000 different persons on 1,410,000 individual projects until it was officially terminated June 30, 1943.

21. Saint Paul Independent Baptist Church was founded March 1, 1922, with 127 charter members. Initial meetings were held at the home of Rev. T. J. Carr, then moved to a tent in his backyard, and then into a storefront at Rondo and Kent Streets. Land was purchased at 505 Central Avenue where the basement was built. Services were held in the basement from 1927 to 1951, when the building was completed. In 1932, the church's name was changed to Mount Olivet Missionary Baptist Church.

22. Mechanic Arts High School was located between Central, Robert, and Aurora streets from 1911 to 1976. It was sold to the state and then torn down in 1978.

23. The Public Safety Building was located at 100 East Eleventh Street on the edge of downtown.

24. The New Han-Kow Café was located at 385 Robert Street.

25. Hallie Q. Brown Community Center, Inc., was opened in the Union Hall at Aurora and Kent Streets in 1929 as a community center specifically to serve the Black community when the Black YWCA closed in 1928. Hallie Q., as it is affectionately known, has served all ages through child care, youth and senior clubs, athletics, music and social events. In 1972, Hallie relocated in the Martin Luther King Building at 270 Kent Street at Iglehart in Saint Paul. The center's namesake was an educator who pioneered the movement of Black women's clubs in the late 1800s.

H. JANABELLE MURPHY TAYLOR

I began to play sports with Hallie.

I'M JANABELLE MURPHY TAYLOR.[1] My parents were long members of Hallie Q. Brown[2] themselves. And Mother[3] belonged to a club as a teenager, although Mother was born in the Rice Street area. But she still associated with the folks who lived in what is called the Rondo area. My parents always lived at 1354 Thomas, and I've lived there all my life. I used to attend Hallie Q. Brown just like I lived in the neighborhood. When I wanted to go to Hallie Q. Ma said, "You want to go, get your feet on the road and go right ahead." I'd walk there and back home. Now, if I was going to be late, then she might come pick me up. I began to play sports with Hallie. I was very much a tomboy in the neighborhood.

Before Hallie Q. Brown came along. I think my first experience with the YWCA[4] would have been when I was around five or six years of age. I had an older cousin who was like a sister, and I always wanted to be her age. So she'd have me as a tagalong. The Y was on west Central and Dale. As I recall, there were staff members from the community that were Black, but the heads of the staff were all White. We used to go to the Y downtown[5] for the swimming because there was no kind of swimming up in this area. And so it was more for the basketball, modern dance, club meetings, that sort of thing.

Myrtle Carden[6] was the first director of Hallie Q. Brown. She made a great impression on all of us kids. She didn't take anything off of any of us. We knew when we walked in that door, you mind, because Myrtle Carden is gonna put you out if you didn't mind! Yeah, she was a terrific person. Myrtle Carden herself came from out East. I think Pennsylvania if I'm not mistaken.

Dwight Reed, at one time, was on the staff. I think I was still in high school then, because his brother was my age. Dwight was a famous football player at the University of Minnesota among the Blacks. You'd have to know our history to know who he was though.

And there weren't that many places where the kids could go. There was the Ober Boys Club,[7] Hallie, and very few after-school programs. And so we had programs there at Hallie for the kids from kindergarten on up. In fact, there was a nursery school in Hallie. My brother used to be a part of that. Mother would take him down there for the nursery school.

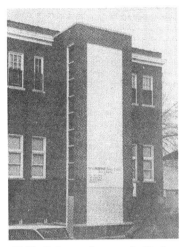

Hallie Q. Brown Community Center
553 Aurora

I grew up there at Hallie with club groups. You didn't just hang around, not with Miss Carden. I mean you are either going someplace or you're going home. Because she said her philosophy was, someone who's just hanging around is looking for trouble. So you're here for activity. And it might be just the game room. It didn't have to be a club, but you are going into some activity. In the game room they had board games. They had a pool table. Mostly boys, because they took over. You know, not going to let girls have a pool table. There was activity there for the kids to do after school. And teenagers, at night, they'd have clubs and things like that.

As I grew older, maybe late elementary and on into high school I became very active at Hallie. Between Hallie and Phyllis Wheatley—because I can't even deny the fact that I was also a very active member at Phyllis Wheatley in Minneapolis. At Hallie we'd have sewing. Miss Hazel Butler used to be the sewing teacher, and I never did learn how to thread a needle. I hated sewing with a passion, even when I had to take it in high school. I think I still have that white cap and white apron that we had to make. Hated sewing!

Oh, I think I had my first fencing lesson at Hallie. It was a fellow from the University of Minnesota who used to come and he taught us fencing. Boys didn't like it, but we girls did. There were a lot of Black volunteers who would come to Hallie to teach us from the various colleges.

We had a connection with the YWCA, so we had the Girl Reserves.[8] I don't know whether you've heard of the Girl Reserves. That's an outgrowth of a YWCA program. And they used to have a group that would meet at Hallie. In fact, I think I became a part of the Girl Reserves when I was in high school myself. But the Y would have programs at the center.

My ma used to say, "You just live down there all the time." At first I volunteered, then I was a part-time staff member when I was at the U. And later became a full-time staff member in the 1940s. I was known as one of the social workers, but I didn't graduate in social work. I'm a phys. ed. major from the University of Minnesota. My first paying job was at Hallie. I was Girls Worker. We were called the Girls Workers and I had all the girls' clubs. I organized clubs for girls and then I had girls basketball.

As a Girls Worker there were not very many times when I would start in the morning. I'd start at noon or one, two o'clock, something like that. And we'd work through till 10:00 at night. And there would be club groups for boys and club groups for girls. There was gym, and girls would have a certain time that they could have the gymnasium for basketball. Boys had more time than we had, and we kind of fussed about it. And then we'd have dances. There was a Boys Worker that organized the boys basketball. They played with teams from other areas. I organized the girls teams. We didn't have that many because parents weren't too great on girls playing basketball. We played Neighborhood House. We'd play St. Bernard's[9] team. They had girls teams. Sometimes it was just teams within the neighborhood. And often though, Phyllis Wheatley would come over and play. There was always a rivalry between Phyllis Wheatley and Hallie Q. Brown, both in the men's department as well as the women's department.

Hallie Q. Brown Community Center staff: (left to right) Hazel Butler, Jane Murphy, Kenneth Wilson, Prentice Stannis, Lucille Hargrave, (seated) Myrtle Carden

I never will forget. I was a staff member by this time. I was feisty. People used to take unfair advantage of us little people, you know. I always had to show that I was as hefty as any of the bigger people. As the Girls Worker at Hallie, I had organized a basketball team for girls. And when I got to the gymnasium area to put the girls on the floor so we could do some practicing, there sat the gym instructor, and the boys are all up and down around the floor. And I said, "What in the Sam Hill do you think you're doing?" "Well, what do you mean, Jane?" I said, "You know this is our day!" "Well, you girls weren't here." I said,

Janabelle 1944

"Get those boys off the floor. We're here now." And at the same time, I picked up an inkwell that he had sitting on his desk and I said, "If you want a head full of ink, you're gonna get it if you don't get out there on that floor and get those boys off of it." I guess he thought I was crazy enough to do it, because he went out there and got the boys off the gym floor. And we girls took over. But the girls didn't have too much of an opportunity in the gym.

I was camp director for a number of years for Hallie. Hallie Q. Brown and Merrick Community Center[10] from the East Side, they combined their kids and went to camp. The camp was up in the St. Croix State Park. I was beating the bus that was returning the kids from camp. I got to Merrick Center, and I just went breaking through these mothers who were standing out there waiting for the kids. And I later learned this from one of the mothers. When I went through a waiting group of mothers, the one White mother said to the other, "Who in the hell is that?" And says the other mother, "Oh, you don't know her? That's Jane, the camp director." "You mean that's who my daughter wants to be like?"

This was the perfect job for me. I love people. I wouldn't have had any other kind of a job.

◆ ◆ ◆

H. JANABELLE MURPHY TAYLOR is compassionate, honest, memorable, and able to build community within diversity. She began at Hallie Q. as a participant, was then hired as a Girls Worker, and retired as the program director around 1985. She was married to James L. Taylor for twenty years and is very proud of her sons and their wives: Lanny; Glenn and Myretta; and Garry and Terri Taylor; and her husband's daughter, Martha. Janabelle delights in her grandchildren: Jeffrey, Carla, Jason, Jade, Janae, Jayme, Casey, Tess, Dazhia, Jae, Abel, and Peter; and great-grandchildren Kayleigh and Carter. Important to her are her brothers and their families: John Edgar "Bud" Murphy, married to Kitty, and Richard Murphy, and nieces and nephews Edgar and Sue Murphy, David and Josephine Taylor, Clarence "Tate" and Diane Taylor, and Vant Washinton and families; and Colleen Russell. Mrs. Taylor appreciates her renewed relationship with Carolyn and Kenn Schmies and their families.

◆ NOTES

1. H. Janabelle Murphy Taylor was born December 3, 1920.

2. Hallie Q. Brown Community Center, Inc., was opened in the Union Hall at Aurora and Kent Streets in 1929 as a community center specifically to serve the Black community when the Black YWCA closed in 1928. Hallie Q., as it is affectionately known, has served all ages through child care, youth and senior clubs, athletics, music, and social events. The original location was in the Union Hall at Aurora and Kent Streets. In 1972, Hallie relocated in the Martin Luther King Building at 270 Kent Street at Iglehart in Saint Paul. The center's namesake was an educator who pioneered the movement of Black women's clubs in the late 1800s.

3. Mother Ida Mae Murphy.

4. A Colored YWCA/YMCA opened in 1923 with a limited Colored program at 598 West Central Avenue. It closed in 1928.

5. The Saint Paul YWCA was opened in 1906. Their first building was constructed in 1911 at 425 West Fifth Street in downtown. In 1961 a new facility opened on Kellogg Boulevard in downtown, with a final move in the 1990s to 375 Selby, four blocks south of the Rondo corridor.

6. Myrtle Carden served as the first director of Hallie Q. Brown Community House from 1929 to 1949. Her efforts on behalf of children, working mothers, and senior citizens led to the creation of a variety of social services from home nursing and dental clinics to summer camp programs for children.

7. Ober Boys Club at 375 St. Anthony at Western was begun during World War II by the Union Gospel Mission. It was named for Edgar Ober of 3M who was active with the Gospel Mission. This recreation club taught Christian values. Boys who participated also attended Snail Lake Children's Camp. There was a Girls Club located at Welcome Hall. Sometime after 1960 the club became part of The Boys and Girls Clubs of America, but the building is still owned by Union Gospel Mission.

8. The most popular and successful YWCA club program was the Girl Reserves, begun in 1918 to foster patriotic war work. After the war, the Reserves grew. The club system, including the Reserves, was the main way in which the YWCA accommodated the needs of women and girls of color. Black, Japanese, and Chinese girls organized themselves into Reserves, often finding a sponsor among women in their churches or schools to guide and encourage them.

9. St. Bernard's Catholic School has stood in the North End Community of Saint Paul for more than 100 years. German immigrants who had moved into the North End founded St. Bernard's Parish Community in 1890. The grade school was founded in 1891. In 1957, St. Bernard's became one of two parishes in the archdiocese to open a parish-based high school. In 1998, the high school and the grade school were united, creating the first and only coeducational pre-K through grade 12 school in the Archdiocese of Saint Paul and Minneapolis. The campus is located between Rose, Geranium, and Woodbridge Streets.

10. Merrick Community Services operates community centers, food shelves, and a job bank at 715 Edgerton.

BERNICE GREENFIELD WILSON

We had a lot of fun.

I'M BERNICE WILSON,[1] mother of Patricia Wilson Crutchfield, Butchie, Steve, and Tim Wilson. In 1949 we moved from Chicago to Saint Paul. We lived at 633 Iglehart, and in 1953 I moved to 892 Rondo, then to Carroll before the freeway came through.

My husband[2] was a railway mail clerk. He had worked for the post office. There weren't many Blacks in the railway mail, in the post office at that time. Most of the people he worked with were White. He took the test and then he went into railway mail. And he didn't want his children growing up in Chicago, so he asked for a transfer. He did run on the Milwaukee Road, from here to Chicago, not as a railroad man, but as a railway mail clerk. He threw mail, sorted mail from Saint Paul to Chicago. He'd go to work about four hours before the train left Saint Paul. They would sort mail for the little towns so that as the train left Saint Paul and you hit the little towns, they had the mail packs ready. The train kept going, they had one of those things with the arm out that takes the mailbags. He would usually spend the night and come back the next day.

When I first came to Minnesota, I thought this was one of the hardest places that I ever had the misfortune to go to. This reminded me of what they were talking about Georgia, Mississippi, the Deep South for the Negroes. I worked at Montgomery Wards in Chicago as an assistant supervisor in an office. They had a Montgomery Wards[3] here. I thought because they had Wards here I could get transferred, maybe not in my same position, but at least a comparable job, and they would not transfer me. And so they said, "When you go there, go to the office and tell them that you were employed with us. Just go to the office and tell them." So I did. What it was, they didn't have Negroes at Wards at that time doing anything but maid work and janitors. In Chicago I was assistant billing supervisor. It was just a title, nothing to get excited over, but it wasn't maid's work.

Although my husband was working, I always was independent, liked to make my own money. And so I went to work at Wards as a maid. Oh, and I was so insulted, but I wasn't that insulted. I worked there, I think, for Christmas. I wasn't there a month and I was ready to go back to Chicago. I was the maid in the furniture department, which meant when the new furniture came in it was full of chalk and white, and everything. The mirrors and everything had white stuff all over it. So you had to wash the mirrors, wash the furniture, the tables, like this. You would have to wash it and then you would simonize[4] it. I think they were paying me $19.50 a week, and you got a little brown envelope and it had a little window in it. They would put the cash in there, the dollars, and they would put a little round paper over it so you couldn't see it.

After a while in Saint Paul, I got used to it. When you've lived somewhere and everybody around you has accepted it, then you just go along with them. But every chance, every excuse I could use, I left. It wasn't that great. Anytime I had a chance to leave I would go, yeah, and I've been doing that ever since. I love to travel. And I would go to Chicago a lot! I always went to Chicago 'cause there was always something going on with my friends.

Then I met some folks here that knew some people I knew in Chicago. So after I was here, I called them. Everybody was in clubs[5] and so they invited me to the clubs and oh, I just had a ball. I danced. I was one of those that would rather dance than eat. So I would go to the club's parties. So I guess they kinda liked me a little bit, because they were asking me to join the clubs.

One club I joined was the Cameos and another one was the Aquarian. I think I started out with one, then it was two, then it was three. I did belong to about nine there for a while, but I kinda cut down. But two or three of them, they disbanded. Folks didn't want to meet, fix food and stuff.

You see, we Blacks couldn't go so many places that were for the Whites. They

Cameo Club: Bee Wilson is seated first on the left in front row.

didn't welcome the Blacks. So then a group of compatible Blacks would get together. We mostly met in our homes, but for special events would have to pool
money together to rent party rooms. Maybe an anniversary party for when
the club first started. Maybe it would be Christmas. They would have maybe a
Christmas dance or Christmas party, and they would rent very nice rooms out
at the University of Minnesota. It was very, very nice and it was in the evening.

I remember how shocked I was when I first went. I don't remember if it was
a formal[6] or just a dance 'cause they had an awful lot of formals here. In Chicago,
socially, you could go out to a formal or party and if it started from 10:00 to
2:00, 11:00 to 3:00, 12:00 to 4:00. Then in Chicago, of course, you didn't go
home then because you'd have to stop somewhere and have something to eat.
So you go home in the wee, wee hours, by the time the sun was coming up.

Then we came here and I was invited to a party and I think I was still
working at Wards. I came home at 4:00 P.M., had dinner with the family, and
then I was pin curling my hair. My friends were gonna come by and pick me
up, but they hadn't told me what time. So I think this was around maybe 7:30
and I'm gonna take a couple hours nap before they pick me up. So just before
I got in bed the phone rang and this was the wife of the couple that's gonna
pick me up. I said, "Oh, hello. How are you?" And whatever and so forth, and

she said, "Hello. How are you? Are you ready?" And I said, "Ready? Ready for what?" And so she said, "Well, you know, it starts at 9:00." And I said, "What starts at 9:00?" And I'm not trying to play crazy, but I know she's not talking about this affair. So she said, "We're gonna pick everybody up, and I was wondering if we should pick you up first 'cause we're just about ready to leave." And I looked at the clock and I thought, "Where?" "Are you going to the affair?" She said. "Yes." And I said, "Tonight?" But anyway I said okay.

I went ahead and threw my rags on. When her husband came to the door to get me—I think my husband, he was babysitting, and so I went. And I remember how floored I was and I said to myself, "My God. Nobody goes out this early." I think they picked me up something like twenty after eight. I thought, "My God. I never heard of such a thing." But then I got used to it and I found out that there were times. They were from 9:00 P.M. to 1:00 A.M. 'cause everything closed at 1:00 A.M. or at 12:00 midnight. That's why we always had the community after-hours joint, so that people, Black folks, could continue partying. They had to stop at 1:00, so we went to the after-hours joints after that.

If the club was going to meet at my home I used to always try to have my house decorated. We wanted to get it painted and make the house clean because we were having company. I'd redecorate the curtains and the windows, and the floors, and the rugs, and have new pretty tablecloths. Maybe you'd take a day off. We redid the bathroom the same as when we had out-of-town company. Whenever we had out-of-town company, we always painted the room, did the curtains. Because we had so many club members, you'd only have the meeting about once every two-and-a-half years or something like that. So we painted sometimes about once every two years, and after that then I got so I would paint maybe once a year. Our club got smaller, so we entertained more often.

Then you would maybe have one or two turkeys and a big whole ham, and maybe a big thing of spaghetti, a big thing. In the summer there would be a big thing of potato salad. I mean a big thing of potato salad! I'm not talking about a little thing like that. You had something like a big bowl—eighteen- to twenty-four-inch bowl, maybe two or three medium-size bowls. What happened—sometimes you would have at least twenty-eight to thirty-some members. I think at one time we got up to forty members.

Husbands and wives belonged to the clubs, or if you were single and wanted to be a member, you could. If it was a man and he wanted to be a member, he could. And of course, he brought his girlfriend when he came. You can see if we met once a month, then you don't have it at your home but once every so many years. You go alphabetically.

And everybody back then drank a lot. I would maybe get a half a case or so of whiskey, a bunch of mix. Then you would have this huge thing. The meeting usually started about 9:00 P.M. That meant you didn't serve until about 11:00 or 12:00.

During the club meetings we had a business meeting to plan where they're going to have the next affair, how much is it, where is it. When I first came we were mostly in our homes. But later they let us rent rooms at the hotels outside of the neighborhood. We would discuss different places we'd been to, see if we could purchase such-and-such a room on such-and-such a date, how much was it. If we were going to have an orchestra, what orchestra, what are their rates, how much are they gonna charge, and whatever. And then how much money do we have in the treasury? Can we afford this, can we afford that? So then sometimes, if we didn't have enough money for an event, we would tax. Tax maybe ten to twenty bucks or so per member. Because if you had a nice room, like at the Radisson[7]—it's called the Hilton[8] now—then we'd have to have flowers all around the bandstand with the band and the singer. We would have to decide which band. We didn't always have the same groups. I don't remember who they were. It's been so long ago. We would get them through the union—the Musicians Union.[9] Well, they couldn't play if they didn't belong to the union. Percy Hughes's Band[10] was one we had.

So then what happened was a lot of the members invited guests to the club meeting, so you would have a couple of extra folks besides the members. So after the business meeting was over, the extra guests would come.

Clip from the newspaper coverage of Cameo Club's cotillion Ball in 1957

Sometimes the hosts would have a piano and somebody would start playing the piano. Depending on whose house you were at, they would roll the rug back and everybody would come and dance. And at that time they were doing the jitterbug[11] or something like that and you throw somebody out, you know, and hope they come back. And everybody's dancing.

So then maybe you'd have somebody in the club that had a new organ. So we jumped in two or three or four cars and we'd go over to John or Mary or somebody else's home and would play their organ and we'd sit there and we'd sing. Didn't have enough chairs, we'd sit on the floor and we'd sing "Peg of My Heart"[12] and some of the other oldies.

Now, I'm talking 2:00 or 3:00 in the morning. Nobody thought about going home. So then, when we'd leave there, then they say, "Let's not go home. It's too early to go home." "So okay, I'll tell you what. Let's go by Jeff's house." And he said, "Well, you can come over if you want to." Someone would say, "I'm hungry." "I am too. I've got a dozen eggs." "I've got a loaf of bread." Okay. Different ones went home, got a loaf of bread, got a couple dozen eggs, some bacon and whatever. Came back and the cooks got in Jeff's kitchen and started cooking and they put the record player on. We would have breakfast and we would eat.

So then a couple of the ladies would go in his bedroom and pull his drawers out and find his pajamas, so then they would model his pajamas and whatever. And he was a single man, so he had some real pretty pajamas. They would model his pajamas.

After breakfast, the sun's getting ready to come up. Then we said, "Well, maybe we should go home." So we get ready to leave and someone says, "We can't go home. Have to go to church." We're Catholics, right? So we said, "What time is it?" We know St. Pete's[13] has 6:30 A.M. mass. If we hurry, we can go there. So then we'd get in there, those of us that were Catholic. Get in the car and go. There's no sense in sitting in the back. Nobody will see. So you get there and you go all the way down the front and you're sitting up there and it's quiet. The priest's voice is *mmmm*, and then all of a sudden you started sliding, and just before you keeled over the one sitting next to you would almost knock you off the seat. Oh, that was terrible. We used to do that and then finally we'd get home.

I would come in. If I had a scarf, I would throw my scarf in, and I would follow with a leg in the door and say, "Well, honey, I'm back again." And he said, "Oh, Mrs. Wilson, come in and have a cup of coffee." And I was so disappointed! But we had a lot of fun.

My husband was working. He was very reserved. He was a party pooper. I liked to party. I was real friendly and made friends. I think I was really too friendly for him. But he was very reserved and I would meet you and I would hug you and, "Come on over to my house." My husband belonged to the club. I paid his dues and he would come when he was in town, once in a while. He tried to stick with us one time and I think it was 4:30 A.M. and we were going someplace else. We hadn't even started to hiccup, and he got tired of us and he told me that so-and-so could bring me home 'cause he was going, leaving. And he did. He left me. And he went home and I came in about three hours later. But he tried to stick with us because he said, "What in the world are you all doin' so late? Why are you all so late?" There's not a husband living that would have a wife that would come home between 3:00 and 5:30 A.M., sometimes 6:30 in the morning, and wouldn't want to know what is she doing all night long.

And it was so cute when I had out-of-town company. Everybody was running up to Saint Paul and they would come up here and my husband was so shocked. I was taking them to the after-hours joint. He was looking at me real funny 'cause he didn't know I knew about after-hours joints. And I was taking them, and after I took them, the next day you heard about that they had raided the place. And the police had come and taken everybody downtown. We just missed them. I was so embarrassed. I thought, "Oh my God, what did I do?" The social clubs made Minnesota life okay. It was a fantastic social life!

John "Butchie" Wilson Jr.

The people here were very supportive when my husband died in 1958 and when my son died in Vietnam.[14] It was December 10, 1965, and he was only twenty-one. An awful lot of folks that came from Chicago. I was shocked. When Butchie died and they shipped his body back from Vietnam and I had to set a date. The funeral director was pushing me to set a date and I hated to set a date because the navy hadn't given me a date yet to when the body was due. I didn't know when the body would come and I was hating to set a date and he wouldn't be here. And so then I did. I think it was December 28th. So he did come. That was a bad time back then.

Just like when my husband died, it just seemed like

almost every other friend I had in Chicago came. And then I was shocked because so many of my friends here opened their homes to the people that came. They gave them rooms and had breakfast for them in the morning. They would bring hams and turkeys and whatever over for us to eat. One lady, she brought the turkey over but she didn't want to stay home. She cooked it in my kitchen. And she was walking back and she was tasting the turkey. It was cute.

My oldest son was a very nice kid. I know people have a tendency when people die, they canonize them. They make them saints. But my son was a nice person. He wasn't a rough kid. John, he was a different kettle of fish. He liked to dance. He liked classical music, he liked operas. He never liked to buy anything on sale. He liked to dress well. I mean, he liked to dress well! He liked clothes. He was a nice kid. He was an escort for a lot of dances and debutante balls. That happened. Life goes on.

◆ ◆ ◆

BERNICE GREENFIELD WILSON, daughter of Etta and Edward Greenfield, is proud of her kids and their marriages. She has a strong sense of the importance of keeping family together. She is a member of Pilgrim Baptist Church, active in the Jolly Seniors of Pilgrim, several social clubs, and has her own private ministry helping people who are down and out. She has instilled in her children responsibility and the importance of never forgetting where they came from. She retired from Minnesota State Statistics Department, where she worked for thirty-five years. She is the proud mother of Patricia Wilson Crutchfield (Charles), Steven Anthony Wilson (Mona), Timothy Kenneth Wilcon (Pam), and grandmother of John Walter Jr., Steven Wilson Jr., Raushana Crutchfield, Alison Wilson, Rashad Crutchfield, Alexis Wilson, Marcus Wilson, and great-grandmother of Steffan Wilson.

◆ NOTES

1. Bernice Greenfield Wilson was born January 21, 1921.
2. Husband John Wilson Sr. was born May 13, 1915, and passed April 1958.
3. Montgomery Ward & Co. was located at 1400 University Avenue.

4. Simonize: to polish or wax.

5. Social clubs were formed out of necessity, since recreation and entertainment facilities for Black people were limited in the 1920s and '30s. None of the better restaurants served them, nor did the major hotels rent rooms to them. By 1935 there were two dozen clubs of various kinds in the Twin Cities. By the 1940s the hotels began to rent party rooms to these social clubs. These clubs included the Sterling Club, founded in 1919; Credjafawn (the name came from the first name of each of the original woman founders); Cameo (which were rivals with Credjafawn); Ludatin; Zodiac Club; En-nous; Forty Club; Regaletts; and DYWYK, which stood for "Don't You Wish You Knew." Club Adelphi was a women's social and civic club; Omicron Boule of Sigma Pi Phi Fraternity was founded in 1922; the T.S.T.C. Club was founded in 1896.

6. Formal dress attire required.

7. The Hotel Radisson was located at 455 Seventh Street, Minneapolis.

8. The Saint Paul Hilton Hotel, located at 11 East Kellogg Boulevard, became a Radisson Hotel in 1975–1976.

9. The Musicians Union was located in Saint Paul, between Seventh and Eighth Street, next to the Tower Theatre. The union was fully integrated.

10. Percy Hughes broke the "color line" for Black bands in Minnesota as a pioneer jazz "big band" leader after World War II. He continues as an active musician and band leader in the Twin Cities.

11. Jitterbug was a popular dance in the early 1940s performed chiefly to boogie-woogie and swing music. This strenuously acrobatic dance consisted of a few standardized steps augmented by twirls, spins, and somersaults.

12. "Peg O' My Heart" was written by Alfred Bryan and Fred Fischer. In 1947, it reached number one on the charts and was recorded by both the Harmonicats and Buddy Clark & The Three Sons.

13. St. Peter Claver Catholic Church began in 1889. A new building was erected for the segregated Black congregation at Aurora and Farrington Avenue in 1892. After the new school and convent were built, the new church building was completed at 375 Oxford at St. Anthony in 1957.

14. The Vietnam War was fought in southeast Asia from 1954 to 1975.

JAMES STAFFORD GRIFFIN

Those were the things that went on.

MY NAME IS JAMES STAFFORD GRIFFIN.[1] I was born July 6, 1917, and raised on Rondo. My grandmother[2] came to Saint Paul in 1906. We've been here ever since. And when my grandmother first came to Saint Paul she lived on Rondo about two doors west of Farrington on the north side of the street. They stayed there for three years and they bought a house, 587 Rondo,[3] in 1909. When my grandmother first came here, of course, my mother[4] was a young girl. She went to McKinley School,[5] and later on she got married in 1912 here in Saint Paul. I lived in our family home until 1955.

When I was a small boy, on that particular block on Rondo Street there might have been maybe four or five Black families at the most. And only one family had any children, so when I was real small the only kids I played with were White kids, because they were the only ones in the neighborhood. A lot of people don't understand that in those days the majority of people on Rondo Street were White.

When I went to Central High School[6] in the fall of 1932 there were, oh, I'd say about 2,400 kids there. We were the boom kids from World War I.[7] The largest number of Black students that was ever at Central in my four years I was there was thirty. And the year I graduated, 1936, there were 2,900 kids there. There were over 700 kids in the graduating class, and out of those 700 and some kids, there were eight Black kids. And out of those eight Black kids that graduated in my class, five of them were on the honor roll. I wasn't one of them! And five of those eight ended up college graduates. I *was* one of them. But you see, those are the things that went on.

So as I said, I lived in Saint Paul all my life, and I was very fortunate.

My dad, William Griffin, was in the hospital for a couple years, and then he passed, and of course that caused a difficult financial situation. Before my father died he was a dining car waiter for the Northern Pacific Railway. After they got married he was transferred to Seattle, Washington, and he worked on the Northern Pacific train that ran from Seattle, Washington, to Portland, Oregon. He stayed on the West Coast there for a couple of years. Maybe three years. My mother was not satisfied with things in Seattle, so they came back to Saint Paul. I was born in the house at 587 Rondo in 1917.

In Saint Paul most of the Black people worked on the railroad, but they only worked in two areas of the railroads. They worked in the dining car department of the railroads or they were sleeping car porters[8] for the Pullman Company, a Pullman Porter. And I think that's the thing that gets mixed up all the time. They were a separate entity. A waiter like my dad worked for the dining car department, you work for a railroad company. Although the duties were similar to the Pullman Porters, the waiters worked for one railroad and often had the same run all the time.

If you were a Pullman employee, you work for the Pullman Company, and the Pullman Company had the monopoly on all the sleeping cars in the whole United States. Those Pullman cars went with all kinds of railroad companies. Say if you bought a sleeping car ticket to go to, say, to New Orleans, why you got on the same sleeping car and you stayed in that. It might change trains someplace, but you didn't necessarily stay with the same railroad company. Because the railroad, they only ran on their own tracks. So it was real complicated. Those are some of the things that went on.

You know, a lot of people say Saint Paul is a railroad town. Railroads built Saint Paul. And they used to say, when I was a youngster, one family in every five in the City of Saint Paul worked for the railroads or something that's connected with it. There was the Northern Pacific and the Great Northern and Chicago Northwestern, the Soo Line, and a couple other real small railroads. But the only place Blacks could work on that railroad was on the dining cars. And another thing that was different in Saint Paul than in most places, say, like on the Northern Pacific, all the cooks were White and all the waiters were Black. And on the Great Northern they might have had maybe one or two crews of cooks that were Black, but ninety-five percent of the cooks on the Great Northern Railway were White. And the Chicago Milwaukee that came through here, they hired out of Chicago and had all Black cooks and waiters. Soo Line had Black waiters and mostly White cooks. And there was another big railroad came in that ran from here to Kansas City. All the cooks on it were Black. But in this section of the country, out of the Twin Cities, Saint Paul, most of the cooks were White and the waiters were Black. With other railroad jobs, of course, maybe there might have been one or two that would get in, but they didn't hire Blacks as section hands, switchmen, conductors, brakemen. So there was always some token, one or two jobs. Those are some of the situations that you had to deal with growing up.

And you see, years ago, before my time and when people had telephones, they had a job called the Call Boy. If they needed somebody for the railroad, they'd send this guy out to his house and tell him to report to where he was needed.

My dad worked for the railroad, and in those days, after you'd been on the railroad a year you could get a pass to ride the trains. We had relatives in Seattle and California and Michigan, so I've been riding trains all my life all over in the North in places like Washington, Montana, Minnesota, Michigan.

I was supposed to have been an athlete years ago when I graduated from Central High School in 1936. A guy named Ellsworth Harpole,[9] that used to play football for Minnesota, took a job as assistant coach at West Virginia State College,[10] an institute in West Virginia. As I said, my father was a dining car waiter. My dad, the last couple years before he had been in the hospital and died, had worked on a private car for the vice president of Northern Pacific. My mother went to see the vice president and told him I had a chance to go to college, if I could get there. I got a pass from him and I went to West Virginia.

On my first trip down to college in West Virginia I was nineteen and I had never ridden a Jim Crow[11] train before. The first time I'd ever come into any real concentrated discrimination was when I got on the train in

Cincinnati. Cincinnati is right across the river from Covington, Kentucky. When I got on the train, I didn't notice the signs at the door. People were getting on at the same place. I looked at the one car. There were about two or three people in there. And I looked in the other side, and it was pretty full and I didn't pay any attention to the people there. So I went on in and sat down. After I sat down waiting for the train to leave, the porter came up to me and said, "Son," he said, "you can't sit here." And I said, "Why not? There's plenty of seats!" He said, "Do you see that sign up there?" I said, "No, I didn't. What sign you talking about?" "Well," he said, "there it is up there." Well, I looked up, and there it was, *White Only*. I was nineteen years old then, and that was the first time I'd ever ridden in a Jim Crow car. So he said to me, "I can't put you off here. But if you don't move," he said, "soon as we cross this Ohio River into Kentucky, if you don't move, the conductor will put you off." I was seven hundred miles from home. What am I gonna do? So I moved. I went and sat in the Jim Crow car. That's what they called it, Jim Crow laws.

I sat there for a while. I only had one suit. I spread a newspaper down on the seat because it looked like it was a little soiled, and I sat down and rode a while. After I'd been riding about an hour or so, there was an elderly Black woman and—of course, we were called Colored in those days, and she said, "Son, where are you from? You must be from up North somewhere. I've been watching you." I said, "Well, yeah." She said, "Where are you from?" I told her Minnesota. "Well," she said, "I knew that." Well anyhow, we rode along for about another hour, over an hour, and that porter came back and tapped me on the shoulder and he said, "You can go back to where you were before." And I said, "Well, why can I do that now?" He said, "Well," he said, "we just passed into Kenova, West Virginia." He said, "In West Virginia there's no Jim Crow laws on the railroad." So that was kind of new, but he told me, "I don't know how far you're going 'cause I haven't looked at your ticket, but if you're gonna eat in the diner, you've gotta eat before you get to White Sulphur Springs, West Virginia, 'cause then you cross into

James Griffin
Central High School
graduation picture, 1934

Virginia and then the Jim Crow goes back into effect." Even before I got to college I had learned a lot. And those were the things that went on.

They had had a scandal in the police department in the Thirties. The department closed their eyes to the Dillinger[12] and the Barker[13] gang activities around here. Two or three guys got killed in the neighborhood, so they had to clean up the town. My brother[14] had a paper route, and I was his helper, so I was very familiar with the crimes and scandals because paperboys—in those days, we'd read the paper before we delivered it.

At one time during the Twenties, there had been eight Black policemen. Of course, we've had Black policemen in Saint Paul since 1881. Lewis Thomas[15] was the first Black policeman. He was appointed in June of 1881. Seventeen black officers were appointed to the department from 1881 to 1921, but then we went from 1921 until 1937 and not a single Black was appointed to the police department. They had a commissioner at that time. He had gone on record. As long as he was commissioner, there'd be no more colored policemen. Well, after they had this scandal they said that they were gonna hire these men, then they said they weren't gonna skip anybody. So if you were on the list, why you'd get hired when your name came up.

And in 1939, when I took the police examination, they had a huge turnout. And you must realize the Great Depression was going on. From 1929 until 1941 the job situation was rough, so when I went down to take that examination, over a thousand guys came down to take it. They had the test May 9, 1939, at Mechanic Arts High School.[16] There were so many people there, they were in the auditorium, and they filled up the auditorium and they started using the classrooms. They had the police examination in the morning and the fire department examination in the afternoon. When I got there and I saw all those people there, if I'd had a job or someplace to go, I would have gone home. But I had nothing to do. So I took the test and I took the test for the fire department that afternoon. I passed both tests.

When I got home the headlines of the *Saint Paul Dispatch*[17] said over a thousand men took the police and fire examination this morning, and there's no money to hire them. I passed the test and they established a list in August 1939. There wasn't a single appointment made off of that list until March 1st of 1941, and they hired twenty-five men off this list. They had to take 240 hours of training, and when the training was through they hired fifteen of them, and ten of them they made reserve officers, and as an opening came they would fill it.

In June I got a letter to report for a medical examination for the police department, and I went down to take it. I was twenty-four then, in good physical shape, and when they failed me on the medical examination I was very, very surprised. As a matter of fact, I was shocked.

They said I had albumin[18] in my urine, I had an overlapping toe, and I was running a temperature. I went to see my own doctor, the late Dr. J. W. Crump.[19] He was a Black doctor who was around here years ago. He says, "There's nothing wrong with you. Go back and take that test again." Well, I went back to take the test again and the guy said I didn't have a temperature, the albumin in my urine was gone, but I still had an overlapping toe. So I went to see my doctor again, and he said, "There's nothing wrong with you. Go back again." So I went back again and the guy said the specific gravity in my urine was too high, and I still had the overlapping toe. So I went back to my doctor again. He said, "Don't go back right away. You have to wait awhile." Finally I got a call, I went back, and they said this time I still had the overlapping toe and the gravity in my urine was too high, and they failed me.

So I didn't know what the heck to do then. In the neighborhood where I grew up the councilman, they were called commissioners in those days, lived not too far from me—the Peterson family. I went down to see Mr. Peterson and he looked at me and said, "Don't I know you?" And I said, "Yes, you do." He said, "Is your name Green?" I said, "No, my name is Griffin." He said, "That's right." He said, "You went to school with my boy Axel, didn't you?" I said, "That's right." He asked me how my family was and all that sort of thing, and then he said to me, "What's on your mind?" And I told him. He says, "I'll look into that." He says, "I'll talk to the commissioner about that." He never made any promises, and he didn't tell me anything.

Well, I was gonna take one more shot at taking this test. In the meantime, they were deciding to hire seventeen more policemen. So I went down to take the test. That time there was nothing wrong with me. And so then I got a notice to report to the police station on August 6, 1941, two days before the list ran out. They appointed seventeen of us, and they were going to take the same route those others had, 240 hours of training. We got through with that. They'd put us on the reserve list for when an opening came. While we were going to this training school they only paid us fifty cents an hour. In those days, you bought your own uniform, your own gun, paid for your own hospitalization, and there was no overtime pay, no holidays. The only thing you got was fifteen calendar days sick leave.

They were starting to build the Twin City Arsenal[20] out in New Brighton, so they were advertising for guards. I went out there. I went to see Cecil Newman. He was the editor of the Black newspaper on the *Saint Paul Recorder*[21] and the *Minneapolis Spokesman*. He encouraged me to go out there and put my application in there. So I went over to the Foshay Tower[22] to put in my application, and the guy who was taking the applications told me that they were only hiring guys who could qualify for the police departments in Minneapolis and Saint Paul and the surrounding areas. I told him, "Well, I've already done that." And he said, "What do you mean?" I said, "I'm a reserve officer on the Saint Paul Police Department." But he wouldn't even give me an application. So I left there and I went to see Cecil Newman and told him about it. He said, "Well, don't worry about it. You go back there tomorrow and they'll take care of you." So I went back the next day to the Foshay Tower. The same guy was sitting there. He dang near broke his arm trying to give an application. You see, Cecil Newman at that time was a very good friend of Charlie Horn of the Federal Cartridge Company. They hired me and I was the first Black guard they hired. Well, in the next thirty days or so they hired about eight or ten more Black guys, give or take a few. I can't remember the exact number. And so I went on there and I stayed there for a year.

As a Black officer you always got the dirty details. They never assigned me to a squad car. I use to walk beats like Seventh and Wacouta. That was skid row. They had a lot of flophouses around there. You could get a bed, what they call a cot, for a quarter. A lot of D-horns[23] drinking. Come to work in the morning there would always be four, five, or six guys laying in the street, paralyzed

Officer Griffin, 1941

drunk. You'd have to call a wagon, haul them in, things like that. Of course, in an area like that you had fights. Guys would go in those bars and cause trouble, and you'd have to go in and straighten it out. And if there were any disagreeable details, I got them.

When I first went on the job, most of the job, most of the assignments I had, I dealt with Whites. I walked a beat, Seventh and Wacouta and places like that, always in low economic and educational levels neighborhoods. Most of those people were White. Some of them resented it, some of them didn't. I think that's the way it is. If you were out in a neighborhood and you pinched[24] a guy—as a rule when the police were there that would always draw a crowd. You'd tell a guy in the crowd to call headquarters and tell them to send somebody out here on this corner or this address.

So in the meantime, my buddy LeRoy Coleman, who I had grown up with here in Saint Paul and he and I had been roommates down in West Virginia State College—he was on the fire department. He was a real smart guy. He told me that Minnesota had the strongest veterans preference law in the whole United States for civil service jobs like police and fire. You got absolute preference over nonveterans in a first-class city in Minnesota. The first-class cities were Duluth, Minneapolis, and Saint Paul. He says, "I'm gonna enlist for the veterans preference." He says, "You better do the same thing." He went in the army. He wrote me a letter and he said, "Jim, if you get an opportunity you better take the navy." He said, "Boy, it's rough down here in Fort Lee, Virginia. Sometimes you got to wait to take a bus, the bus will go by and they won't even pick up the Black soldiers." I thought about it for a couple of days. After I signed up, I told them I'd take the navy. I was in the navy about a year.

I got back home from the navy in World War II[25] and I went to work the first shift at 11:00 on that Sunday night. I was sitting around there shaking hands with all the guys, and we were laughing and talking. They called off the roll call and I was assigned to Seventh and Wabasha. Years ago, Seventh and Wabasha was the crossroads of Saint Paul. And right around Seventh and Wabasha there were five theaters and I'd say a dozen bars. So I was standing in front of the St. Francis Hotel and a guy ran down to me and said, "Boy, you better get around to the Drum Bar."[26] I said, "What's the matter?" He said, "Boy, they got a real donnybrook going over there." I walked on down to the corner. I got over towards the Drum Bar, and I looked over there and there must have been 150 people out in front of the Drum Bar. It was, oh, I'd say about 12:30. All the shows were turning out and the bars were empty, so they had a big crowd. I said, "Well, geez, what am I gonna do by myself with all these guys." I kinda pushed my way through the crowd and the bartender and another guy was having a big fight. I said, "Come on, let's break this up." These guys were still wailing away, so I grabbed the bartender from the back, pinned his arms to him, and kind of raised him off his feet. He was kicking and carrying on. I said, "Come on, let's kinda get yourselves together. We don't want to have any trouble. We don't wanna have anybody go to jail here or nothing. Let's kinda calm down." And of course the other guy was wailing away. And he turned around and said, "Jim." I looked at him and he was a guy, Dick Kool, I knew from playing football. So we broke the thing up. Finally, one guy said, "Boy, is that guy tough. Did you see him break up that fight?" The only reason I was able to break it up was 'cause I knew one of the guys. Of course they didn't know that. So those were the things that went on.

It was always easier to arrest a White person than arrest a Black person. Easier to arrest a tiger than arrest a Black woman! I was on the job two years before I arrested a Black person. If you walk into a White tavern, everyone would back up. Walk into a Black tavern, everyone would try to get into a fight. When you are the only Black guy it is a lot easier, a lot easier. Easy to be well known, not 'cause you are very smart, but because you are Black. People remember you. How are they gonna miss you?

Walking the beat you deal with a lot of drunks and domestics, fights, disorderly conduct, things like that, disorderly houses, bootleggers. When I started walking beats, the guys walking beats didn't have radios. Not only me, nobody did. They had two-way radios on most of the cars when I came on. Being a Black officer, I was there five years before they put me in a squad car.

They didn't start putting Blacks in squad cars until after the war. That was in 1946. When I first got my first assignment as a squad man, why, there was no problem 'cause you didn't have a partner. And of course, a lot of those White guys supported the idea of no Black officers in the squad cars cause they didn't want a Black partner. When I first went into a squad my partners were Black. Then after a while we had Blacks and Whites in the squads.

When I got to be a sergeant in 1955 there wasn't a whole lot of Black sergeants in the country. There were only three other Black police officers on the job in Saint Paul. Let's see, there was Turpin and myself. That made two. Thomas[27] made three. Remember, back in the 1920s they had eight Black officers.

When I made sergeant they had the top six guys off the sergeant's list pictures in the paper. I got a charge out of that. That was on September 15, 1955. There was one big question on everybody's mind. "Will they put Griffin in charge of men?" Most White officers didn't want to report to a Black. Well, I was assigned as desk sergeant. I didn't have any men to supervise, because I was Black. But I decided I was going to be the best desk sergeant the Saint Paul Police Department ever had. And with time it changed.

I made captain in 1970, and we were the same three Black officers. About 1971, Lieutenant Huss[28] assigned a White man to a squad with a Black man. The White man said he wouldn't go out. I was a captain at that time. I was a station commander. and it came to my attention, so I said, "Well. there's no option here for you. Either go on out with that guy or you'll have to go home." So he went out. He was a real popular guy. That caused lots of trouble, but he never said anything to me about it 'cause he knew I wouldn't go along with that.

I studied extensively and took the deputy chief exam. When the results came out I was number one on the test, but Chief Rowen[29] told me he was going to appoint McCutcheon, who was White, younger than me, and scored number two. And it kinda raised the hackles there a little bit. I said, "What do you mean, you're going to appoint him?" They had never passed a number one guy before. I hired an attorney and took it to court. It's a long story. The paper came out in my favor and the union, too. They finally decided to appoint two deputy chiefs that year. I was appointed in 1972. My hard work had paid off.

My favorite memories with Saint Paul PD? Well, of course, the first one when I passed high enough to get a sergeant job. They appointed six sergeants that year and I was in the top six. That was it. Then I guess the next biggest kick I think I got was when I was number one on the deputy chief's exam. So those are the things that happened. The job I enjoy the most was, well, actually was the highest rank—deputy chief. I retired in 1983. I was sixty-seven years old, and had forty-two years with the Saint Paul Police Department, and these are some of the things that went on.

Police Day, 1979

♦ ♦ ♦

DR. JAMES STAFFORD GRIFFIN, born to Lorena Griffin Harris and William Griffin, said awards and honors are wonderful to receive, but it was his family and his many friends who were life's real treasures. Edna and Jim Griffin were married sixty-four years. He was the proud father of Vianne, Helen Anderson, and Linda Garrett, and grandfather of five grandchildren and one great-grandchild. He joined the Saint Paul Police Department in 1941, and became Saint Paul's first Black deputy chief. Chief Griffin served on the Saint Paul School Board. He was a founding member of NOBLE—National Organization of Black Law Enforcement Executives. Jimmy received an honorary doctorate from Concordia, was inducted into the Minnesota State High School League Hall of Fame, and was on the board of directors of the Sterling Club. In 1988, Central High School's football field was renamed the James S. Griffin Stadium in his honor, and in 2004 the Saint Paul Police headquarters was named the James S. Griffin Building.

♦ **NOTES**

1. James Stafford Griffin was born July 6, 1917, and passed November 23, 2002.

2. Grandmother was Leonora Waters Cox, Mrs. James Cox.

3. 587 Rondo was near Dale and Kent. This residence was maintained as the family home until 1956, when the state purchased it to build Interstate 94.

4. Mother Lorena Waters Griffin Harris passed in the late 1950s

5. McKinley School was located between Carroll, Mackubin, and Rondo from 1903 to 1966. Fire destroyed the building in 1977.

6. Central High School began in 1866 and consisted of two rooms in the Franklin Building in downtown Saint Paul. By 1872 it was known as Saint Paul High School and was moved to Seventh and Jackson. In 1883, a twenty-seven-room building on Minnesota Street in downtown Saint Paul was completed, and the school was named Saint Paul Central High. Because of space needs, a new school was built at 275 Lexington Avenue in 1912. In 1977, the building was reduced to its structural form, then rebuilt into the current building.

7. World War I was fought in Europe against primarily Germany and Austria-Hungary, 1914–1918. The United States entered the war in April 1917.

8. Pullman Porters worked for the Pullman Company and carried baggage only for Pullman sleeping car passengers. The Pullman sleeping cars would be transferred between different railroads and traveled all over the country.

9. Ellsworth Harpole was an outstanding football player for the University of Minnesota varsity football team in the 1930s.

10. West Virginia State College is located in Institution, West Virginia. It is now known as West Virginia State Community and Technical College.

11. Jim Crow Laws enacted in the late 1880s and 1890s supported practices of segregation or discrimination against Blacks in public places, public transportation, and employment.

12. John Dillinger, well-known bank robber in the early 1930s, spent time in

Saint Paul, since the Saint Paul Police Department often ignored the presence of out-of-state hoodlums.

13. The Barker-Karpis Gang rampaged throughout the Midwest from 1931 to 1935, often finding refuge in Saint Paul. The gang was known to have committed murder, kidnappings, and bank, mail, and train robberies, but they didn't conduct their crimes in Saint Paul in exchange for the police ignoring their presence.

14. Brother Billy (William) Griffin passed in 1932.

15. Lewis Thomas's career in the Saint Paul Police Department is documented in David Vassar Taylor's *African Americans in Minnesota* (Minnesota Historical Society Press, 2002).

16. Mechanic Arts High School was located between Central, Robert, and Aurora from 1911 to 1976. It was sold to the state and then torn down in 1978.

17. *Pioneer Press Dispatch* newspaper: in 1849 the weekly *Pioneer* began, becoming a daily paper in 1854. In 1861 the *Saint Paul Daily Press* appeared. In 1868 the *Saint Paul Dispatch* appeared. The *Pioneer* and the *Press* merged in 1875 to become the *Pioneer Press*. In 1909 the *Pioneer Press* and *Dispatch* merged. The *Pioneer Press* was published as a morning newspaper and the *Dispatch* as an evening paper. In 1985 the name became only the *Pioneer Press*.

18. Albumin: sulfur-containing, water-soluble proteins occurring in blood.

19. Dr. James Crump's medical office was located on Rondo between Kent and Mackubin.

20. Twin Cities Army Ammunition Plant of the Federal Cartridge Corporation covered a four-square-mile area in New Brighton. In 1942 it began production of four billion rounds of ammunition for war efforts. It was placed on inactive and standby status from 1950 to 1965, and again began production of ammunition for the Vietnam War. The facility was placed on shutdown status in 1971. In 2002, some land was transferred to Ramsey County Parks. The Ordinance Plant, as it was known, hired Blacks at all levels according to their skills, education, and training. At one point it employed twenty percent of the state's adult Black population.

21. The *Minneapolis Spokesman* was founded in 1934 by Cecil E. Newman and is the longest-lived Black newspaper in Minnesota. The *Saint Paul Recorder* later began publication under Newman. The newspaper remains under the same family ownership and is now known as the *Minnesota Spokesman-Recorder*.

22. The Foshay Tower was the tallest building in Minneapolis at that time. It is located at 821 Marquette Avenue South.

23. D-horns: perpetually drunk person.

24. *Pinched* is a colloquial term for arrested.

25. World War II was fought between the Allied powers (England, the Soviet Union, the United States) and the Axis powers (Germany, Italy, Japan) from 1939 to 1945. The United States entered the war in 1941 following the bombing of Pearl Harbor by the Japanese.

26. The Drum Bar was located in downtown Saint Paul and served White patrons.

27. Mahlon H. ("Roy") Thomas began serving with the Saint Paul Police Department on July 25, 1949; he passed in 1974. Thomas had been denied the opportunity to play in the Police Band because he was Black. For years he walked a downtown beat. After his death, *Saint Paul Dispatch* columnist Oliver Towne collected funds and had a bronze plaque erected honoring Thomas on a building at Ninth and St. Peter Streets in downtown Saint Paul.

28. John Huss began serving with the Saint Paul Police Department in 1948; he was promoted to detective in 1954, and lieutenant 1965. He retired January 1982, and passed in 1991.

29. Richard Rowen served with the Saint Paul Police Department from 1947 to 1979. He was promoted to detective in 1965, deputy chief in 1964, and chief in 1970. He retired in 1979.

MELVIN WHITFIELD
CARTER SENIOR

Whatever the main theme is, the baritone kind of answers.

My first remembrance of Rondo is everything horse and buggy. MY NAME IS MELVIN WHITFIELD CARTER SR,[1] I remember the milk cars, and the things would be pulled by horses. And I remember it was a very smelly town at that time because the horses weren't—they had crews that would come around with the little shovel and shovel that up, you know, as fast as they could. It was very smoky and everybody burned coal. It left a kind of haze over everything, like a mining town or something.

But everyone knew each other. It was a typical small community. I think the Black community was from about Rice Street up to Lexington, and I would say on either side of that was where the community extended about two blocks on either side. I would say there were about a thousand in that area.

We lived at 305 Rondo and the community was about ninety percent Black. Not that they couldn't move somewhere else, but people tend to congregate where other people are like them. I noticed when I worked at the train station. Blacks would come up here from the South, the first thing they would ask you, "Where is the Black neighborhood?" And that's where they would head and ultimately they would end up staying there somewhere. So it was mostly Black. There were a few White though—about ten percent. There were businesses all up and down the street. In fact, across the street from me was a tailor shop. His name was Mr. Love,[2] and he was Black. And he tried to teach me the tailoring business, which I was all thumbs at.

I had two uncles here, Uncle Mac and Uncle Foster. Mac Carter lived on the same block that we did, about three houses east of us, and Foster lived on Chatsworth. They were my father's[3] brothers. They came here before us and actually sent for my dad when they found out that Paris, Texas,[4] had burned down. People were scared to stay there. There was always some controversy whether the fire was intentionally set in the Black neighborhood, and nobody wanted to stay around and find out at that time. So they sent him to come up here and said there was plenty of work in Minnesota, which there was. I had one uncle who was working for the train station at the Union Depot[5] in Saint Paul. He was what they call a Redcap.[6] And another one working at the packinghouse[7] in South Saint Paul when it was very good work for unskilled people. So he came here and found work right away. I am not sure which place he worked because it was before I was born. I am the only one born here. I think he got here in 1917 or 1918, and I was born in 1923. My folks were married in Texas. My dad was a musician and had been traveling with different circus bands for years. Ma[8] said he was in the best band in Paris, Texas, that everybody always raved about. He was a big dog there.

I had one brother and one sister, and I am the only one left in that original family. Here I'll show you a picture. My sister Tubie or Leantha, and my brother Mym was about ten years older than me.

My mom, she was a typical mom, but she was the breadwinner in the family. So she spent much less time with me than my dad. She worked at the Federal Building[9] as a cleaning woman. It was a civil service job cleaning up the Federal Building, dusting, stuff like that. Cleaning. She worked

Mym Grundy Carter Sr., Mym Grundy Carter Jr., Melvin Whitfield Carter, Leantha Carter Zeno, Mary Whitfield Carter

from five in the morning until afternoon sometime. We would go pick her up all the time. And she said she saw all those gangsters come through there, and they had to go on trial. That was a big thing. I remember when Dillinger[10] was in town. Just before they caught him he stayed in the Rondo district because he was hiding. But all us kids knew this because you know how kids are—we snoop around, running errands for people and stuff like that. "Dillinger's in town!" That was the big news, and we all knew where he was staying.

Then she would also do day work, as they called it, which was going to people's fancy houses and cleaning for them on the weekends and stuff like that. So she was on the go most of the time. She began working when I must have been around eight, nine years old—something like that. I wasn't even aware that we were poor. I didn't really understand that, because I had the necessary and important things in life going for me. I didn't know what poor was. I thought we were just normal. I remember my mother saying she made $33 a month. That was the basic income, and out of that we managed to live. We had an old car, and Dad managed to buy an old truck he found somewhere. He would make a little dough with that.

We were a musical family. My dad's mother was a music teacher. That's why he was so well acquainted with music. In Paris, Texas, she use to play organ for the church choir, and teach music at the same time out of their home. So that's why he got so well grounded in music.

My dad played at some places they called chicken shacks around, and they were the nightclubs of today. And guys would take the girls there, and they would dance and eat fried chicken. Every chicken shack would have their own recipe for chicken—you know, a thousand different ways. They would always have a two, three or four piece band playing there of local talent, which was very lucrative for the local musicians in those days. We don't have that now. We have canned music. It put a lot of musicians out of business, most of them. Whites and Blacks both would kinda go to those places. Dad played the guitar and my brother played piano, then they would have a horn player like a trumpet or saxophone. And it was a very musical environment that I came in. There was no way for me to avoid it really.

Then my brother was also playing a lot on Rice Street near McCarron's Lake.[11] I remember that my father had been on a job playing with my brother, and they were driving home on Rice Street and they either hit something or—anyway, my dad went through the windshield of the car and landed on his knee and cracked his knee. And they had to wire it together. That was the procedure in those days. He had a wire in his knee for the rest of his life to hold his knee bone together. I imagine they would just replace it nowadays. But he was crippled up forever after that. He had to always use a crutch. He must have been in his sixties by that time.

We use to have jam sessions at our house. When my brother and his group would get through playing at night he'd bring the cats over. We use to call each other cats in them days. He brought the cats over and they would take the top off the piano and have a big jam session at one o'clock in the morning. Wake up everybody! That's when I first got aware of jazz. He'd bring a lot of the musicians home, and I'd meet them and learn from them.

My dad, well, he was the most important person to me because my mother worked and he was a cripple. After his car accident he couldn't do any physical kind of work. He wasn't qualified to do any other profession than play music. So we spent a lot of time together. To compensate he got a truck and we hauled furniture, hauled rubbish and ashes, move people, and odd jobs. I would do the work and he would do the bossing. My dad could lift a certain amount, but what he couldn't lift, I would do. So I had plenty to keep me busy after school. We would always have a job or two to do. Without me to help him, Dad couldn't do anything. I would do the driving.

He also bought a half an acre down on the Mississippi River, which is now the Saint Paul airport.[12] At that time a lot of people lived along the river because they could live there tax free, and there's a lot of little shacks there. And you could get the land for little to nothing, and he knew how to—he was a farmer, too, in his younger days, so he knew how to garden. So we would use that quarter acre and plant stuff down there during the summer, and Ma would can it for the winter.

He played all the instruments. So that's why when Father Keiff, who was the second priest at St. Peter Claver[13]—he found out about my dad's talent and he said, "Well, Mr. Carter, how would you like to start a band of young boys?" He said, "That would be fine, of young boys and girls." And he said, "Well, if you get them together, I'll talk to the people in church and have them bring you some instruments." So he announced one day that he needed instruments and for people to look in attics and basements and places like that. If you have any old instruments, bring them to church, and Mr. Carter is going to go and pick them up, which he did. One day he came home with a truck-

St. Peter Claver Band, 1935: Melvin Carter with baritone (third from right),
W. D. Massey with trombone (leader Mym Carter not pictured)

load of used instruments all bent out of shape and everything. He worked on
them for weeks until he got them all polished up and repaired. And he started
this band. I think I was about in seventh grade. We became the toast of the
neighborhood.

Then I played the baritone horn in that band. They were all buddies of
mine that lived around the neighborhood. Two or three of us went into the
service and were musicians in the service, including me. I was a musician
in the Navy during World War II.[14] And some of these kids became nationally known musicians in big bands of the days, after they grew up. Albert
Cotton was a dear, dear friend of mine. He went on to play with a band
called Erskine Hawkins that was a recording band. That was just before
World War II in the late 1930s and early '40s. Teddy Massey and his brother
is in this picture also. He went on to play with a big band, but I can't call the
name of it right now. So the work that my dad put into the kids all paid off.

The main reason he started the St. Peter Claver Band was because I didn't
play football, or basketball, or baseball 'cause I was too skinny. And he was

always afraid I would get hurt. So since I didn't go anywhere he brought all the kids to our house. Against my mother's best wishes, he had all of us in the living room just like this. After school he had us blowing horns, and my ma would be trying to sleep in the next room.

He would write all the music, unbelievably or not, for each instrument. Stuff that he would remember from days when he was playing, and so we played marches and military marches. He would write the notes down. Each member had their own pamphlet with their music in it so they could remember.

But my dad did a lot of good in the neighborhood because these young kids would play at all the neighborhood functions. They would say, "Where is St. Peter Claver Band? We want those kids to play for us!" Then if anyone in the community had a picnic, or any of the parishes or churches had some big doings, Pa would put big placards on the sides of the truck to advertise it. Then people would say, "Oh there's a big picnic going on at Como with such-and-such a church." All the girls and boys would show up out there. We had a good time. And we would parade from Rice Street up to about Chatsworth, which is about a two-mile run. We didn't go beyond Chatsworth 'cause beyond that was a pretty roughed-in area at that time, kind of woody and there wasn't much going on. We would make two or three passes up and down the street. People would run out to see what was going on. We'd march up and down Rondo for special days on parades. And we would parade from Rice Street up to about Chatsworth: "What's Mr. Carter and his . . ."—they called us the St. Peter Claver Brass Band, incidentally, and it's the first and only band I think they've ever had.

Our big deal every year was to play at the Holy Name Parade at the fairgrounds. And we would play every year in the school parade. And I think Lieutenant Hetznecker[15] was the head of this particular part of the police department who would get my dad to have the kids come and play. We would march from the Capitol[16] down to Harriet Island,[17] which was a long way. All the different schools would march and they would have their bands. All the kids would look forward to that big day at Harriet Island. And they would give us all free tickets for the rides and all the pop and junk you could eat. That was a big day. That was one of the biggest days.

This would have been before World War II, about 1935 to '40, 'cause the guys started getting drafted, ya know. We all got about draft age at the same time, which was eighteen, I think—out of high school, which broke up the old family band. My dad would give music lessons to the people who could afford them and he would charge fifty cents if the parents had it. If they didn't have, he'd give lessons free. So some paid and that was enough to buy gas for the truck.

My dad was jovial and had a good sense of humor, which I wish I would have inherited. But he gave me his music knowledge, and I am thankful for that. He had the enthusiasm and had a little knowledge of every instrument. He could take you so far, then you had to go the rest of the way on your own. And a lot of these people went to other professions after he started them off.

My band director wanted a baritone player. Kids didn't just naturally gravitate towards playing baritone 'cause it wasn't a very popular instrument. They wanted to play the popular instruments of the day, like today everybody's a guitar player or a drummer. And in those days trumpet was the dominant instrument—Louis Armstrong,[18] Harry James,[19] and all those guys were making it well known. So I wanted to play trumpet and he wanted me to play baritone horn. So I played baritone horn a couple years, then my last year he let me switch over to trumpet. But baritone is a very beautiful instrument. I thank God to this day that my dad started me out on the baritone because it teaches you music theory, because it answers the dominant—whatever the main theme is, the baritone kind of answers. And it spells out the core that the main theme is based on. So in an unusual way you are getting to learn theory of music.

After playing in my dad's military style band, which was marches and stuff, the first music I heard was jazz. And my brother, the piano player, he had an old windup victrola.[20] I think one of the first records I heard was Louis Armstrong's "West End Blues." And I was hooked on it ever since.

This is kind of a different story. I was drafted by my own request. And I think it must have happened to a lot of guys. Guys that I use to play music with, would run the streets with—they all started disappearing from 1940 to 1943. Pretty soon there was nobody to hang out with. All the guys were going. And they'd come back and talk about what units they were in, what they were doing. So I just said, "Well, hell, I'm not going to stay here." I called up the draft department. A month later they sent me a letter. Boy, that's really youth for you. That is really youth. So that's how I got in the service.

In 1943, I went to Great Lakes. I've been a musician, that's what I wanted to be in the Navy because I heard they were taking Black musicians, which they'd never done before. The Navy being of southern tradition, saying, White officers and all the Blacks did was cook. And so when I went up there I told my commanding officer I wanted to be a musician and he says, "Son, you're here to fight a war, not to play music." I took it in my own hands. I ditched the company at the risk of going AWOL, and I found out where the musicians hung out. I was at Robert Smalls Training Station.[21] It was all Black and so I went to the band shack and I said, "I want to be a musician." So they said, "Well, come in." And they went and found a horn. Two official guys came up. "Here. Can you play this?" They put some music. I played it. "Here's another one." Played that. "Can you play jazz?" I said, "Yeah." I played some jazz. He said, "Well, we could use you." He said, "You go back to your company and don't worry about it. We'll take care of your commander for you." They were making up Black bands and shipping them around the country wherever there was a Black naval base. Almost every base has their own band. That was standard in the war days, I guess for morale purposes. I was shipped out to San Diego.

In the Navy there was a military band and a dance band and a concert band out of about twenty guys. And we'd always rotate. If there was some military events going on, we would always put our uniforms on and play for that. Like guys returning from overseas or going overseas. We go down to the beach and play for them to leave. There we would play the military stuff. Then when they have something for the guys on the beach, like a dance or something, we would form the dance band and play for that. And if there was a parade or something we had to play for, we put on our military stuff and play for that.

In the Navy you could get music as your full-time assignment. I was a musician second class, second class petty officer. Just as the war was over I made first class, and next would have been chief, but I didn't stay in. I think in the army they called it special assignment, but they didn't have the insignia like we had. So we thought we were pretty damn special! That's where I met my wife,[22] and I was discharged in San Francisco in 1946.

After World War II in 1946, I came back to Minnesota. Music was always a sideline with me because I had a family[23] coming in. Every year we'd have another kid, so I had to have a day job. Trains and the packinghouses were the place where you could get a job just walking in, and people were coming from the South by the busload and trainload to get these jobs because they had heard about them. Shortly after that they started petering out because airplanes took over. It was just a natural thing to go where it was easiest to get the job at that point in time. And I tried to go to school at the same time, but that didn't work too well with raising a family.

I was a Redcap at the Union Depot during the days, that's how I paid the rent. My number was thirty-six. You had the same number on your cap for as long as you worked there. I worked as a musician at night. A Redcap was a guy that worked in the train station, and he wore a red cap so the people would know who he was. He would carry the luggage for passengers down to the train or bring it back. You'd live off your tips, which were considerable. It wasn't a big paying job, but it was job that you could do well, depending on how much effort you put into it. You worked hard, you'd get

Redcaps 1952
James Rideaux (Redcap night captain, front on right).
From the Rideaux Collection, Minnesota Historical Society

paid good, and if not, you didn't. He also parked cars under the building for travelers, and we were responsible for cleaning the public areas and office. Polishing the brass was a daily job we all hated. We had to clean the bowling alley on the second floor. Nobody liked that job.

When Black travelers came to town they were not welcome in most hotels, and they'd ask Redcaps where the Rondo neighborhood was or where they could find a room. Generally there was always somebody who had rooms for rent, so we'd tell them go see Mrs. So-and-So, she's got rooms for rent. We'd generally know where to steer them.

I did a lot of piecing work. I would be a waiter on the railroad, often in the winter when it was slow at the depot for Redcaps. I ran an elevator for a couple years at the First National Bank Building[24] and worked at the packinghouse, too. You had to support your family, and often you worked several jobs to piece enough money together. I pieced all jobs together, like a quilt, to make some time to work as a musician and to support my family.

I worked on that for, oh, about twelve years until the railroad folded up and they started laying off people. So I saw the sign posted and I said, "Well, I better get another job." I worked long enough to get a basic pension from them. That's when I got with the Saint Paul Schools. Then I worked with the schools as a janitor for twenty-seven years and I got a pension from there. I started off as a janitor and worked up to an engineer-four, which is over a period of twenty-seven years. When I retired I was head custodian at Humboldt High School[25] for the last six years. It was a good job and it helped pay the bills. I always had my nights and weekends off so I could play music, which supplemented my income pretty good.

I still play. I played with Beasley's Big Band when they made a CD. Our CD is in the big band in the Forties tradition. They cut the CD when I was ill last summer and waited for me to play the solos to mix it. I look forward to playing in the Rondo Oratorio. It's still an honor to play.

Good Age Photos by Stephanie Shaw

MELVIN WHITFIELD CARTER SR. is a musician. The only aspect of his life for which Mr. Carter has more pride than for his music is his family. He is the proud father of Teresina, Melvin Whitfield Jr., Paris, Mark, Matthew, and Larry. He has twelve grandchildren and six great-grandchildren. He was also the loving husband of Billie Carter for forty-four years. After working twelve years as a redcap porter, Mr. Carter served twenty-seven years in the Saint Paul Public Schools, retiring as head custodian at Humboldt High School. Because of his commitment to his family, he worked day jobs to pay the mortgage and then celebrated his skills and love of playing music at night.

◆ NOTES

1. Melvin W. Carter Sr. was born September 8, 1923.

2. Love Tailor Shop was located at 310-312 Rondo.

3. Father Mym Grundy Carter was born September 30, 1877, and passed November 25, 1958.

4. A 1916 fire in Paris, Texas, burned out most of the Black community's homes.

5. Saint Paul Union Depot is located at 214 East Fourth Street on the southeast side of downtown.

6. Redcap Porters worked at the Saint Paul Union Depot. The uniform included a red cap, so as to be easily identifiable by passengers. Redcaps' salaries were minimal and they supported their families mostly through tips. Responsibilities included carrying baggage for travelers, mopping floors, polishing brass, parking cars, and cleaning offices.

7. Armour Packing Plant was located on Armour Avenue, about two blocks east of Concord Avenue in South Saint Paul. The plant was open from 1919 to 1979, and covered about forty acres. Because this was one of the few industries that hired Blacks, many from Rondo took the streetcar to South Saint Paul.

8. Mother Mary Whitfield Carter was born July 7, 1886, and passed July 14, 1952.

9. The Federal Building, now known as the Landmark Center, is located at 75 West Fifth Street in downtown Saint Paul. In 1978, this building was desig-

nated a National Historic Monument and became a cultural center for music, dance, theater, exhibitions, public forums, and special events.

10. John Dillinger was a well-known bank robber in the early 1930s. Gangsters regularly spent time in Saint Paul, as the Saint Paul Police Department often ignored their presence.

11. McCarron Lake is located in Roseville, Minnesota, with public access at 1795 Rice Street. The Lake has 9,000 feet of shoreline (eighty-one surface acres) and a maximum depth of fifty-seven feet—small and deep by metro norms. The lake is surrounded by single-family homes, except for a fifteen-acre park located on the east shore that includes beachfront, recreational amenities, picnic shelter, play area, a fishing pier, and a beach building. McCarron Lake was named for a farmer who lived beside the lake, John E. McCarron. He served in the Fourth Minnesota Regiment during the Civil War.

12. Saint Paul Downtown Airport/Homan Field is located at 644 Bayfield Street. This field is southeast of downtown and is surrounded on three sides by the Mississippi River.

13. St. Peter Claver Catholic Church began as a mission in 1889, initially meeting in a rented church on Market Street in downtown. A new building was erected for the segregated Black congregation at 322 Aurora at Farrington in 1892. After the new school and convent were built, a new church building was completed at 375 Oxford at St. Anthony in 1957. The church is named for Peter Claver (1580–1654), who was canonized by Pope Leo XIII in 1888 for his work with the African Negro of Spanish America.

14. World War II was fought between the Allied powers (England, the Soviet Union, the United States) and the Axis powers (Germany, Italy, Japan) from 1939 to 1945. The United States entered the war in 1941 following the bombing of Pearl Harbor by the Japanese.

15. Frank J. Hetznecker was appointed patrolman June 18, 1917, with the Saint Paul Police Department. He went on military leave 1918–1919 to serve in World War I. He was assigned to direct the School Patrol December 22, 1922, and promoted to sergeant that same date. He was promoted to lieutenant October 1, 1926, and Superintendent of the School Patrol March 1, 1937. He retired December 1958.

16. The Minnesota State Capitol is located at 75 Dr. Martin Luther King Boulevard, formerly Constitution Avenue.

17. Harriet Island was acquired by the city in 1929 and is located at 75 Water

Street, across from downtown Saint Paul. It is named after Harriet E. Bishop, the first school teacher in Saint Paul, and is two miles from the capitol.

18. Louis "Satchmo" Armstrong (1901–1971) was a Black cornet and trumpet player, jazz singer, bandleader, and entertainer. Born in New Orleans, he began leading his own band in 1925, recording with some of the most renowned blues singers of the time. He performed all over the world as an unofficial ambassador for the United States. He won a Grammy award in 1964 for "Hello Dolly." Queens College, in the New York City borough of Queens, maintains a museum in his honor.

19. Harry James (1916–1983), a famous trumpet player, grew up playing in circus bands and played with the Benny Goodman Band early in his career. He discovered Frank Sinatra as a waiter and had him perform with his band the Music Makers in New York City. James may be best known for his 1943 version of "You Made Me Love You." He was inducted into the Big Band Jazz Hall of Fame in 1983.

20. Victrola is the trademark for a brand of phonographs.

21. Robert Smalls Naval Training Camp was named after slave Robert Smalls. On May 12, 1862, the White Confederate officers of the steamer *Planter* went on shore in Charleston, South Carolina, for a party. Smalls and other slaves quietly took the ship to the mouth of the harbor and turned it over to the Union Army. This was a considerable prize for the Union because of the number of guns on the *Planter*. Smalls went on to become a major general in the South Carolina Militia and served in the U.S. Congress from 1875 to 1886.

22. Billie Dove Harris Carter was born in 1927 and passed in 2000.

23. Mr. Carter's children are Teresina (1946), Melvin Whitfield Jr. (1948), Paris (1952), Mark (1953), Matthew (1955), and Larry (1962).

24. First National Bank was located in downtown Saint Paul between Minnesota Street, Robert Street, Fourth Street, and Fifth Street.

25. The original Humboldt High School was built in 1879, at the southwest corner of Colorado and South Robert. From 1888 to 1911, Humboldt High School was located at the southeast corner of East Delos and Livingston. In 1909 a new building was constructed at Humboldt, Elizabeth, and Livingston for Humboldt Junior and Senior High Schools. This building became the junior high in 1976 when a new senior high was built. The schools share athletic fields.

VENTRESS LAROE
JACKSON ROBERSON

Active in the community.

MY NAME IS VENTRESS JACKSON ROBERSON.[1] In 1923 my parents got married in Mississippi, and then came back to Minnesota because my father[2] was running on the road.[3]

He was a Pullman Porter[4] for the Pullman Company.[5] You know, when you are young, you don't observe all what your parents do, but I do know that my dad had to work five years before he was a Pullman Porter. And at that time, they were only getting $25 a month. So the tips meant a lot. His legal name was Dewey Jackson. But when he ran as a Pullman Porter, he had to be called George, or George Dewey. Most of his runs were between either Seattle or Portland. And then a lot of times, if someone wasn't available, they would call him and he would have to make another run. Some of the fellows, if they didn't want to, they wouldn't answer the phone or anything. He always went whenever he was called upon.

He belonged to Pilgrim Baptist Church[6] and he was in the Gospel Chorus up until the time when he got sick. He was always active with his church and with the union, the Brotherhood of Sleeping Car Porters. And even with the NAACP[7] he did what he could, and Dad had a very good sense of humor. He loved to tease and he was good at it. His nieces and nephews in Chicago just loved it. A lot of times his nephew would pick him up when he had an overnight stay in Chicago, and they would take him back for his run the next day. Dad was kind of quiet but mischievous in a way, in a loving way.

My dad had a car and he would take us all around in Minnesota. It was just fantastic. He would always take us out, Mother[8] and I, for a ride, and sometimes we would get lost but he could find a way back. And then we traveled South where his and my mother's home are, down to Coahoma, Mississippi, where they were born. Usually we would stop in Saint Louis because he had relatives there, or we would stay over in Memphis because he had a sister there and cousins. At that time, we couldn't stay in motels, hey, no way. No, no, no. Black people weren't allowed in hotels, and especially when you got South.

Once when we were south I went to the drugstore and the person was waiting on someone, and I just went over to the chair and sat down to wait. But what did I do that for? Because they said the "n" word and, "You got to get up." And I couldn't understand that at that time because being from here in Saint Paul sitting would have been acceptable. But it wasn't in the South. I didn't encounter that too much because, after all, the majority of who I was around down there were all Negro anyway.

Mother didn't work out of the home until I went into high school. She did day work, housework, for an affluent White person. She did cleaning and ironing and all of the usual things that you do in your own home. She belonged to the

Dewey Jackson

Lela Mae Braugher Jackson

Ladies Auxiliary of the Pullman Porters. She was secretary for quite a few years. She was very active in that because when they had conventions, she was one of the delegates who would always go to them. My mother was very involved in her church, of course. Even when she passed away, she was a deaconess at Pilgrim Baptist Church and belonged to the Ladies Aid there. She was in the Gospel Chorus. And also, she was active in the NAACP. And Mother belonged to the Eastern Star.[9] She belonged to the Princess Oziel Chapter. The majority in the chapter was Black. I don't know if any Whites ever joined. She loved to do needlework and all that. She had a personality that was superb because everybody loved her, and she loved to cook and she could really cook.

My parents would go fishing and catch whatever they could get—crappies, sunfish, bullheads. Oh, they loved to fish. Mother and Dad, they went fishing all the time. She would go out in the boat with him, but she wouldn't go in the boat with anybody else. They went to Centerville[10] mostly, and some of the other lakes—Buffalo, Minnesota.[11] He was a very good family man, and he loved to fish and hunt. He would go hunting for deer, rabbits, and squirrels, mostly for rabbit. I like rabbit myself—domesticated rabbit. He would hunt with some of his friends, but he stopped that. He would bring home venison, which was really nice. It is. It's good.

My parents lived in the community and were active in the community all their lives. We lived on University and then we moved to 642 Rondo and then from there, it was 731 Rondo, then to 739. We were still at 739, Rondo at Grotto, when I got married. Our house was taken because our side of the street was destroyed by the freeway. Then my parents moved to 1012 Rondo. But then they renamed the street Concordia for Concordia College. That was a done deal before anybody knew about that. A real blow to the community! And like my parents, I still remain active in the community.

—— ◆ ◆ ◆ ——

VENTRESS LAROE JACKSON ROBERSON describes herself as a low-key woman who works from her heart. She worked for Burlington Northern for nineteen years and volunteered at the Senior Federation for ten years, reading to children at elementary schools. She continues to do community work as her parents did, usually serving as an officer of the organizations she contributes to. She is or was involved with Railroad Business Women, Hallie Q. Brown Community Center, Inc., Board, Credyafawn Club, Pilgrim Usher Board, Jolly Seniors, NAACP, and continues to be the president of the Golden Agers. Ventress has also been a member of the Elks Club # 128 for well over half of her life and has served in many positions from the top down.

♦ NOTES

1. Ventress Laroe Jackson was born November 22, 1925.

2. Father was Dewey Admiral Jackson, born January 13, 1899, and passed in 1979.

3. "Running on the road" refers to serving travelers on trains as a waiter or porter.

4. Pullman porters worked for the Pullman Company and carried baggage only for Pullman sleeping car passengers. The Pullman sleeping cars were transferred between railroads and traveled all over the country.

5. The Pullman Company was founded by George Pullman right after the Civil War and provided a standard for luxurious travel. Beginning in 1867, the earliest staff were the genteel servants of the plantation South. The early Porter worked receiving passengers, carrying their luggage and making up their rooms, serving beverages and food, keeping the guests happy and making themselves available at all hours of the day or night. In Saint Paul, the Pullman Company was located at 214 Fourth Street.

6. Pilgrim Baptist Church was first organized as a prayer group before 1863 and formally organized as a church November 15, 1866. Their first house of worship was constructed in 1870 at Twelfth and Cedar Streets in Saint Paul, and it moved in 1918 to the current location at 732 West Central Avenue, Saint Paul.

7. The National Association for the Advancement of Colored People (NAACP) was founded in New York City in 1909 by a multiracial group of activists. The NAACP believes that all men and women are created equal. Attorney Fredrick McGhee of the Rondo corridor was invited by W. E. B. Du Bois to attend the second meeting of the Niagara Movement. When he returned to Saint Paul, he organized the Twin City Protection League, which become the Twin Cities Branch of the NAACP in 1912.

8. Mother was Lela Mae Braugher, born December 25, 1903, and passed in 1990.

9. Eastern Star is a Masonic fraternal organization made up of men and women in which strong spiritual values are practiced. While this is an order composed of people of deep spiritual convictions, it is open to all faiths, where relationships of sisterly and brotherly love are brought about through common vision and rituals. The purposes of the organization are Charitable, Educational, Fraternal, and Scientific.

10. Centerville is on a lake about fifteen miles north of Saint Paul.

11. Buffalo is a lake region about fifty miles northwest of Saint Paul.

GLORIA ELLEN
GILBREATH WILSON

If they needed help, I assisted.

I remember growing up on Rondo. MY NAME IS GLORIA ELLEN GILBREATH WILSON.[1] I've been here seventy-seven years. I was born here at St. Luke's Hospital.[2] We lived at 667 Rondo on the second floor.

My mother[3] worked for Donaldson Company[4] on Pelham. They made air cleaners. She was a matron there. My mother had a personality that didn't make any difference what color you were. My mother got along with everybody. She was six feet tall, weighed 320 pounds, and was a beautiful woman. She was trained as a beautician. So if a friend or somebody would come by and needed their hair done, she would do it. She was too heavy to stand on her feet doing hair all the time. When she did mine she had a stool to sit on.

My father[5] was a Redcap[6] down to Saint Paul Union Depot.[7] A Redcap Porter is an individual that works for the train station,

Parents Elbert and
Isabella Starks Gilbreath

who takes the customers' bags, picks them up, and takes them down to the train. They had a salary and received tips. He was there for forty-two years. And the day before he passed, he had a heart attack and he wouldn't leave work because he was off the next day. He never went back.

I loved to play basketball. I played basketball at Hallie Q.,[8] I played for St. Peter Claver,[9] and I had friends that played basketball from the West Side,[10] so we'd ride over there and go on the playgrounds and play with the children over there. We had friends over there. See, I played for Hallie Q. Brown and St. Peter Claver. We did just fine until we played each other. Then I couldn't play. They said I had to make up my mind which team I wanted to be on. So I took St. Peter Claver, because they had less girls. Hallie Q. Brown had a boatload. So I went to St. Peter Claver. It was a girls' team, just a girls' team. And St. Peter only had six, seven players. Of course, we won!

The depot wouldn't hire me as a matron until I was thirty-one. I worked there for sixteen years. A matron is one that cleans the restrooms, takes care of the travelers as they come through, see to their needs, help them, gives them all the assistance she can. My mother never knew what I was going to bring home, people, animals, or whatever. In the winter sometime passengers didn't have any coats or things like that. I'd call my mother and tell her to send me down a coat or a jacket or something, shoes. We had a four-bedroom home. Full attic, full basement. It was real nice. There was no problem with room. I brought one young lady home with her daughter. They got off the train and all their things had been stolen. So I took them home with me and they stayed with us until she got a job at Saint Paul Companies[11] downtown. When she got enough money, she left. Another young lady, she got stuck and we kept her, too. My mother would always say, "I never know what she's bringing home." I brought home anyone, Black or White. I have no color preference. None whatsoever. If they needed help, I assisted.

◆ ◆ ◆

GLORIA ELLEN GILBREATH WILSON is the most proud of her children, Deborah (Debbie), Dwayne, and Dale; her grandchildren, Matthew, Robert Jr., Dawn Marie, Mark, and Gloria D'Lynn; and her great-grandchildren, Jordan, Bryce, Blake, Bryce, Sydney, Lauren, Wayne, Robert, and Deshana. She worked at Honeywell for thirty-six years, for the Union Depot for sixteen years, for Office Max for thirteen years, and is now working at Cub Foods. Working with and helping people is what Mrs. Wilson finds most fulfilling. She contributes to the police fund and to the sheriffs because her daughter was a police officer for twenty-eight years, to the American Cancer Society because they need all the help they can get, to the Red Cross, Veterans of Foreign Wars, and to Catholic Charities.

♦ **NOTES**

1. Gloria Ellen Gilbreath Wilson was born August 7, 1925.

2. St. Luke's Hospital was located at 333 North Smith Street. In 1972, St. Luke's, Miller, and Children's Hospitals merged to become United Hospital at the same location.

3. Mother Isabella Starks Gilbreath was born in August 11, 1894, and passed January 5, 1981.

4. Donaldson Company, Inc., was located at 666 Pelham. They manufactured air cleaners for tractors, trucks, and automobiles.

5. Father Elbert Gilbreath was born October 18, 1889, and passed January 18, 1961. In World War I he was a corporal in Company Thirteen of the 366 Infantry, Ninety-second Division. He was the head Redcap at the Saint Paul Union Depot.

6. Redcap Porters worked at the Saint Paul Union Depot. The uniform included a red cap, so as to be easily identified by passengers. Redcaps' salaries were minimal, and they supported their families mostly through tips. Responsibilities included carrying baggage for travelers, mopping floors, polishing brass, parking cars, and cleaning offices.

7. The Saint Paul Union Depot is located at 214 East Fourth Street on the southeast side of downtown Saint Paul.

8. Hallie Q. Brown Community Center, Inc., was opened in the Union Hall at Aurora and Kent Streets in 1929 as a community center specifically to serve the Black community when the Black YWCA closed in 1928. Hallie Q., as it is affectionately known, has served all ages through child care, youth and senior clubs, athletics, music, and social events. In 1972, Hallie relocated in the Martin

Luther King Building at 270 Kent Street at Iglehart in Saint Paul. The center's namesake was an educator who pioneered the movement of Black women's clubs in the late 1800s.

9. St. Peter Claver Catholic Church began as a mission in 1889, initially meeting in a rented church on Market Street in downtown. A new building was erected for the segregated Black congregation at 322 Aurora at Farrington in 1892. After the new school and convent were built, a new church building was completed at 375 Oxford at St. Anthony in 1957. The church is named for Peter Claver (1580–1654), who was canonized by Pope Leo XIII in 1888 for his work with the African Negro of Spanish America.

10. Saint Paul's West Side is south of downtown and the Mississippi River, west of South Saint Paul, and north of West Saint Paul city limits.

11. Saint Paul Companies was incorporated in 1853 as Saint Paul Fire and Marine Insurance Company. Offices have always been located in downtown Saint Paul.

BUELAH MAE VIVIAN BAINES SWAN

They said, "We'd like to hire you, but nobody will work here if we hire you because you're black."

I AM BUELAH BAINES SWAN.[1] I was raised out near Como and Dale by my parents, in my parents' home. My father[2] came here after the start of World War I[3] as a timber cutter for the war movement from Arkansas. He had been seeing my mother[4] as young people, and he brought her here as his bride. They married here and purchased a home out at 1094 North Kent Street. There were about three other Black families in that small community at Como and Dale. My parents lived and died in that house. They always had a nice vegetable garden to the back, which my dad took care of. My mother loved flowers, and she raised flowers in the front.

I'm the oldest child. My sister, Elmercia, is a second girl and my brother, Walter Benjamin Baines

Walter and Nina Baines, and Buelah at age one, in the front yard of their home at 1094 Kent in 1928.

Pilgrim Baptist Church Sunday school class, mid-1920s

Jr., is the youngest. I was born—as my brother and sister were—at the old Ancker Hospital[5] out West Seventh Street.

I can remember when Pilgrim Baptist[6] had a little shack educational unit with a horrible toilet system next to the building there. When I was eight and ten years old, my dad and I used to go on Saturday night and start a fire in the furnace and all that, and provide coal and wood and kindling so there would be some heat in the building on Sunday during the winter when people would come. They always had a big garden, and Reverend L. W. Harris, who was a very prominent minister in the community, used to walk from his home. The minister's home used to be at 719 St. Anthony. He would walk out to my mother and dad's in order to get greens and other vegetables from their garden to take home to his family, because the church did not pay him. I can remember that very well.

During the Depression[7] I remember mostly being aware of the commodities my dad got in exchange for money. I believe it was orange and blue food stamps during the Depression, and I can remember he took all sorts of odds and ends of food in exchange for fuel or ice or whatever people needed. My mother was a very good cook, and she learned to make many things with odds and ends and make do.

Besides our own garden Dad was very good about doing the—he used to do the grocery shopping. Both my parents were farm raised. I can remember Dad buying like a hundred pounds of flour, hundred pounds of sugar. As a matter of fact, he used to bring home lard, and then Mother would render it and things like that. So I don't remember being hungry. I can remember my mother going to places like the Goodwill[8] and the Salvation Army[9] and getting other people's clothing and making it over into clothing for us, but I didn't feel deprived by the Depression. My mother had a sewing machine, and my mother was a beautiful quilter and crocheter. I have a very beautiful quilt that my mother—my mother died at seventy-nine, and at age seventy she was working on this quilt. And it's beautiful.

My father Walter Benjamin Baines Sr.'s business[10] was at 554 Rondo, and he was very well known in the community. He was between Kent and Mackubin Street. McKinley School[11] was up on a high bank behind the business. His lots ran back to the alley on Carroll. This is just off of Rondo and Kent. His business was coal, wood, ice, kindling. That was for heating and for the refrigeration at that time. Rondo was the front street where his office was. People would remember him for passing out chips of ice to the children and carrying ice up steps for iceboxes. People often didn't have money to pay for fuel, coal, wood, kindling, or fuel oil, and when my dad died, just before he died, he gave me a book listing people in the community who owed him money, and he said to me, "Daughter, perhaps they will pay you." And I said to him, "Dad, if they didn't pay you, they won't pay me."

I have a picture of him by probably a 1918 Model T Ford truck that he was very proud of. He had many trucks and eventually—I think he probably started out hauling and moving people, and then he eventually got the land and started the business there. His business was enough that he employed several people. At one time he had a woman that I became very familiar with employed as a clerk in his office. He employed my uncle and some of my cousins. His business—he was very well known in the community. His business grew well enough that he had promotional items that he gave out, like fans

Walter Baines with his Model T truck

that said W. B. Baines Sr. Coal and Wood. And then he had a baseball bat lead pencil that he would give out, so he did quite well.

Yeah, I used to work with my dad. I was very crazy about my dad. He wasn't so crazy about women or girls. I used to go with my dad out to Square Lake. It's just off of Rice Street, where they used to cut ice in great big chunks, and I helped him cut ice and load it on the truck and bring it back in town. My dad was very ambitious. At the back of his lot was a real high clay bank off of Carroll Avenue, and he and my Uncle Jett [Jettson Scott] took shovels and cut that out, cut that clay out. The clay insulated and they put straw in it and then they would put the ice in it. They would get the ice in the winter and it would last well into the summer.

He and Uncle Jett cut that out with shovels, and I would say it must have been fifty by fifty and maybe ten or twelve feet tall. Coal was sold sometimes by the sackful. It depended on how much money he had to pay. He used to go to Thorne Coal,[12] which was on the Mississippi River bank. The coal used to come up the river by barge, and he would go there and buy coal to supply his customers, and I used to go with him.

He had sheds for the different type of products. Whether it was hard coal, soft coal, kindling, he had different sheds. I would say for coal he probably had four sheds, for wood maybe a couple sheds, maybe a couple sheds for kindling. He had a little building for the office and the ice storage place. At that time the lots were very small in Saint Paul. I would say he had a minimum of two or three lots that he had his business on. The woodsheds were like twelve feet across and twenty feet deep. They were not locked like today. They were open because he always kept German shepherd dogs to watch, to keep people out of it at night. I don't remember a fence.

And then he had an icehouse where the ice that was cut up was ready for the public and he used to have little wagons. People would come and get ten and fifteen cents worth of ice and then pull it home in his wagon, and then they would bring it back when they wanted another piece of ice. Oh, let's see, I remember ten or fifteen cents of ice would be ten inches, maybe eighteen by twelve by maybe ten inches deep or something like that. If it was a good one, maybe it would keep four to five days.

He stayed within the Black community for his customers. When I was maybe like eight years old and his business was going well, I can remember one time my dad came home and ordered my mother, brother and sister, and

I into the basement and got his shotgun. He had gone into a White ice, coal, and wood dealers' community and they were after him, and he ordered us into the basement until he felt it was safe to come back upstairs. I could see that my dad was very frightened. He was afraid of being lynched or harmed or his family harmed. After that he just didn't go out of the community.

There was a Renchin Drug Store[13] on University and Dale, and I believe that Mr. Renchin owned part of Citizens Ice Company.[14] That was on Selby and Dale, and my dad used to do business with them occasionally, but when they would get in their anti-Negro moods, they would cut him out. He was a competitor of theirs. There were other companies that sometimes then would serve the Black community. He didn't have it exclusively.

When I got older my mother did day work—housekeeping, cooking, cleaning. She worked for Baron Desnick who had Desnick Drugstore,[15] and they had a home in town. I never was there. And then they built another home out in Mendota Heights[16] and she worked for them for a long, long time. She would use the streetcar to get to work. Streetcars were the transportation mode then. And then the buses came and all that. We used to have a big black lab dog—his name was Footy—at home, and he was crazy about my mother. He was my dad's dog but he was crazy about my mother. And he used to walk her up to the Como line to catch the streetcar, and then he would leave home when he thought she should come and sit up there and wait until she came home.

I went to Gorman Grade School, which the City of Saint Paul destroyed and put in housing at Front and Western. That was my elementary school. I was one of the first Black children in there. There was only one incident that I can remember with my elementary school. My mother had prepared an outfit that consisted of a sweater and a skirt with some kind of top on it, and she said, "When you go to gym"—so it must have been like the third grade— "don't take off your sweater. Tell the teachers not to take your sweater off." I didn't like my gym teacher. Her name was Miss Secord, and I told a lie. I went home and told my mother that she made me take it off and it was a lie. My mother went up to school and raised hell and found out I had lied and all of

HAPPY SCHOOL DAYS
1937

Buelah's high school graduation picture, 1945

that. I really, really regretted that. I graduated from Washington High School,[17] which is still out at 1041 Marion Street, and had a wonderful time in high school. I did very well.

In 1945, when I graduated, everybody said that I should have been valedictorian, but I guess because of my race, I didn't make it and all of that. As a matter of fact, about six, eight years ago, one of the last living teachers in our school, Washington High School, was at a class reunion, and she apologized to me because she had done wrong. They did not let me get in the National Honor Society[18] and I should have been. I didn't realize that I had been not even submitted for National Honor Society. I didn't realize that until after graduation. And they did not let me be valedictorian of our class, and I should have been. Her name was Grace Benz and she came to me at our class reunion and apologized. I can remember two teachers came—I didn't realize what they were doing. They came to me and said, "There's been some error made in your grades and we are changing the records." Of course, I was young and foolish and didn't pay any attention, but that deprived me a lot of things. I wanted to go to the University of Minnesota. I started at the U and I wanted to be an M.D., but I didn't have the financing. It hurt that they would do that, because some of my best friends are my high school classmates until this day.

Well, the last time I was at the class reunion, Gwendolyn Schlichting is her name, and her dad was a police officer in Saint Paul. She sort of acknowledged that things weren't the way they should be and she was the valedictorian. A boy, Dick Crum was his name, he was salutatorian—I used to work with him on class reunions. But they were the two. It didn't make me angry until way later in life, when I realized what had been done about that. I don't think my parents realized. I think they just accepted what was handed down.

My father preferred to keep us out of the Black community, so most of my friends in elementary school and high school were White. He didn't approve of a lot of the activities in the community, and he just thought we'd have a more wholesome life. He was rural raised and he thought—at that time, 1094 Kent was considered out in the country. We were near the end of the Dale Street streetcar line, and he just felt it would be more wholesome for us.

I was never particularly race conscious. We were in a White community. The first boy I kissed was White. We went their way when they went to church and socialized.

And otherwise, we got along. I don't think I really became conscious of the differences in race until sometimes in seeking employment. S. Vincent Owens was head of the Urban League.[19] In addition to college prep courses, I took business courses. I was capable of stenography, and he would send me to various places trying to crack the employment. That was kinda hard. He was trying to get me a job and then after I got in there, the plan was I would work for a while. He would look for a replacement for me, and I would go to another place and I'd be replaced by somebody else Black. And that's the way we'd get different employers. I was one of the young people he would place, not the only one. I had that ability and they used me like that. I can remember I went to one place on University Avenue at what used to be a big insurance company, right at the city limits. I started out there. I rode either the streetcar or bus out there. And I started there and applied for employment. They said, "We'll see ya" and all of that. And I walked to University and Raymond. There was a place there that was advertising for typists. Oh, I can't think of the man's name. I went up there and they gave me a typing test and they said, "We'd like to hire you, but nobody will work here if we hire you." And that hurt my feelings. So then I was walking and then I walked all the way down to the State Office Building and took a test there and did very well. I got hired immediately by the state, and so I worked for the State of Minnesota. I worked on the project that planned the freeways as a research analyst.

I worked for the state for a while, and then I worked in private industry. I was at the unemployment office and they had a bunch of college graduates there, so it would be June, telling them about different jobs that were available. I was sitting there, waiting to take a test or something, and I listened to what they were telling them. And they told about a statistical job at Simon and Mogilner.[20] They were children's clothing manufacturer. So I just got up from my seat and hightailed it down to Simon and Mogilner ahead of all the college graduates. Told them what I'd heard and that I wanted to be hired.

And they hired me. I worked there—I have an analytical mind. I worked there and I used to take all the salesmen's orders, tabulate what needed to be manufactured and what delivery date. And I worked out a system whereby we could schedule incoming orders, delivery date, what material needed to be ordered, what accessories need to be ordered, how many people you needed to work on it. I got my salary doubled. I've had my salary doubled twice in my life. Yeah, because it was a good plan and they used it until they moved to Birmingham, Alabama. They moved south when costs got to be kind of high here. They were the second-largest children's clothing manufacturer in the United States. This would have been 1955.

I got a little money together. I learned to keypunch. I was a good typist, learned to keypunch. I went to Control Data Institute.[21] I had $600, and I went there to learn how to be a programmer. When my money ran out, they kicked me out. The institute was over on France Avenue and at that time I drove. When my money ran out, they said you can't be in class anymore. I had gone over there during the day to go to a class, and they said you are absolutely out, turn in the books and all like that. So I just drove up France Avenue and Control Data had a big plant at 4201 Lexington. Drove up there and applied for a job, and I said I just spent six hundred bucks at your institute, and they kicked me out and I want a job. I got a job, and I got my salary doubled there too.

I had a boss—he started me out as a Weekend Warrior and I was supposed to do very minor tasks, and he soon discovered that I knew more than minor things. I'll tell you something funny. I was working one weekend and I used to have the guard lock me in. They had a big glassed-in lab—lock me in there. And we had I think it was four computers, and I don't know how many printers and other computers. I was in there doing work. I had taken off my blouse, I think I was in my bra and one of them fluffy petticoats and stockings, and I had all the computers going and the printers going and I was running around. I liked the challenge. I was running around, my boss came in and said, "What on earth is going on?" And I said, "I'm getting your work out." And I said, "Don't bother me now, I'll be right back." And when he saw the amount of work I did, that's when I got my salary doubled.

I was working at the post office.[22] Oh, I made a foreman in the post office. First Black woman foreman. I had a career there twenty-six years, and I had fifteen years where I clerked, I carried, I worked in the stations.

I did all that. And I had eleven years as a foreman. I retired at sixty. I often would have three jobs—one full-time job and two part-time jobs.

After I was divorced from my husband, I bought a home in the Black community. I bought a home that was one block from Maxfield School,[23] one block from the church because I wanted my children not raised out in Saint Paul Park.[24] That's different from my father, but since I would be raising the two children[25] by myself, I felt that it would be much better in the Black community. I'm very satisfied, but they're not part of the community either. There must be some intangible difference. They have friends and all that. Well, like my son says, "I'm Buelah's boy. I'm not a Baines, I'm not a Swan. I'm Buelah's boy." And that makes a difference.

◆ ◆ ◆

BUELAH MAE VIVIAN BAINES SWAN is the loving mother of Virgie Mae Swan and Everett Nathaniel Swan. She worked for the post office for twenty-six years and became the first Black woman supervisor, retiring in 1987. Always working several jobs at a time while raising her children, she was well respected for her outstanding skills, often recognized for her speed in her data. Early in her life she played piano for Pilgrim Baptist Church. In November 2004, Mrs. Swan was inducted into the National Honor Society through Saint Paul Public Schools.

◆ NOTES

1. Buelah May Vivian Baines Swan was born September 13, 1927.

2. Father Walter Benjamin Baines Sr. was born May 14, 1893, and passed February 1978.

3. World War I was fought primarily in Europe against Germany and Austria-Hungary, 1914–1918. The United States entered the war in April 1917.

4. Mother Nina Aris Estelle Brown Baines was born August 2, 1898, and passed July 27, 1977.

5. Ancker Hospital opened in 1872 as the City and County Hospital. In 1923, it was renamed in honor of its late superintendent, Arthur B. Ancker. Over the years it encompassed twelve buildings over several acres with a mailing

address at 495 Jefferson. In 1965, it moved to 640 Jackson Street and was renamed Saint Paul Ramsey Hospital, then renamed again in 1977 as Saint Paul–Ramsey Medical Center. Since 1997, it has been called Regions Hospital.

6. Pilgrim Baptist Church was first organized as a prayer group before 1863 and formally organized as a church November 15, 1866. Their first house of worship was constructed in 1870 at Twelfth and Cedar Streets in Saint Paul. They moved in 1918 to the current location at 732 West Central Avenue, Saint Paul.

7. The Great Depression in the United States was a period of economic instability. It began in late 1929 with the stock market crash and ended in 1941 with America's entry into World War II.

8. Goodwill Industries had locations at 596 Cedar, 150 East Thirteenth, and 848 Payne Avenue.

9. The Salvation Army has locations at 49 West Tenth, 51 West Kellogg, 1471 Como, and 1019 Payne Avenue.

10. W. B. Baines Sr. Coal and Wood was located at 554 Rondo between Kent and Mackubin.

11. McKinley School was located at 481 Carroll Avenue, between Mackubin, Arundel, and Rondo from 1903 to 1966. Fire destroyed the building in 1966.

12. Thorne Coal had a location on the Mississippi River and at 1429 Marshall Avenue, Saint Paul.

13. Renchin Drug was located at 621 University Avenue at Dale Street, Saint Paul.

14. Citizens Ice Company was located at 600 Selby Avenue, Saint Paul.

15. Desnick Drug was located at 1098 University, Saint Paul. This store was opened in 1942 as the Lexington Drug Company, became Desnick Drug in 1955–1956, and closed in 1995.

16. Mendota Heights is a Saint Paul suburb south two miles south of the city.

17. Washington High School became a junior high in 1976, and is located at Cook, Lawson, and Galtier.

18. The National Honor Society began in 1921 as the nation's premier organization to recognize outstanding high school students for extraordinary leadership, service, character, and scholarship.

19. The Urban League has served the Black community since 1923 as a human service advocacy organization. The Urban League address issues of quality employment, housing, education, and health care. Initially, it was located in vari-

ous buildings downtown. In 1967, it moved into its own building at 401 Selby Avenue, four blocks south of the Rondo Corridor.

20. Simon & Mogilner was located on the sixth floor of the Lindeke Building, 332 Rosabel (renamed Wall Street), Saint Paul. It is currently located in Birmingham, Alabama.

21. Control Data Institute is a computer company and educational institute.

22. The Saint Paul Post Office Building is located at 141 Fourth Street East in downtown.

23. Maxfield School was originally at 363 St. Albans at St. Anthony, and was built in 1890. In 1955 a new school was built at 680 St. Anthony at Victoria, Avon, and Central.

24. Saint Paul Park is a suburb located twelve miles southeast of Saint Paul.

25. The children are Virgie Mae Swan and Everett Nathaniel Swan.

GLORIA JEANNE
LINDSTROM LEWIS

We had no problem on Rondo whatsoever.

MY FULL NAME IS GLORIA JEANNE LEWIS.[1] I grew up, actually, two places: in the Como Park[2] neighborhood and then from Como Park we moved over to Marshall Avenue. I met my husband[3] at the Catholic Youth Center, at a dance. I was seventeen. At that time it was not a very good time to be dating Black and White. I mean that was actually a no-no. And I'll tell you, we had some experiences, please believe me.

People did not accept Black and White, including my family. My family was not happy at the time that I married my husband. But after my family realized that I had a good husband, they accepted him. But it was a shock for them, naturally, because that was not the regular line to go. And, of course, my father was Irish. His birth name was Malone before. Why we have the name Lindstrom was because he was adopted into a Lindstrom family. But he was Irish, and he couldn't see why I couldn't find an Irish man. But everything turned out fine. The public did not really accept it like they do today.

We were in a theater one time, at the Faust Theater,[4] and a police officer came down to where we were watching the movie. A White policewoman came down and she said, "I would like to see you." I said, "Yes," and she had me go to the back of the theatre. And she said, "Do you always go, with a"—at that time, they were *Negroes,* you know. I mean, she didn't call him the other name—she said, "Do you always go with Negroes?" And I said, "I haven't always gone with a Negro, no." I said, "In school I didn't, but," I said, "now I do." And I said, "I've only gone with one, and that's the gentleman that I'm sitting in the theater with." I said "And why are you asking me this?" And she said, "Well, we just want to know." Oh, and then she had the nerve to ask me did I work on the street? And I said, "I beg your pardon." I said, "No, I don't." And I said, "And I don't appreciate you asking me this, I'm a lady." And so that was that. And I said, "And furthermore, I'm through talking to you." And I went back and sat back down and watched the movie.

But there was another police officer, Skally,[5] that knew who we were, and he told her, he said, "This lady is very nice. You should not bother her. You do not have to worry about this couple. This couple is very nice." And that was it.

And then, of course, you had the people that when you would go down the street they would gawk at you and look at you and have smart-aleck things to say, you know. But we never paid attention to that. We never did.

So when I would bring Dee Dee,[6] for instance, when I had her down for her first Holy Communion dress at Rothschild's[7]— because that's where they had the long dresses for Cathedral.[8] And the woman says, "What nationality is she?" I mean that kind of thing. You expected it because it was something that they didn't have every day, they didn't see every day.

Gloria with husband, Sonny, at a social event

Dee Dee in First Communion dress on the steps of Saint Paul Cathedral

We got married in 1946. I had five children. My children were born in '46, '47,[9] '48,[10] and '49[11] and '52.[12] Our family history was mixed. My husband was mixed Black and White. And his father[13] was Black, but his mother was a mix of Black and White parents. And all my children are all very, very fair. And my grandchildren.

When we first got married we lived at 222 Rondo, with my mother-in-law, Cecelia Lewis, and then we moved across the street to 235 Rondo. That was at Louis and Rondo. There was a whole complex. There was one apartment on one side, and then across there was another apartment on the other side. I think there were about four sections like that where they had two apartments on each area. Downstairs were business. Across the street from that was a tire place, and then across the other street was a grocery store,[14] and then across from it was another little grocery store.[15] But there were three corners that we had businesses on. It was a great big long complex. We had two bedrooms. We had a living room, no good-sized living room. We had a dining room. We had a kitchen and a bath. And we had three children.

I would take my children and I would give them their baths, and then we would sit out on the porch. We had a little porch with steps. We could sit out there and nobody would ever bother us. It was very peaceful. We didn't have to lock our doors. I still say, why they called it Lower Rondo I don't know, because it wasn't rough. We had an Indian woman that lived on one side of my mother-in-law, and then we had a mixed family, the Jackson family, who lived on the other side. They were both very lovely people.

Then down further there were White people. She worked for the priest at Cathedral, and then the other one just was a housewife. And then on the corner was a shoemaker who was White. There was a little tailor shop below, actually, right across from my mother-in-law's, which, again,

In front of 222 Rondo: brother and sister-in-law Andrew and Ruthie Hartshorn, Mother-in-law, Cecelia Lewis, and nieces Theresia, Jowanna, Estelle Hartshorn, with streetcar in background, c. 1945–1946

Sonny Lewis with the Silver Top Cab

was 222 Rondo. Her name was Mamie Jackson, and his name was Bunk Perkins. He had this tailor shop[16] and then he got a cab company.[17] And then he talked my husband into driving for his cab, and so my husband drove for his cab. And I don't think that cab turned out too well. So then there was another cab company and it was called Silver Top Cab,[18] and then my husband worked for that gentleman. He was Black also. It served the whole community. They would go all over.

Both of these companies only had one cab. If the owner wasn't working, then my husband might be working. They served the Black community, but they also had a lot of White people that they would take too, so it was a mixture really. He would even go out of town and take somebody someplace. A lot of people from Jim Williams[19] would call him. A lot of people from Walker's Tavern.[20]

The streetcar would be going up and down. It was like, every half hour, every forty-five minutes, something like that. It wasn't real bad service. And you could stand out on the corner, nobody bothered you. You didn't have to worry like you do nowadays.

When I got married and moved to Rondo people were very kind. The families associated with us. We had no problem on Rondo whatsoever. It was after we moved out that all the problems came. On Rondo everybody practically knew everybody. Everybody spoke to everybody, and we weren't really uncomfortable there. Everybody accepted me. I never had a problem.

But people said things that hurt my children when they were young. Very much so! Destroyed my children, really. Not on Rondo. We had no problem on Rondo. It was when Rondo was taken away from us, that's when everything started hurting.

We moved up on Aurora and my mother-in-law bought a duplex at 710 and 712 Aurora. She lived upstairs and we lived downstairs. And we lived next to a police officer, an ex-police officer on one side. They were Polish. And on the other side was some kind of Scandinavian, Olson. And the one on the one side I had to end up taking to court because he just was so terrible. He would call my kids *niggers*. Tell them we need to go back down South where they hang us, and all that kind of carrying on. We had a dog that was called Beauty, that was black, and he'd take a pitchfork after him.

And then, when I finally took him to court, that's when my little girl was toddling. She was maybe just barely walking. And she had walked on his grass. And he took the hose and washed her down with the hose, and I was so angry. I said, "Now this is a little tiny child, just barely toddling, and because she stepped on your grass . . ." He put the hose on her. So then on top of that, the kids would play music when they were in the bathroom, and he would holler, because of course in the summertime we didn't have air conditioning, and they would have the windows open. And he would say, "Will you niggers turn that radio off?" and that kind of stuff.

In front of 710–712 Aurora: Sonny and Gloria with Debbie, Bobbie, Dennis, Dee Dee, Darrell, and cousins, 1961

Then they would go out in the alleyway and they would be playing ball. At that time the other neighbors, on the next street over, they were all playing with my children. They were all White, and they practically lived at my house. I mean, because we always said we would rather have our children at our home, where we knew where they were, and so we had the whole bunch down our basement. And they were fine. But when they would go into the alley, this police officer, ex-police officer, would holler and call them niggers, and "get them out of here," and talk to the other people and say, "What are you playing with them for?" This was in about 1953.

They told him that if they had anymore reports about that, that they were going to lock him up. They never did, but they told him that. And after that, I mean he just constantly—here's a street that he does not own, okay? But if we had our car parked just this far [holds hands up about a foot apart] into the front of his house, he would put the hose on it, he would call us all kinds of names, he'd tell us to move our car, that we were on his property. That was not his property, that was the public street. He would do that even if we had friends come and they would park their car, maybe only a foot into the front part of their place and he would get out there and call us all kinds of names, you know. So we lived with that for a long time. A long time. And it was very painful. And it was very harmful to the children. Very, very harmful to the children. We didn't have those painful experiences on Rondo.

I took my children to Hallie Q. Brown.[21] And Dee Dee was Queen of Hallie Q. Brown one year. I still have the picture where the Snow Queen of the Winter Carnival[22] crowned her. She must have been about thirteen or something like that, fourteen.

After a while my husband was working at some upholstery shop. Mr. Garelick had heard about my husband doing very good upholstery work. We were living at the projects at that time. And he came to that place where he was working, and he asked would

he consider working for them? So my husband came home and he asked me, he says, "Honey, I got an offer to go to work for Garelick Manufacturing Company."[23] And I said, "Well, what do they make?" And he said, "Boat seats." And I said, "I don't think that would be a very steady job." Which I was wrong. So I said, "I think you better hang on to your job that you're on, okay?" So he said he would. So then, he went to the Garelicks and he told the Garelicks. So then they said, "Well, would you consider working at home for us?" So then we talked it over and he told them, yes, he would do that. But he had to work at his regular job, too. So he did that. He carried the boards—my kids carried them down the basement, helped him unload them from his car. And we did that for quite awhile. And then we realized that this was a real big company. That they were shipping all over the world. And so I thought well, you know, this is a stable place, so we stopped doing the work down in the basement and then he was hired as a supervisor of the upholstery shop. He worked for Garelick Manufacturing Company for eighteen years as an upholsterer supervisor in Saint Paul Park. Then he decided he wanted to go into his own business, so that's why he left there.

I helped in the business, and we did very good work, but still experienced some racism. For instance, in about 1976 I went to West Saint Paul. I would do the estimate and I would get the job. My sons worked with us, they would pick up the furniture, and when they saw these Black people . . . This one woman, she told my husband, she said, "My husband is an attorney." As she's letting them take the furniture out. It isn't that she's not letting them take the furniture out. She's letting them know that "my husband's an attorney, and I hope that you don't tear up my furniture." I mean, that's what she was thinking. And so when my husband came back and he told me this and I called her up. And I told her, I said, "What made you insult my husband?" I said, "That was my husband you insulted." And she says, "Well, I just wanted to make sure that my furniture was going to be done right." And I said, "I beg your pardon, lady." I said, "But you know, even if he's Black, the work isn't going to change. And he is a very good upholsterer. In fact, he's one of the best." So it ended up that that particular woman gave us so much business. Everybody that she knew she sent to us.

We were the only Black business that they had and, of course, I was bidding against these White people businesses and I did a lot of business. Lots. I got a lot of business. I upholstered the state highway department, I upholstered the judge's chambers, I upholstered colleges, even St. Peter[24] Hospital. And of course, I got the bid because I knew how to bid right.

We had Lewis and Son Upholstery.[25] And then it was called Lewis and Son Interiors afterwards. For over twenty-five years we were in the upholstery business. It was a good business.

Lewis and Son Upholsterers, 502 University Avenue

◆ ◆ ◆

GLORIA JEANNE LINDSTROM LEWIS, married to Robert "Sonny" Lewis Sr. for forty-four years, has deep pride in her family and their family-owned and -operated upholstery business. She did all of the estimates, bids, and bookkeeping. All of her children went to St. Peter Claver School, and she continues to be involved with the church and community center. When she and Sonny married, they lived with her in-laws, Cecelia and Harold Lewis, from whom she and her children learned what family and community mean. Sonny's nieces and nephews also lived with them, so Estelle, Jowanna, and Theresia were like siblings to their children: Dee Dee Ray, Robert Jr., Dennis, Darrell, and Deborah. She always tells them, "Wherever there's a will, there's a way!" Mrs. Lewis also loves her eleven grandchildren, ten great-grandchildren, and Brandy, her Yorkie.

1. Gloria Jeanne Lindstrom Lewis was born September 18, 1927.

2. Como Park is located around Lake Como and between Lexington Avenue, Hoyt, and Como Avenue. It was initially planned in 1872. In 1873, $100,000 was donated to purchase land for a park, and the city acquired 300 acres around Lake Como. In 1848, Lake Como was named by Charles Perry, who farmed a tract of land on the shore of the lake. Today there is a pathway 1.67 miles long surrounding the lake. The park includes picnic shelters, tennis courts, ball fields, swimming pools, fishing, paddleboats, a conservatory and gardens, zoo, amusement rides, a golf course, and a historic streetcar station.

3. Husband Robert "Sonny" Lewis Sr. was born June 2, 1924, and passed June 12, 1990. He was, among other things, a Knight of Columbus at St. Peter Claver Catholic Church.

4. The Faust Theater, built in 1911 as a family movie theater, was located at 626 West University Avenue near Dale Street.. The theater closed in the late 1960s when the building became an evangelical church. In 1970 it reopened as a sex-oriented movie theater until the city purchased it and closed in March 1989. The building was razed in 1995.

5. Bill Skally served as a Saint Paul Police patrolman from 1941 to 1973. During his assignment as a beat officer on Rondo he had a reputation of taking youth to their parents before arresting them. He was well respected for his knowledge of the community and its members.

6. DeVelma Jeanne, known as Dee Dee.

7. Maurice L. Rothschild and Company was located at Seventh and Robert Street. It began business in 1938 and by 1960 was acquired by Young Quinlin, another department store.

8. The fourth Cathedral of Saint Paul is located at Selby and Summit Avenues and was finished in 1917.

9. Robert Winston Jr., known as Bobbie.

10. Dennis Anthony.

11. Darrell Craig.

12. Deborah Marcella.

13. Mr. Lewis's father was Harold W. Lewis.

14. Julius Fooksman Grocery Store was located at 243 Rondo.

15. Sam Kanun owned a groceries and meat store at 241 Rondo Ave.

16. J. Bolch Perkins's Your Tailor Shop was located at 225 Rondo.

17. Radio Cab, also referenced as "Bunk's Rondo Cab Company."

18. Silver Top Cab was owned by David J. Payne and Lee Miller. Silver Top operated out of a garage at 463 Fairview Avenue. Their motto was "Fully Insured, Prompt, Safe, Courteous Drivers."

19. Jim Williams's was at 560 St. Anthony. Jim Williams's was notable for being the first Black restaurant in Minnesota to have a legal liquor license.

20. Walker's Keystone Bar and Hotel was at 379 Carroll.

21. Hallie Q. Brown Community Center, Inc., was opened in the Union Hall at Aurora and Kent Streets in 1929 as a community center specifically to serve the Black community when the Black YWCA closed in 1928. Hallie Q., as it is affectionately known, has served all ages through child care, youth and senior clubs, athletics, music, and social events. In 1972, Hallie relocated in the Martin Luther King Building at 270 Kent Street at Iglehart in Saint Paul. The center's namesake was an educator who pioneered the movement of Black women's clubs in the late 1800s.

22. The Queen of the Snows of the Winter Carnival is chosen each year from young women in the community at a pageant. In the mythology that surrounds the carnival, Queen Auroras is the wife of King Boreas.

23. Garelick Manufacturing Company is located at 644 Second Street in Saint Paul Park. Garelick is still in existence and manufactures boat seats, as well as other marine products.

24. Saint Peter is seventy-five miles southwest of Saint Paul.

25. Lewis and Son Upholstery opened on Selby Avenue in 1968 and moved to 502 West University. They closed after Sonny Lewis's death in 1990.

DON GOUGH WILSON

I've been treated better there than I was in Saint Paul, on Rondo.

MY NAME IS DON WILSON.[1] I'm seventy-four years old. I was orphaned. I had a sister, Fontella, she was two years older than I was. We were in the Owatonna State Public School when I became conscious of anything. I was moved to 575 West Central. It was my first foster home. Her name was Mrs. Archer. Mamie Archer to be exact. In fact, it wasn't my first foster home as I look back. It was my second. But the first one was—well, I couldn't have been over two years old. It was Mrs. Melcher at 419 St. Anthony. I remember that vaguely in my mind. I started school with Mrs. Archer at McKinley Grade School.[2] And I remember being in the first grade. Mrs. Dunn was my teacher.

And then I was moved to 403 Carroll with the Jameses, Roscoe James and Dorothy James. And I went to McKinley School from there, of course. I stayed there until I was—I must have left Mrs. Archer's about six-and-a-half, and I stayed with Mrs. James until I was about ten. 403 Carroll was as far east as I lived. That was between Western and Arundel in Cornmeal Valley.[3]

I remember the first fight I ever had. I was very young and I couldn't understand it. I moved to 403 Carroll, and I was in the first grade. And there was a girl in the classroom, her name was Eva Scroggins, and she smelled like urine. She sat right next to me. We had these rows of desks that

Don's sixth-grade class at Maxfield School in 1941. Don remembers almost all of his classmates' names. Front row: ____, Earl Dngue, Don Wilson, Harvey Erlich, ____, Richard Sayles. Second row: ____, Verlene Price, Rosemary Jones, Evelyn Lewis, Gloria Parker, Gladys Hobbs, Betty Lewis, Rita Shaver. Third row: Betty Bobo, ____, Marlene _____, Georgia Russell, Margaret Brown, Mary Collins, Sarah Hill. Back row: Billy Archer, Jerry Slavn, Raymond Danges, Harry Estes, Billy Goins, ____, Nelson McCoy

were tied together, I guess. I don't know how to describe it. And she was just right there. And I said to her, "You smell like urine." And boy, she whipped me so much after school. I mean, she beat me up good, and I had never had a fight before. I didn't even know what it was. Well, I'll never forget that. I went home crying. That stood out!

When I was still at Mrs. James's I had a sled, a brand-new sled I had gotten from the orphans' Christmas party, which was always held every Christmas at Brown and Bigelow[4] for all orphans. You got three gifts and all you could eat. And I got a new sled. So I'm sliding down the hill from Carroll to Rondo, behind my house—403 Carroll—on my new sled. And two or three guys were at the bottom of the hill. One of them was named Gentress O'Neill. He took my sled and I didn't understand that. "You can't take my sled!" So I tried to get my sled back. Next thing you know, we're fighting. And he's got one of these big welfare coats on. We called them welfare coats. And all he did was bundle up in this coat, and I kept beating on this coat until I got tired. And he's holding my sled and he's laughing. When I get tired, then he turns and beats me up and walks off with my sled. Those are the experiences I remember!

Then I was moved to Mrs. Josephine Todd on St. Anthony, 491 St. Anthony. She bought a house after that up at 659 Rondo. I stayed with Mrs. Todd until I was fifteen or sixteen. I don't remember exactly. I was in the tenth grade. She was a huge impact on me, and taught me how to take care of myself, and manners. She was very strict, but very loving, and a tremendous cook. Those were some of my best years. But Mr. Todd died. He was a packinghouse worker[5] and he died.

One of my best friends was Ted McDay. He lived on Central, near Grotto, right across from Pilgrim Baptist Church.[6] But I'm not sure Ted was really a member of the community in that sense. Him and I were close, because his parents were alcoholics and never home. At that time, Mrs. Todd was gone and Ted and I were buddies and kind of hung out together. People would call me a name and he'd fight them quicker than I would. He was Irish. Very tough kid. I liked him. But other than that, I can't think of any White kids in the neighborhood.

I went to Maxfield Grade School.[7] I went to high school from Mrs. Todd's place. She was a housekeeper, a domestic I guess they call them these days. She worked for a lady, Mrs. Tans, who lived on Summit, somewhere up there. And anyway, Mrs. Tans offered her an opportunity to go to Florida with her, and Mr. Todd had died and she decided to take that opportunity. I really don't remember how I ate, how my clothing was taken care of. I started skipping school. I think I missed seventy-three days of school my freshman year.

I remember getting a little bit lost then. I was moved to Mrs. Mamie Graves. That was her name. His name was Mr. E. P. Graves, Earnest Preston Graves, and they were elderly people relative to Mrs. Todd and they lived at 756 Iglehart. I lived there with a foster brother by the name of Ronald Wagner, and went to high school, John Marshall High School.[8]

Before I got married I was in eleven different foster homes. I think I gave you four of them. It got so bad there at Mrs. Todd's, they moved me to Minneapolis. I ran away from there. I used to go get the mail and never come back. And finally they said, "Well, he's not going to do well in Minneapolis." So they moved me back to Saint Paul.

I don't remember a home I was in where they didn't ask me repeatedly to call them Mom and Dad, and I never did. I couldn't. I would be out playing with my foster brother or whatever. I would be on the playground. I would be anywhere and the social worker would come by and say, "Pack your box." You know, you're gone! Just like that. No warning, just bingo, you're gone! That happened more often than not. So it was very difficult. Very difficult.

Then they came and moved me after my freshman year in high school. I think maybe I was waking up then to my real situation, my condition. My sister had become a prostitute. They had separated us. When they moved me from Mrs. Archer's, they moved her to Mrs. Siesmore's on St. Anthony and moved me to 403 Carroll. I'll never forget that as long as I live. I can't hardly handle that now. They separated us, and it was difficult. I was left to imagine that they couldn't find a home for both of us. I don't think people wanted a boy and a girl. They just wanted one or the other. And then there were some people who didn't want dark-skinned Black people. Fontella was lighter than I was.

I was sixty-two years old and I find out that she was my half sister. But I always considered her my whole sister. How did I find out? Well, I got the records at my wife's[9] insistence. I had never done that. But I'm getting ahead of myself there, and I don't want to confuse you.

Fontella left. We were separated, rather, and she kind of went to pieces. But I think she was kind of unsettled about the whole situation more than I was anyway. She started chasing around, becoming anything but a decent person. I don't know if I'm using the right words. She was confused and she got lost. She got into the wrong crowd and bingo, that was it.

About age eleven until age eighteen, she spent the majority of that time in Sauk Centre.[10] And if she wasn't in Sauk Centre, she was living with some older man, and he was putting her on the block or whatever you call it. Of course, I tried to talk to her. I didn't know anything. I'm just the younger brother, right? But it hurt, yeah.

She's all I had, and it was out of control. I couldn't do anything. It was terrible. Very, very sad. Always in turmoil I was. You know, she even forced me to do some things. We used to steal doughnuts when we'd go get doughnuts from the ladies who made the doughnuts, and we'd steal money out of the collection plate at church. She finally overdosed at age forty-five, and that was the end of that.

I was not doing good things. I was fighting in school, for example. I started boxing, too, by that way. I was very talented athletically, and boxing was probably my gift. But I hated it! I didn't dislike it, I hated it. I did it because Mr. Brown, my trainer, told me I was ten feet tall. Nobody else did. So I boxed for eleven years. I had 111 amateur and professional fights. I lost nine. But I hated the sport.

Mr. Horace Brown. There was just nothing about boxing, fundamentally speaking, that I didn't know and I could execute. He saw to that. He was strict. I went to the Golden Gloves and I won and went from there. I just kept doing it. Again, I really disliked the sport. I didn't tell anybody that, but I disliked the sport.

I started when I was twelve. They put my age up to fifteen to get in the Golden Gloves. I was fighting guys eighteen years old and I was twelve. I was kicking butt! I retired at twenty-three, I think it was. Yeah. I fought at 127 and 135 weight. Most of the time 132. I was in between lightweight and a featherweight.

Out of the nine fights that I lost, six of them there's no question I could have beat the guys. I just didn't feel like it. And they used to ask me, "What happened? You've got no guts?" And I said, "No, guess I don't." I just didn't feel like it. I kept it to myself. But I could have whipped those guys. The other three, I don't care if I ever see them again! They were just too much for me, that's all there was to it. I mean, they really were too much!

I met my wife, Bobbie, in the seventh grade. She told me I was ten feet tall. She couldn't get rid of me after that! We were married for fifty-five years. I was eighteen and she was fifteen. She was pregnant, of course. She told me one day on the way to Sunday school, and I said, "Fine! Let's get married." So we got married in September, with her parents' permission. I was eighteen then and I was free from the state, so I got a job. The evening we got married, we went to watch the fights after the ceremony.

We were married on September 26, 1947. Reverend Skelton, who was a reverend at that time at St. James AME Church[11] on Central and Dale, married us. We lived in a one-room, share the kitchen place at 491 St. Anthony. His

Don about eighteen years of age

name was Jim Burke and her name was Esther Burke, and they were friends of Bobbie's mother's. They had three or four kids, and it was not a nice place, but it was a place. So we rented a room there for $7 a week, and Bobbie had use of the kitchen. I quit high school in the eleventh grade, to get married. I worked at Western Electric,[12] wiring switchboard connections, in those days for telephones. And then I got in a fight down there and they fired me. Then I was unemployed for a while. Then I mopped floors for a while, for twelve bucks a week. I got so sick of that. Then I got a job at Hayden Ford Company[13] polishing cars, and I worked there for about a year-and-a-half, and I made $125 a week. That was a lot of money in those days. Then I came to Honeywell[14] and moved to Minneapolis in 1958.

A thing I remember is 1953 we went to California. We drove out there. Bobbie's sister had moved out there after she graduated. She was younger than Bobbie. Took us four days and three nights before the days of the freeway. It was tough, tough driving. And you can't stay any place. This is why I'm bringing it up. You're Black. You can't stay in any place, and you can't eat in any place. I remember stopping at a restaurant in Nebraska and asking them if my family and I could eat there. They said, this is a quote, "No, you cannot. Your dog can, but you can't." And so we went from there to a drive-in. I had my wife's little brother, my son, and my wife and I. And we got a malted milk at a drive-in, and they gave it to us in Mason jars. Well, we were so hungry I didn't notice. So we ate, and I'm the only one who got sick. I got terribly sick, threw up green stuff. I had ptomaine poison.

Anyway, make a long story short, we couldn't eat anyplace. We ate at these fruit stands, people selling fruit on the road. And that's all we ate. We're finally in Las Vegas. We ran into a guy in the gas station where they wouldn't let me go to the bathroom, and we found out that there was a place in Las Vegas that would let you stay there. Owned by a Black woman. So they gave us the address and we were going through Las Vegas. Oh, it was hot. We had no air-conditioning in the car in those days. And we were just angry with each other and we were tired and it was terrible.

So we went down the strip in Las Vegas, and we saw this guy walking down the road. He was Black. I stopped the car. I said, "Where can I find so-and-so and so-and-so." And he says, "Well," as he leans into the car he says, "you go down here about two blocks. You make a right-hand turn, you go underneath the Iron Curtain. And then you do this and you do

Wife, Bobbie, at nineteen

that and you'll find it. It's a big white and green house." Iron Curtain? I go down and turn and sure as heck, there's an overpass over this road as it goes down, and on it is written The Iron Curtain. On the other side of this strip, which is gaudy, of course, there's dirt roads. There's tin shacks. There's pigeon coops. There's chickens. There's clotheslines hanging from house to house. It's the desert. Tin shacks, and then there's this big green and white house. So we went there and we took a shower. She was a Black woman. Big house. Then she wanted to charge us an outlandish number to stay there, and I said no thanks and left, and we just drove on. By the way, we ate there, too. We had okra. Okra, only it was not fried. I forget how it was fixed, but it was slimy. I don't know, boiled it or something. We couldn't eat it. It was terrible. Okra and cold liver and cold gravy and rice. I got to California, I weighed 119 pounds. When I left, I weighed about 135.

From all this I learned to wear the mask. There were definitely scars. But the foster homes were all good homes. I lived better than a lot of my friends did who had parents. The houses were clean. Insecurity was a scar that I received. Not knowing who I was. I mean my parents—nobody ever told us anything, and we had no opportunity to contact our mother. We didn't know anything, so we just assumed that she didn't care about us. That was a scar. So we kind of tried to forget about that. I did. I'm sorry. Fontella didn't, I did. And so I went on with that mind-set until I was sixty-two years old. My wife asked me at sixty-two years old. She kept after me. Bobbie was a very gentle, loving person. She was a Libra: scales, balance, you know. She asked me to get my records and stuff, and I said, "Nah, nah, nah." Because I felt nobody—they didn't care. What the hell did I want that for? I guess I didn't want the pain of it either.

But finally, I don't know why, I finally consented and I did call. Ramsey County welfare. And lo and behold, they said, "Sure, Donald. We've got all your records. Yours and Fontella's." Well, Fontella was dead then, but I said, "Send me hers, too." I think it cost me fifteen cents a copy. I must have got 300 pages, because the social worker would come out and visit us once a month, wherever we were, and she'd have to write a report on how we were doing. I got every bit of that. I also got information about my mother and how we became orphans.

She left us with a Mrs. Battle, who I don't know anything about. I was two. Fontella was four. She went to Omaha and asked Mrs. Battle to watch us and she'd be back within a week. I guess she had done this before and she was back. Well, anyway, this time Mrs. Battle turned us over to the state. She betrayed my mother. And I don't know what else, but the records said she turned us over to the state and said that no one would take care of us, and that she wasn't going to do it. Anyway, that's what started it all, and I guess my mother contested it and they ruled against her because she was a prostitute. She was described in the records as being "tall and good looking for a Negress." That's a quote. And then she was also described as being very, very vulgar by the people that she stayed with when she was a foster child. She lived with a Reverend and Mrs. Webb, and her name was Ruby Webb.

That hit me like a ton of bricks, because I had to get an affidavit when I got my first job, from Omaha. That's where I was born. And I of course asked for my birth certificate. I went under the name of Don Wilson and my birthday of April 8, 1929. They sent me an affidavit, which essentially said the person described in your letter has a birthday of April 4, 1929. Well, lo and behold, if I would have asked for my birth certificate using the name of Donald Webb, I would have got one. I didn't know about Webb until I was sixty-two years old.

She was living with a Mr. Wilson when they picked us up. So I had the wrong birth date and the wrong name, I find out at sixty-two. What really hit me, though, was that I had never, never thought—and Fontella died thinking the same thing, that she didn't care about us.

I read five letters in her handwriting in those records begging the courts to let her have her children back, saying that she had finally settled down, she was married, her husband had a good job. They had a home they were renting, and she had a dog and she knew Donald would love the dog. And I've always had dogs. So that myth was cleared up, and I'm saying that to keep from breaking down, because that really hit me.

Oh, boy. I can't describe the feeling. I kissed my wife a long time, I'll tell you that. That's about as close as I can come to verbalizing that feeling. So I guess there is a bit of anger there, too. But like my life on Rondo, bittersweet.

That's the way that experience was. I don't know how to describe it any other way. It's like I'm bitter at the authorities for not at least telling us how we could get in touch with her once we became of age, or something. Tell me something. But they didn't, and so I'm bitter about that. And I do mean bitter. But the sweet part was reading her letters.

I've thought about it a lot, and as best I can describe it I had an attitude that I'm sure I acquired from my childhood on Rondo. I wanted a nice fast car. I wanted to be a playboy kind of thing, I guess. Drinking never bothered me. I didn't drink. I didn't smoke. Girls were the thing, and dancing. That was my whole idea of the future, I guess. School, I was smart enough. My grades were good when I went. But that didn't apply to me. All I would end up doing was shining shoes somewhere. That's kind of Rondo, see.

I have an idea that a lot of people will try to make Rondo into something that is all grand and glorious, and I may tell you, I'm a rebel. I'll tell you that that's not the case. It wasn't my experience, nor the experience of people I knew. There was Deep Rondo,[15] there was Cornmeal Valley, and there was Oatmeal Hill.[16] And Cornmeal Valley and Oatmeal Hill had character, but none of it had the character of Deep Rondo.

I was down in Deep Rondo, and I couldn't have been a day over eight years old, and I was coming from Welcome Hall,[17] which was like a Hallie Q. Brown for those who lived in Cornmeal Valley. And we'd come from there, me and John Gardener and Richard Gardener. John was my age and Richard was younger. And George Lawson was my foster brother. He was younger. As I say, I couldn't have been a day over eight. I will never forget this. We came down Farrington, and on the corner of Farrington and Rondo was a place we knew as the Bucket of Blood,[18] which was a bar. It was a Sunday morning, after Sunday school. John and Richard were peeking in the Bucket of Blood. People drinking and swearing and music and all that stuff. These were unemployed and unemployable people. But anyway, there is a gentleman sitting on the curb. And he's laying back on this curb and he's got a bottle of wine that's half open and I notice him. I don't even know what John and Richard are doing, and George, but I'm watching this person. And it's warm out, and he's sitting there, kind of just—well, he's had way too much to drink. And he's singing this song. [Sings] "*Dooooowwwwwwn on Rondo. Oh-ooooh dooooowwwwn on Rondo. Smoke my reefer.*[19] *Drink my gin and act just like a fooool.*" He was one of many.

I have never forgotten that man on that curb, and his image was re-inforced throughout all of my years on Rondo as I grew up. I left there in 1958, so I was about twenty-nine years old. I moved to Minneapolis. That was a powerful image, and that was more like the Rondo, the Deep Rondo, that I knew about. Now, in Cornmeal Valley there was the same thing, but not as overt. Of course, as you get up to Oatmeal Hill you don't see that. You see people going to work and they're dressed a little nicer and they make a little more money.

This gentleman had a tremendous impact on me. I didn't understand the impact. It's just that I will never forget it. It has in very strong, overt ways guided my life to do what I later did. I detested it greatly, if I'm clear. And I know he was a symptom, not the cause. I later began to know the cause, and I became very angry. I'm still very angry.

It's colorism. I refuse to use the term racism, because I think there's only one of those and that's the human race. It's colorism. It's powerful. It's just as powerful in Saint Paul as anywhere I've ever been in this country, and I've been all over this country, so far south you can't go any farther unless you can swim. And I've been treated better there than I was in Saint Paul, on Rondo.

◆ ◆ ◆

DON GOUGH WILSON is proud of his fifty-five-year marriage to Bobbie before she passed in 2002. He has children, grandchildren, and great-grandchildren: Don Jr., his daughter Cicely and her five children; Glorie and her two children; and Vanessa (senior human resources manager of the *Star Tribune*). Without a high school education, Mr. Wilson taught seminars, including one for the White House staff on the psychology of White male racism. Working for Control Data and Wilson Learning, his seminars took him to Tokyo, where he taught through an interpreter for seventeen days, Brussels, London, Johannesburg, and across the United States. Any successes he had, Mr. Wilson attributes to his wife, Bobbie, because (although he is five foot seven) she always told him he was ten feet tall. He lives in the North Woods of Wisconsin, where he and Bobbie used to fish in the Brule River. Their German shepherd, Sufie, keeps him company whether he is out hiking or at home reading about the history of Sufism, the Gnostics of Islam.

1. Donald Gough Wilson was born April 4, 1929.

2. McKinley School was located at 481 Carroll Avenue, between Mackubin, Arundel, and Rondo from 1903 to 1966. Fire destroyed the building in 1977.

3. Cornmeal Valley, also known as Lower Rondo or Deep Rondo, was east of Dale Street. This was a lower-middle-class residential neighborhood with predominantly single-family homes. From the 1930s, this part of the community struggled with growing poverty.

4. Brown and Bigelow was located at 1286 University Avenue.

5. Armour Packing Plant was located on Armour Avenue two blocks east of Concord Avenue in South Saint Paul. The plant was open from 1919 to 1979 and covered about forty acres. Because this was one of the few industries that hired Blacks, many from Rondo took jobs at Armour and rode the streetcar to South Saint Paul daily.

6. Pilgrim Baptist Church was first organized as a prayer group before 1863 and formally organized as a church November 15, 1866. Their first house of worship was constructed in 1870 at Twelfth and Cedar Streets in Saint Paul, and it moved in 1918 to the current location at 732 West Central Avenue, Saint Paul.

7. Maxfield School was originally at 363 St. Albans at St. Anthony, and was built in 1890. In 1955, a new school was built at 680 St. Anthony at Victoria, Avon, and Central.

8. Marshall School was built in 1925 at Grotto, Holly, Ashland, and St. Albans. It was Marshall Junior High from 1926 to 1937. In 1937, tenth grade was added; in 1938, eleventh grade; and in 1939, twelfth grade was added, with graduating classes from 1940 to 1953. It returned to junior high only in 1954. Webster Elementary School was built on the same site in 1926. The two buildings were connected in 1975 and become Webster Magnet Elementary School.

9. Bobbie Jean Haskin Wilson was born September 30, 1932, and passed September 14, 2002, from lung cancer.

10. Sauk Centre Facility in Sauk Centre, Minnesota, was the State of Minnesota's Juvenile Female Correction Facility.

11. St. James AME (African Methodist Episcopal) Church existed as a prayer group as early as 1870. Formally organized in 1878, they purchased a permanent

home in 1881. The current church was built in 1926 at 624 West Central Avenue at Dale.

12. Western Electric was located at 333 Sibley in 1948.

13. Hayden Motor Sales, Inc., was located at 1800 University Avenue in 1948.

14. Honeywell was located at 2753 Forth Avenue South and had a downtown location at 420 North Fifth Street in Minneapolis.

15. Deep Rondo was considered between Rice Street and Western.

16. Oatmeal Hill was a term referring to Rondo west of Dale Street toward Lexington, sometimes known as Upper Rondo. More affluent residents tended to move into this area, giving the impression the residents had a higher social standing. This middle-class neighborhood consisted of predominantly single-family homes.

17. Welcome Hall Playground was at Western, Rondo, St. Anthony, and Virginia.

18. A tavern was located at 318 Rondo at Farrington.

19. "Reefer" is marijuana.

CONSTANCE JONES PRICE

They were going to have to learn to live together.

I remember growing up in Rondo's Oatmeal Hill.[1] I'M DR. CONNIE JONES PRICE[2] and I'm a native of Saint Paul, Minnesota, and a member of a family that's been here over a hundred years.

My grandfather[3] was recruited from Tennessee by Saint Paul businessmen. He didn't just decide to come here on his own. He was what they call a master craftsman, a bricklayer, and he was recruited here along with nine other African American craftsmen, to work on the Capitol,[4] the Landmark Center,[5] which was the first federal building, and a number of the other buildings around Saint Paul. They lived for the most part on the East Side and the North End. Then when African Americans came here, they didn't move to this Rondo area first. A lot of people don't know that, but they lived on the East Side and in the North End and the West Side.

My family moved to Summit/University/Rondo in 1920. Actually, it was my grandmother,[6] my father's mother, that bought the house at 1021 Rondo. This was the last block there's houses on Rondo, and that's where we lived, between Oxford and Chatsworth.

My grandfather had left Saint Paul before that, because they would hire him to work on these buildings. He's what they call a corner man, dig the foundations up, and then the foreman would come along and say, "Jones, I've got to fire you." He'd say, "Why? Isn't my work satisfactory?" He'd say, "Yes, your work is great, but you're not a member of the union." He says, "Well, I've been trying to join the union." He says, "You can't join our union." It was for Whites only. So they would fire him and then he would be off work. He'd have to go get work someplace else because he had a family to support. Finally, he got so frustrated, he told my grandmother, he says, "I think we should move to Chicago. I know I can work there and I know I can join the union."

She wouldn't do it, because she said, "I have these young children and I'm not going to move them." That was years ago that she thought Chicago was not the place where they should grow up, so she didn't go. So they were not separated because they didn't love each other or anything. It was racism and discrimination that broke up their marriage. You know, that's a terrible thing to do. So he went, helped form a union in Chicago, and worked there for years.

He was a beautiful dresser. He'd wear the three-piece suits, the spats, everything. He was a very nice-looking man. But the sad thing about it was that when he came back to visit, he had—do you know what a grip looks like? A suitcase and on one side of his grip he'd have all of his suits, the fine shirts and everything. On the other side he'd have his bricklaying tools, because he always hoped he'd come back and get another job in Saint Paul.

One of the things I remember, my sister and my brother and one of my cousins, was that he would tell us, "Pick up my grip." Well, we were little skinny kids, and we'd try really hard and we couldn't do it. Then he'd laugh and he'd say, "Here." He'd always bring a silver dollar for each one of us every time he came back, and that was one of the things that we remembered, that even though we couldn't pick up the grip, we would still get our silver dollar.

My grandmother worked at the packing plant[7] in South Saint Paul. Terrible

Grandfather Ernest T. Jones

work! My father[8] was one of the oldest children in the family, so he did anything he could to help support the family, but they all worked very hard. The packing plant was one of the few places that would hire Blacks. They gave jobs to Hispanics and Mexicans, too. And they made, for the time, pretty good money, and she needed that because she had a family to support. So she bought the house at 1021 on her own and lived there until she died. And the sad thing about it was, she was working in the yard. It was a hot summer day. She had a sunstroke and died.

My father then continued to live in the house because he had some sisters who were teenagers. My grandfather invited my dad down to live in Chicago. My dad wouldn't leave. Well, he had responsibility and so he never left, although he wanted to. He married. He moved back in because he had these younger sisters and somebody had to be able to pay the mortgage payment and things like that. So he moved back and stayed in the house until they demolished it with that freeway.

My mother[9] was born in Butte, Montana. They had come out in the Underground Railroad before the Civil War. The Underground Railroad took them as far as Indiana. Then the family went on their own to Colorado. My grandmother[10] was born in Indiana. Her sisters were born in Colorado. The family moved at some time during that period from south Kentucky to Indiana to Colorado to Montana. My grandmother's father was Indian, and he owned a ranch and he got exploited out of it. I mean, really, he was just distraught. He never really got it together after that. But these White ranchmen, you know.

I lived at 1021 Rondo. This was Oatmeal Hill. A lot of people didn't like us because

Connie, brother Ron, sister Shirley

they thought we thought we were something special. We didn't know what that was. You know, if you were on the east side of Dale, that was Cornmeal Valley.[11] We were a block off of Lexington. Oxford, Lexington. There were houses in this neighborhood. Most of them were Dutch colonial with the kind of rounded roof that looks sometimes like a barn. Most of the houses are that and so was ours.

I was born in 1930. It was predominantly a White neighborhood at that time. The neighbors on my block, for the most part, were African American homeowners. As I say, the only one that didn't own their house was a White family that lived up the street from us.

This was during the 1930s, the 1940s. Mr. Jones, who lived next to the Smiths—they were 1022 Rondo. Mr. Jones had a bachelor's degree in economics and a master's degree in economics and worked at the post office. Mr. Smith worked at the post office. Mr. McFarland, and I'm not sure what his degree was in, ran on the railroad.[12] So you had all these well-educated people. That's why when White people would say to me, "Well, if you people just get yourself an education . . ." And I'd say, "Wait a minute." I said, "I grew up in a neighborhood where most of the people were educated." My dad didn't have a degree, but other members of the family did. I said, "No, I grew up around college-educated people who could not work in their field, not because they weren't competent or they hadn't prepared themselves, but because they were Black." I just really get angry that it's so unfair. These people, you know, good people, hardworking people, and all they wanted was an opportunity. Don't let me start talking about affirmative action!

My mother died when I was four. My mother's mother moved in and took care of us. Then she had to go back to Butte, Montana. My stepmother[13] joined our family when I was nine.

My dad grew up in Saint Paul. In fact, one of his best stories was that he had gone to Sunday school with Roy Wilkins[14] at St. James AME Church[15] on Dale and Central. My grandmother had been one of the people that had been there when they founded the church and everything. But my dad, because he worked all the time when we were growing up, didn't go to church.

My mother was Baptist. When she moved to Saint Paul, she joined Pilgrim Baptist Church.[16] In fact, I've got a certificate she got for teaching Sunday school there before she died, because she was, I think, pretty active. So she started us at Pilgrim, and we went to Pilgrim until my dad remarried. My stepmother was Catholic, but she didn't think she could get the whole family to convert to being Catholic, and so she decided she would join St. James and wanted all the family back together because it was my dad's church. So then as a teenager, we were at St. James, and that's where we were for years. In fact, we still are at St. James. Our socializing was on Sundays at church.

Schuneman's[17] was a store that turned into Dayton's, but before that it was Schuneman & Mannheimer. Mannheimer was one of my father's best friends. In fact, my brother's second name is Benjamin because of Benjamin Mannheimer.

We shopped downtown because the shops on Selby had shoddy materials. I mean, it wasn't the greatest stuff. The people who didn't have a lot of money, or any real money, would shop there and get exploited. We never shopped there. We went downtown. My dad knew most of the people who had stores downtown. In fact, he could get a discount because of his friendships. Good quality stuff!

In the stores you had to buy anything, and you couldn't even bring it back. There were other things. You never knew when you were going to experience it. Like some places sometimes, they would not serve you or wait a long time before they served you. Well, they knew they had to eventually, but hopefully they thought we'd get mad and leave, and hopefully they hoped we'd be quiet, maybe not say anything.

We would go all kinds of places on the streetcar. Downtown. I know when we were really young, we would go out to Phalen Park[18] to swim and we'd take the streetcar so far and then we'd walk the rest of the way. There were no problems here in riding streetcars or buses. In fact, we were almost at the end of the line for the Rondo bus, and so sometimes the streetcar drivers, the bus drivers, would let us off in front of our house if it was night. These were all White drivers. Then they started getting some Black drivers. They were so pleasant and so polite.

When we went to the movies we went to Selby or University. We went to the Dale Theater[19] on Dale and Selby, the Faust[20] on Dale and University, the Beaux Arts,[21] which was at Selby, and then the Oxford,[22] which a lot of the people who lived further east probably never went to, was on Selby, close to Chatsworth. In fact, we used to go there from Hill School.[23] Now if there was a popcorn drive or something like that and we sold a lot of popcorn for the school, then we got time to go over to the Oxford during the week, during school days, to the movies. But most of the movies I hated. It was like Laurel and Hardy and people like that, who I thought were awful. I didn't like those kinds of comedians or that kind of humor. So even as a kid I thought, "Well, this is not a treat." Then if there was something we really wanted to see, we'd get on the streetcar and go there.

We had things we took for granted, like we had our own little playhouse. We had a swing set in our backyard. People like Mannheimer, their kids were older, and when they outgrew some of their toys that were in great shape, we would get them. I remember we had this little vacuum cleaner. Then my dad bought us this little stove and sink to put in our playhouse. I hated school, but at home it was a haven. It really was. We had to learn good manners. When my stepmother was there, we had to learn how to answer the phone appropriately.

I went to J. J. Hill School. At that time it was at Oxford and Selby. For the most of the time I was there, I had no other African American classmates. I think I got my first one when I was in the seventh grade, and I'd been there since kindergarten. I think in third or fourth grade I had one Chinese classmate, but other than that, they were all White.

The teachers really didn't want us there. Some of them were not bad. But at Hill School we had a process where you went from kindergarten to fourth grade with one teacher. In the fourth grade you had several teachers—a music teacher, an art teacher, a physical education teacher, and then a general core teacher. The music teacher was really probably one of the worst people I'd ever met. I can't carry a tune. I'm tone-deaf. Nobody had told me that you had to sing if you were Black. So it wasn't really a problem, I thought. But she would scream at me. Now, there I am, the only Black child in class and the only one that couldn't carry a tune. You know how you have to learn the scales and all of that? I couldn't even sing the scales in tune. I didn't know that was a major crime until I got in her class, and she'd scream at me in front of all of these kids and say, "Why can't you sing? You're supposed to sing." Until I went home I didn't know why I was supposed to sing. Nobody had said I was a terrible person because I couldn't sing, but she made me feel like I was.

Then she would say things like, "My, your mother sends you to school nice and clean." Well, how else would you go to school? It wasn't my mother at all. She was dead. Shows you how insensitive she was. Like it was a surprise I wasn't dirty and raggedy. We dressed better than most of the White kids in school because that's the way we were. But she would say things like that to me. I just hated going to music class because of that.

When you had to go out for recess and you had to play on the playground, nobody wanted to hold my hand or pick me for a team. I mean, you just knew you were different and unwanted. It was really, really bad. There were a few teachers that weren't so bad. But there were kids that would walk up to you and call you "chocolate drop" and Sambo,[24] and Mambo. I mean, it was blatant. I hated grade school. I really did.

The one thing they couldn't take away from us, we got a good foundation in education. They couldn't just sort us out and say, "Well, the White kids learn this, you Black kids sit there dumb." We learned it the same way they did. We got a good foundation.

There was a library on the third floor of Hill School just lined with bookshelves, and once a week our literature teacher would take us up there and we'd pick out a book to do a book report. You know, a lot of people get to high school before they do a book report. We were doing them in the fourth grade. Reading, we had to memorize stuff from Shakespeare, "As You Like It" and "The Seven Stages of Man," Longfellow's "Hiawatha." We learned all of this in grade school. There's no way from keeping us from learning, because we were in the environment, although it was, for the most part, a hostile environment. So we learned in spite of it. I went to Marshall Junior High[25] for my first year.

My sister went right to Marshall because she graduated before I did. So I went for my first year, and then I went to Central High School[26] because that was the school in our neighborhood.

I've always loved history, and we had a good foundation in grade school on history, so I was the top student in the history class. That was at a time where they gave double A if you were good. I never got one wrong answer on the test, always had my hand in the air if she asked a question, so it even got to the point where the White students would say, when our report cards came out, "Well, did you get your double A?" I never got it. I would get an A, but never the double A I deserved, because she couldn't stand to think that her top student was Black. We went through things like that at Central.

We couldn't go to things like the prom, because you had to go with somebody from the school or an alumni from the school. We had one male student who didn't look very good. Nobody wanted to take him to the prom. Nobody asked us, but we wouldn't have gone anyway. So there was a lot of stuff we missed because we were at Central.

Midway through my junior year, I talked to a friend of mine who also was at Central, and I said, "Listen, this is killing me. We have no social life. We have nothing." I hated it, because I think there were about eight of us in the whole school, White students and us. We decided we were going to take ourselves down to the school administrative office and get transfers to Marshall. We didn't tell anybody. I didn't tell my dad, and she didn't tell her family. We just went down there. The person we talked to said, "Do you know that there are people that are dying to get into Central?" It was the friendliest school in the city at that time. You've probably heard that.

Sister Shirley, brother Ron, Connie

And we said, "We're dying to get out." And so we argued with him. I mean, it was probably pretty aggressive on our part, but we were desperate. We wanted a social life as well as a good environment to be in where there wasn't all this racism, because the kids didn't talk to us. The White girls had all their little sororities and little groups, and naturally the guys weren't going to pay any attention to us, which was okay. So we were very lonely. So we stayed down there and argued with him until he said, "Oh, all right," and gave us our permits. Then we had to go home and break the news.

Now, my dad was the kind of person that was just very quiet. I mean, he'd been through a nightmare losing my mother, because they were just soul mates, you know. But he made a deathbed promise that he would always be there for us. He was very mild-mannered little man who didn't raise his voice. He didn't swear. He'd say, "People are dern fools," and things like that. But he was just very mild-mannered. So he was not happy with me, but he didn't scream or holler or anything. He just was very sad that I had done that, because he knew about the reputation of the school and he didn't want us going to a lot of different schools.

There were more Black students at Marshall. There were some in every class. Two of my best friends were not African American at Marshall, they were Japanese. They had come after the Second World War. They had relocated to Saint Paul, and when I was a junior I met them. They were seniors. We had the best friendships. It enabled me to meet other people. I'd never been taught to hate anybody. I mean, why would I hate the Japanese? They certainly weren't the ones who were the enemy. Some people did, but I mean, that never fazed me.

Connie at eighteen years old

My dad didn't say you had to work, and I had an older sister who didn't most of the time, but I liked to have extra money for clothes. I was always trying to see how many cashmere sweaters—that was a real status symbol, how many cashmere sweaters you have with matching skirts. The only job they would give you was the very menial jobs. When I was fifteen I got a job at Snyder's Drugstore[27] downtown, washing dishes, which is a horrible job. But that was the only thing I could do to get a job. Some of the White kids who weren't even as bright could do other kinds of things, but we couldn't because we were Black.

When I started college, my dad got me a job at a jewelry store. I hated it because you had to put on a maid's uniform and clean the display windows and things like that. I thought, "What if somebody sees me? Here I am a freshman at the University and I'm doing this horrible job." But you did that. You did what you could because you had to work. I mean, you wanted to work and have the money.

I belonged to different clubs at Hallie.[28] I was a Campfire girl there. That was number one. We would make up our own little clubs and then get them sponsored. The No-Name Club, that was one. I belonged to a number of clubs there.

My dad sent us to camp. It was called St. John's Landing,[29] and this camp we went to through Hallie Q. Brown, and that is on the St. Croix near Hinckley, Minnesota.[30] We'd stay ten days there. We had cabins and a counselor in each cabin. We had an outside latrine. You hated to go, especially if you had to go at night and nobody would go with you. The deer used to come up and scratch their antlers on our cabin, and they said there were bears, and so you really hated to go. Half the night you were sitting there, "I wonder if somebody else has to go." My sister wouldn't go with me because she didn't have to go to the bathroom, and nobody else seemed to have to go at night except me. If it got really bad, I had to crawl out of bed and go by myself. That was an experience.

There were four units. We were like Campsite D. There was A, B, and C, who were all White girls. It was not integrated. It was three of them, and they came from some of the other community centers, Merriam Park and Merrick and some of the other community centers in Saint Paul. But they did not integrate us. We were all apart. We ate in the same dining room at the same time. They couldn't serve different times. But their activity was separate from ours, except the last night we'd have a joint meeting. We had the biggest lodge, so all of them would come over to our lodge and then we'd have singing and camp songs and a big fire and things like that. I have no idea if they did different activities. We were busy with our own activity. You know, there was no point in trying to check out what they were doing. But they kept us separate 'cause we were Black. We had a mixed staff. We had some counselors that were not Black.

I became involved in the civil rights movement in the 1950s and '60s. Every time they had a march in the South, we boycotted the Woolworth[31] store, Kresge's[32] store, different places around here. Almost every week we had a march at the Capitol in support. We could go in Kresge's and we could eat at the counter, or Woolworth's, and we could buy our food, we could try on clothes, which they couldn't do in the South. But this was in support of what was happening there. I was very much involved.

In 1962 I went south for the first time in my life, to Atlanta, Georgia. The NAACP had decided that they were going to go south for the first time for the national convention. We met Medgar Evers.[33] One day we got in the car, and he had James Meredith[34] in the car, and this was before James Meredith was going to integrate the University of Mississippi. So we got in the car, and Medgar introduced my friend and me to James Meredith. So he told us he was going to integrate the University of Mississippi. At the time, I was still taking some classes at the U, and I said, "Oh, I graduated from the

University and I'm still taking classes, working on my degree." And we acted like it was the same thing. You know, "Okay, you're there. We're here."

If you remember, when he integrated the University three people got killed, and it was just a nightmare. He was supposed to go in July, at the beginning of the next summer session, and didn't go in until October. But it was a terrible mess. I got a chance to meet him before he integrated Mississippi U. I met Dr. Martin Luther King[35] there and Coretta King,[36] and just all kinds of people were there for this convention. It was really a good experience.

Probably in the Sixties when my kids got ready to go to camp, Hallie Q. Brown was using a camp on the other side of the St. Croix called Head of the Rapids, and they went there as campers, young campers. I believe in camping. They usually went to several during the summer, especially my son,[37] who loved camping. When they were campers at Head of the Rapids, they started integrating the campsites, putting White girls and White boys and mixing them all up. Our kids did not like it. My daughter[38] said they just were not happy. They liked it the way it was, maintain the status quo.

Janabelle Taylor was the camp director and she said, "You will integrate." She just sat my daughter and all those other little girls down and told them, "These girls are going to move in here, and you are going to be nice to them." They did not want to have anything to do with them. But they finally decided they were not going to keep people segregated and separate. They were going to have to learn to live together.

◆ ◆ ◆

DR. CONSTANCE JONES PRICE was born to Emerett L. Jones and Odessa Drake Jones. In 1950 she married Scott Price and was the proud mother of Jan and Scott, and grandmother of Shani, Daniel, and Danika. Dr. Price earned a B.A. in sociology (University of Minnesota), a master's in urban planning (Mankato State), and a doctorate in public administration (Nova University). She served the community working for Hennepin County, Saint Paul Youth Services Bureau, Wilder Foundation, and the Minnesota Human Rights Department; and was active in St. James AME Church, Saint Paul YWCA, Saint Paul NAACP, St. Croix Valley Girl Scout Council, Hallie Q. Brown, Saint Paul

Urban League, Ramsey Action Programs, Genesis II, Operation de Nova, Twin Cities International Center, Life Source, Ramsey County Charter Commission, Limited Thirty Black Women's Network, Alpha Kappa Alpha Sorority, and many others. As Connie said, "There's just so much we need to do."

◆ **NOTES**

1. Oatmeal Hill was a term referring to Rondo west of Dale Street toward Lexington, sometimes known as Upper Rondo. More affluent residents tended to move into this area, giving the impression that residents had a higher social standing. This middle-class neighborhood consisted of predominantly single-family homes.

2. Dr. Constance Jones Price was born May 28, 1930, and passed December 5, 2003.

3. Grandfather Ernest Jones.

4. The Minnesota State Capitol is located at 75 Dr. Martin Luther King Boulevard, formally Constitution Avenue.

5. The Old Federal Courts Building is located at 75 West Fifth Street in downtown Saint Paul. In 1978, this building became known as the Landmark Center and was designated a National Historic Monument. It became a cultural center for music, dance, theater, exhibitions, public forums, and special events.

6. Grandmother Ora Lee Jones.

7. Armour Packing Plant was located on Armour Avenue two blocks east of Concord Avenue in South Saint Paul. The plant was open from 1919 to 1979, and covered about forty acres. Because this was one of the few industries that hired Blacks, many from Rondo took jobs at Armour and rode the streetcar to South Saint Paul daily.

8. Father Emerett Jones.

9. Mother Odessa Drake Jones.

10. Grandmother Georgia McRutledge.

11. Cornmeal Valley, also known as Lower Rondo or Deep Rondo, was east of Dale Street. This was a lower-middle-class residential neighborhood with predominantly single-family homes. From the 1930s, this part of the community struggled with growing poverty.

12. "Running on the road" refers to serving travelers on trains as a waiter or porter.

13. Stepmother Maude Jones.

14. Roy Wilkins (1901–1981) went to the University of Minnesota and lived in Saint Paul. He became executive director of the NAACP. Saint Paul's River Centre complex at 175 Kellogg Boulevard in downtown Saint Paul includes the Roy Wilkins Auditorium.

15. St. James AME (African Methodist Episcopal) Church existed as a prayer group as early as 1870. Formally organized in 1878, they purchased a permanent home in 1881. The current church was built in 1926 at 624 West Central Avenue at Dale.

16. Pilgrim Baptist Church was first organized as a prayer group before 1863, and formally organized as a church November 15, 1866. Their first house of worship was constructed in 1870 at Twelfth and Cedar Streets in Saint Paul, and in 1918, it moved to the current location at 732 West Central Avenue, Saint Paul.

17. Schuneman's, Inc., was located at Wabasha and Sixth Street in downtown Saint Paul from 1864 to 1958. This department store chain had stores throughout the metropolitan area. It succeeded Mannheimer Brothers, becoming Schuneman & Mannheimer until 1958, when it was bought by Dayton's Department Stores. Dayton's Department Stores became Marshall Fields under Target Corporation in 2001.

18. Phalen Park is located between Frost Avenue, Maryland Avenue, Arcade, and East Shore Drive, and was first planned by the Saint Paul City Council in 1872. The city acquired the land in 1899 at a cost of $22,000, and it was opened to the public soon afterward. The park was named after early settler Edward Phalen, who staked one of the first claims to the land around Phalen Creek. Today there are 3.2 miles of trails around Lake Phalen, a playground, beach, golf course and clubhouse, and an amphitheater.

19. The Dale Theater was located at 937 Selby Avenue.

20. The Faust Theater, built in 1911 as a family movie theater, was located at 626 West University Avenue near Dale Street. The theater closed in the late 1960s and the building became an evangelical church. In 1970 it reopened as a sex-oriented movie theater until the city purchased and closed it in March 1989. The building was razed in 1995.

21. The Beaux Arts Theater was located at 391 Selby Avenue.

22. The Oxford Theater was located at 989 Selby Avenue.

23. J. J. Hill School was originally built in 1905 at Selby, Hague, Chatsworth, and Oxford. The school housed kindergarten through eighth grade. This building was torn down and a new building built in 1974 for J. J. Hill Elementary School. Currently, the building serves as Montessori School for four-year-olds through sixth grade.

24. *Little Black Sambo* is a children's book published in 1899 by Helen Bannerman, a Scot living in India. The original book contained racist caricatures and stereotypes. The word *sambo*, partly as a result of the book, has a long history as a racial slur.

25. Marshall School was built in 1925 at Grotto, Holly, Ashland, and St. Albans. It was Marshall Junior High from 1926 to 1937. In 1937, tenth grade was added; in 1938, eleventh grade; and in 1939, twelfth grade was added, with graduating classes from 1940 to 1952. It returned to junior high only in 1952. Webster Elementary School was built on the same site in 1926. The two buildings were connected in 1975 and become Webster Magnet Elementary School.

26. Central High School began in 1866 and consisted of two rooms in the Franklin Building in downtown Saint Paul. By 1872 it was known as Saint Paul High School and was moved to Seventh and Jackson. In 1883, a twenty-seven-room building on Minnesota Street in downtown Saint Paul was completed, and the school was named Saint Paul Central High. Because of space needs, a new school was built at 275 Lexington Avenue in 1912. In 1977, the building was reduced to its structural form, then rebuilt into the current building.

27. Snyder's Drug Store was located at 412 Wabasha Street and 403 Robert Street in downtown Saint Paul.

28. Hallie Q. Brown Community Center, Inc., was opened in the Union Hall at Aurora and Kent Streets as a community center specifically to serve the Black community when the Black YWCA closed in 1928. Hallie Q., as it is affectionately known, has served all ages through child care, youth and senior clubs, athletics, music, and social events. In 1972, Hallie relocated in the Martin Luther King Building at 270 Kent Street at Iglehart in Saint Paul. The center's namesake was an educator who pioneered the movement of Black women's clubs in the late 1800s.

29. St. John's Landing was a camp run by Hallie Q. Brown Community Center and was located in St. Croix Park outside of Hinckley. Later it was renamed Head of the Rapids.

30. Hinckley, Minnesota, is located eighty miles north of Saint Paul.

31. F. W. Woolworth & Company had several locations in the 1940s and 1950s that included 81 East Seventh Street, 438 Wabasha, 1088–1090 University Avenue, 1624 White Bear Avenue, and 969–971 Payne Avenue.

32. Kresge's was located downtown at 57 East Seventh Street and 2167 Hudson Road in Saint Paul.

33. Medgar Evers (1925–1963) was a hardworking field secretary for the NAACP in Mississippi. His assassination in the front yard of his home on June 11, 1963, galvanized the civil rights movement. After thirty years, in 1994, his killer was found guilty and jailed for the murder.

34. James Meredith was born June 25, 1933. In 1961 his admission into the all-White University of Mississippi was denied twice until a federal court ordered his admission. When U.S. Attorney General Robert Kennedy sent federal marshals in to protect Meredith there were riots in which 160 marshals were wounded and two bystanders were killed. Meredith graduated from Old Miss in 1964.

35. Martin Luther King was born January 15, 1929, and assassinated in Memphis Tennessee on April 4, 1968, for his leadership in the civil rights movement.

36. Coretta Scott King was born April 27, 1927, and majored in music and education at Antioch College. She married in 1953 and by 1964 had four children whom she raised besides her active involvement with the SCLC—the Southern Christian Leadership Conference.

37. Son Scott Price, born February 28, 1954.

38. Daughter Jan Price, born 1952.

BARBARA "PETEY" VASSAR GRAY

Being a Vassar girl meant you had a sense of who you were.

MY NAME IS BARBARA VASSAR GRAY.[1] I'm the youngest of the seven Vassar girls. My nickname was Petey. Hardly anybody knew me as Barbara. I grew up in Saint Paul at Mechanic Arts High School.[2] I went to the University of Minnesota,[3] and I went to St. Catherine's[4] for my graduate degree. I left here when I was twenty-three years old.

I was one of seven Vassar girls raised in Saint Paul. Being a Vassar girl meant that you were physically attractive, that you were mentally strong, that you were well educated, that you had a sense of who you were, where you were, and where you were going. And you had this sense of personal integrity and all because of your family background. So being a Vassar girl meant to me that the community knew about me and my family and my father and that there were certain standards that were required or expected of us. Standards like conduct of life, being kind to people, attendance at church and more or less following the Ten Commandments and the Beatitudes. These were the things that were meaningful in life, and this is what you should follow as a guide in your life.

I lived with my sister Lola and Maceo Finney and Corky. She ran Finney's Beauty Shop at the same address.[5] Our home and the business were two separate entities. I never thought of it as Lola running a business out of her home. I mean, there was her business that was part of the house, but it did not infringe on or have any relation to our home. She had a regular beauty shop, a shampoo room and everything. So that was entirely separate.

Lola felt that when women came to the beauty shop, that was a relaxing moment for them and they talked about things that children didn't talk about. I mean, there may be marital problems, there may have been problems with children, whatever. So neither Corky nor I were allowed to work in the beauty shop. That was a profession, that was a business, and we did not work in it. Once in a while, though, you kind of overheard something. My hair was down to my waist and Lola had to wash my hair. It was just horrible, having to wash my hair. And I remember one time sitting under the dryer and hearing something about someone was going with somebody's husband and "Shh, shh, shh!" And I never got to find out who it was, because in our family, when things like that were talked about, it wasn't talked about in front of the children. This was strictly a woman's opportunity to, in effect, let her hair down and relax. And I'm sure that Lola heard many a story, but she was not a gossiper, and you didn't know these things.

I grew up in St. Philip's Episcopal Church.[6] St. Philip's Church meant a lot to me and in my life, to have been part of the Girls Friendly Society, which was one of the groups associated with the Episcopal Church, to have been a Sunday school teacher, to have been part of the choir. We could give dances at St. Philip's Church, and besides St. Philip's and Hallie Q. Brown,[7] there really wasn't any other places that teenagers could get together and enjoy one another under supervised circumstances.

Hallie's Queen of Hearts Ball, Petey representing Los Cabelleros, February 1948

We always had someplace to go and something to do at Hallie Q. Brown. There were the clubs. The boys had Los Cabelleros and the girls had the Doll Club, which started when we were about six or seven years old. We met every Thursday. The Doll Club originally started out as just a social activity for young girls over at Hallie Q. Brown. And it was more or less kind of a cultural thing. We learned music. We learned poetry. We had readings. We did all kinds of things. I think there are only a few of us left out of that original group of the Doll Club. So that was our activity.

Once a year from eleven until about thirteen I went to go to St. John's Landing Camp.[8] Connie Jackson and Janabelle Murphy were the counselors up there. Now they all liked me, but nobody really wanted to be counselor to me because I had such long hair. Nobody wanted to comb my hair! That was fun, but I came home when I was about thirteen and I said I wasn't going back to camp anymore. I'd had enough of seeing baby fawns and deer and bear and picking berries and stuff.

Then we had something that was called Stay At Home Camp. In the summer you went over to Hallie Q. Brown from nine in the morning until about three in the afternoon. And we would start out the morning in the gym and we would sing all kinds of camp songs and things. Then there were different activities, different crafts and things that you learned, and activities outside or in the gym. Then we would have lunch. Then there would be kind of a cultural, quiet time, and then at 3:00 we went home. On Wednesdays, we always went out to Phalen Park[9] to go swimming, and on Fridays it was Surprise Day. We never knew where we were going. There would be a bus that would come that would take us places.

The dances that we had at Hallie Q. Brown were something called The Lounge, and that was on Saturday nights from 7:00 to 11:00. Janabelle Murphy was usually there as one of the chaperones. As little as she was, everybody was afraid of her! She meant business! We would have the records playing, and we could have the lights down a little bit. Once you reached about thirteen or fourteen, you could go to The Lounge. One of my role models was Janabelle Murphy Taylor, who was a social worker at Hallie Q. Brown. She was a strong Black professional woman role model with a college degree. So my social life and my sense of integrity grew out of the experiences at St. Philip's Episcopal Church and the people that were at Hallie Q. Brown Community Center.

At St. Philip's we might have a dance maybe once a month or every six weeks or so, and it would be downstairs in the undercroft. And at that time, Father Llewellyn Williams was the rector. He would sit in the kitchen and he would let us dance with the lights down low, but then every so often he'd come out, he stuttered sometimes, and he'd say, "Uh-uh-uh, I-I-I wanna see some space. I wanna see some light between—Petey, you and Herschel.

William Ziemer

I wanna—you know, I wanna see some space between you." Then he'd go back and sit back in the kitchen and then at 11:00, he'd call out and say, "Last dance! Last dance!" And usually the piece that would be played would be "After Hours," by Coleman Hawkins, and we'd go da-donk, da-donk donk! So it was wonderful.

I went to Mechanic Arts High School. I met my best friend, William Ziemer, when I was thirteen years old at Mechanic Arts High School. He had blond hair, blue eyes, and was from a well-to-do Jewish family, but because he'd had polio, he had to go to a school that had an elevator and a full-time nurse. We were like brother and sister. We called each other, "This is my foster sister. This is my foster brother." I never really gave it any thought about the fact that he was White and a Jew and I was a Black and young woman. We just took to one another and he became very, very fond of my family and was around.

I never really gave a lot of thought to whether there was diversity in my life. It was just my life and the experience that I had from school and being very active and popular in high school. I was a cheerleader, I was president of several organizations, GAA—Girls Athletic Association, Prom Night Committee, homeroom captain, and I never ran into any prejudice so to speak with the attendees at Mechanic Arts High School. As a matter of fact, my class of 1949, every time they've had a reunion—I've missed only one.

My two good friends were Joan Milashius—her father was Lithuanian, her mother was Polish, and then Sandy Lasman, who was Jewish. They both had Polish backgrounds. And we met when we were thirteen years old, and we've been close ever since. And so we've watched one another's children grow up. It's just a wonderful loving friendship. But that does bring to mind how we met. And it was an instance of prejudice.

There was a lady named Catherine Tschida who was dean of women. But nobody paid any attention to this Miss Tschida. She called me in, I think the first week of school, and she said to me, "You don't need to take college prep." She said, "You'll probably never go to school any further than what you are and so you don't need to go to college prep." She felt I wasn't going to be doing anything except maybe cleaning somebody's bathrooms

Mechanic Arts High School

and maybe working as a salesgirl in Bannon's[10] or some of the dime stores in Saint Paul.

I said, "Miss Tschida, my name is Barbara Vassar. Do you recognize the name? Because I understand that my mother came over and spoke to you when Bea went here, and when Lola went here, and when Kitty went here. Where you did not want them to take college prep and you had changed their programs, so my mother came over." I said, "I am one of those people."

Later on, I learned that she had spoken disparagingly to both Sandy and to Joan. I think we met outside Miss Tschida's office. I think we'd been sent in there for misbehaving in gym class. And she spoke disparagingly to them. I think she said to Sandy something to the effect, "Well, you're nothing but a poor Jew and you're never going to be anything." And I think more or less she indicated to Joan, "Your background is Polish. You're never going to be anything." And so here was something. Miss Tschida was known to be anti-Black, anti-just-about-everything, and nothing was ever done about her. And I think there were a lot of people who went through that experience at Mechanic Arts, having this kind of woman who was supposed to be dean of girls and if you listened to her, she would have crushed your dreams. I don't ever know what happened. Everybody called her "that old bitch."

When I graduated the girl that was salutatorian did not take precollege classes. I thought about it. It didn't really bother me particularly, because I thought it was unfair that they calculated the grade point average the way they did. You're taking gym and you're taking business classes as opposed to someone who was a straight A average with all the courses that I took. But then I reflected that this young this girl might not ever have anything else, and I knew that I was not defined by not having received the salutatorian designation. So I didn't harbor any anger or anything about it. It was just one of the things that happened. I addressed it by going to the principal, Mr. Smith, and telling him that I thought they should do something about changing the way that it was determined who was going to be a salutatorian or valedictorian in terms of what their educational course had been. Because at Mechanic Arts, there was commercial, there was cosmetology, there was general and there was precollege and college prep.

I worked at the Saint Paul Public Library[11] when I was sixteen, in 1948. And that in and of itself was a prejudicial, prejudiced experience. I had taken the examination for library page, and I came out number one. I kept wondering why

From the Mechanic Arts 1949 yearbook: Barbara Vassar

I hadn't been called for a job, and one of the girls at Mechanic Arts told me she was the page. I said, "How can you be a page? I took the examination. I came in number one." This is something that I addressed because I knew how to go about doing it, and it was wrong for me to come in number one in the examination and then I don't get the job. And so I just thought it through and I just walked down from Mechanic Arts High School, went right down to Saint Paul Public Library, asked to speak to the director. I asked to see Perry Jones—we called her P. J. behind her back—and told her what my experience had been. She said, "Well, young lady, what do you intend to do now?" I said, "I'm going to go over to the Saint Paul Civil Service Commission and I will tell them that I've come in and spoken to you, who are the Saint Paul Public Library director." So that's what I did. I went right down to Saint Paul Civil Service Department. "I want to talk to the director, Eugene Mathivet." "Well, he's not available." "I'll wait!" And within a week, I had a job. So that's an example of some of the things that I ran into that could be considered prejudice. But I was never going to let it stop me. It was a situation that I thought I could address. I didn't go to my father or any of my sisters or anything. I took care of it myself, and that's the way I've been all my life. Something needs to be addressed or confronted, and I just go on ahead and do it.

I think maybe I knew in some respect that I hadn't gotten the job because I was Colored and that the other girl, who maybe came in number three or four, had gotten it and this was wrong. Also, I didn't think she was very smart. And it was a written examination. It tested your background in terms of speech and following directions, definitions of words, your background in terms of your reading, how would you arrange books on the shelf, what was your experience with the Library of Congress system. So I felt I was an intelligent person, I'd come in number one, the room full of other high school kids, and that I owned the job. I had earned it so I wanted it.

The woman who was head of the children's library in the downtown library, she was not very nice to Black youngsters that came into the children's room. She would fawn all over the White kids and everything. And I noticed that especially when I became a library page and sometimes had to go down to the children's library to help shelve the books. And she would be very loving and effusive if White children came in with their parents. But when Black children came in, she totally ignored them.

Her attitude, even toward me, was that I was "different" because my speech was good, because I dressed appropriately, that I had a sense of who I was, and she didn't like that. I suppose she wanted me to come in and talk with a heavy Southern accent and all, but that was not my life's experience. My family did not talk that way.

I found these experiences empowering. I don't know if that was necessarily the word at the time. I went up through the ranks of the Detroit Public Library and the Wayne-Oakland Library Federation. I've always been proud of who I am and what I am and so I think that reflected in the decisions and the jobs that I performed.

BARBARA "PETEY" VASSAR GRAY, the youngest of the seven Vassar girls, graduated from the University of Minnesota with a B.A. (in English and history) and the College of St. Catherine (with a graduate degree in library science). Mrs. Gray is an active member of Alpha Kapha Alpha Sorority, the Mariners' Anglican Church-Epistlor (fifteen years), and the Richard III Society American Chapter (Mrs. Gray recently presented a paper: "Titles of Royalty in England and France 1066–1485: Battle of Bosworth"); and is a retired member of the Association of Personnel Administrators, the American Library Association, and the Michigan Library Association. Mrs. Gray and Wilfred Gray, the administrator of the Chrysler Corporation and an avid stamp collector, have been married fifty years. She is the proud mother of Portia Lynn Gray, who is a social worker, and grandmother of Layla, a graduate of the University of Michigan in English literature and Afro-American history; Carlos, a computer programmer; and Michelle, University of Michigan class of 2006, secondary education.

◆ NOTES

1. Barbara "Petey" Vassar Gray was born September 2, 1932.

2. Mechanic Arts High School was located between Central, Robert, and Aurora from 1911 to 1976. It was sold to the state and torn down in 1978.

3. The University of Minnesota developed from a preparatory school founded in 1851 and is the largest public university in Minnesota. It has campuses in Saint Paul, Minneapolis, Duluth, Morris, and Crookston.

4. The College of St. Catherine was founded in 1905 by the Sisters of St. Joseph of Carondelet and became fully accredited in 1917. The college was named for St. Catherine of Alexandria, the fourth-century Egyptian lay philosopher who suffered martyrdom for her faith. The college is located at 2004 Randolph at Cleveland.

5. Finney's Beauty Salon was located at 437 Rondo.

6. St. Philip's Episcopal Church was formed as a mission church in 1894, meeting in a home on Carroll Avenue. Later they rented a store on Rice Street, and in 1900 purchased a white frame building at Aurora and Mackubin. When

this was torn down in the early 1950s, the altar and reredos were salvaged and placed in the structure built on the same northwest corner.

7. Hallie Q. Brown Community Center, Inc., was opened in the Union Hall at Aurora and Kent Streets as a community center specifically to serve the Black community when the Black YWCA closed in 1928. Hallie Q., as it is affectionately known, has served all ages through child care, youth and senior clubs, athletics, music, and social events. In 1972, Hallie relocated in the Martin Luther King Building at 270 Kent Street at Iglehart in Saint Paul. The center's namesake was an educator who pioneered the movement of Black women's clubs in the late 1800s.

8. St. John's Landing was a camp run by Hallie Q. Brown Community Center and was located in St. Croix Park outside of Hinckley. Later it was renamed Head of the Rapids.

9. Phalen Park is located between Frost Avenue, Maryland Avenue, Arcade, and East Shore Drive, and was first planned by the Saint Paul City Council in 1872. The city acquired the land in 1899 at a cost of $22,000, and it was opened to the public soon afterward. The park was named after early settler Edward Phalen, who staked one of the first claims to the land around Phalen Creek. Today there are 3.2 miles of trails around Lake Phalen, a playground, beach, golf course and clubhouse, and an amphitheater.

10. Bannon's Drug Store was located at 74 East Seventh Street in downtown Saint Paul.

11. Saint Paul's Central Library is located at 90 West Fourth Street in downtown Saint Paul. The Central Library was opened in 1917.

KATHRYN CORAM GAGNON

My life has been about Rondo!

MY NAME IS KATHRYN CORAM GAGNON.[1] I was raised on St. Anthony and Mackubin, one block north of Rondo, two blocks east of Dale, in Saint Paul, Minnesota. I lived in Rondo in the Thirties, Forties, Fifties, Sixties, Seventies, Eighties, Nineties, and right now!

My mother's family was really settled into the Rondo area. My great-aunt had married a fellow who ran on the Soo Line. They lived only in this

Vegetable vendor's horse cart on St. Anthony Avenue, late 1940s

particular area in Saint Paul for years, from the early 1900s. My mother[2] was born in Ohio, raised in Minnesota. She lived in a number of houses on Rondo and ultimately at 495 St. Anthony. She graduated from the University of Minnesota in 1919. You know the *Crisis* magazine? NAACP's[3] magazine? Well, back in those days, they very often took the pictures of those Black individuals who had graduated from integrated colleges. The year that she graduated, her picture appears in there. So very cool!

She worked at Hallie[4] from its beginning, from 1929. And I think because it is such a demanding job to really put your energy in there, she eventually decided she wanted to change and took tests to work for the state government. Well, now here's a woman with a college degree, but because she was Black, what they hired her to do was push the mail cart. Eventually, she was able to get a position as the employment interviewer. If you wanted to get a job, you were not the person she spoke with. She spoke with the people who were looking for workers, which is why I never had a summer vacation. She always had a job waiting for me the minute I got home from school! But that's basically what she did.

My father[5] came from a family where there was not a lot of education. He was raised in New York. To the best of my knowledge, his formal education didn't go past maybe fourth grade. He was gifted as a mechanic. He came here because they said the Ford Plant[6] needed workers. When he got here, they hadn't laid the first brick for the Ford Plant, but they had advertised for all these people, so he ended up being a nightman with Warren Given.[7] Warren Given had a shop on Grand, and that's where my dad was a nightman. My dad used to work on Dillinger's[8] car when he'd come up here. The stories he would tell! Then he was working over at what was then Hetfield Queenan.[9] It was a Dodge, Plymouth, De Soto, and Chrysler dealership on University and Oxford. And he

Kathryn's father, Ulysses Grant "Duke" Coram, c. 1926

was there almost until he retired. They sort of retired him because it got sold. He was a nightman. He did janitorial stuff and might do some mechanic work, but that's not what he was called, although he did the work on occasion.

My dad, probably he could have been Jewish. He could have been Italian. Both my parents were light-skinned. My mother had no brothers and sisters, but this side of my father's family was probably the lightest and then they shade down. But there are no cousins that I know of who are really dark. Most of us are pretty obviously Black, but my side of the family, no.

This area was never totally segregated. The block I lived on had a smattering of Black families. There were German families, the Adelhelms. There were Polish families, the Tolendouskys. But the whole block on both sides of the street between Mackubin and Arundel on St. Anthony was highly integrated. Most of the grocery stores in the area were owned by Jewish families. The Gottesmans had the one on the northeast corner of Rondo and Mackubin.[10] There were little grocery stores on all the corners, just about. If you wanted good fresh meat, that was about three blocks up on Kent and Carroll. That was a White family that owned that.

I started nursery school at Hallie when I was two and a half years old. It was wonderful. The WPA[11] supported it, and we had the best food. Farmers couldn't sell their butter, so we had spinach drenched in butter. We had cod liver oil laced with a bit of orange juice. It kept us healthy. We learned our alphabet, some singsong, and my prize possession when I graduated at five years old was my purple sunsuit. It didn't make a difference to me that everyone else had one identical to mine, it was my prize position.

Rebecca Moore "Aunt Becky," Mrs. Carroll Vassar "Gramma Vassar" and Kathryn
in her favorite purple and white W. P. A. sunsuit. at Lake Phalen.
Aunt Becky's 1928 Chevy is seen in the right of Grandma

McKinley School 1941—Third Grade
Back row: Lilian Field, Dorothy Clark, Theresa Brown, Virginia Thomas, Juanita Nelson, Elsie Bjorkman, Kathryn Coram, R. Acheson, ____. Third row: Connie Brown, Alice Atkins, Crola Slaughter, Syvilla Price, ____, ____, Audrey Kadrey, Audrey Cramer. Second row: John Fisch, Jerome Sandbloom, Lyle ____, Catherine Norton, Beverly ____, ____, Dianne Freeman, ____, Lyle____. First row: ____, ____, ____, Marlowe Schultz, Joe Ray, Frank Thompson, Fred O'Neal. Sitting: ____, Henry Davis, Albert Tolendousky

McKinley School[12] stood as a bastion there at the corner of Carroll and Mackubin, fortunately or unfortunately, just two short blocks from my house. We never missed a day of school. As a matter of fact, my sister,[13] who was ten years older than me, had been sent to McKinley one day when I think the temperature was well below zero. And as she arrived there, she found the only other person there was the janitor stoking the furnace! Needless to say, she was sent home. But my mother was insistent that we actually spend our time in the school.

My father was one of these people, "Don't come lookin' to me to solve your problems on the street. You got 'em, you got to take care of 'em." He was into the athletics and I loved it. I was really good at sports. And my mother was one of these people who would always encourage the academics. When I was in fourth grade, we had to do a speech about somebody famous. You go home and you—well, Abe Lincoln, George Washington. My mother said, "Oh, no! Oh, no! You're doing George Washington Carver."[14] And in those days, they didn't teach you Black history, and if you were raised in the North, you really didn't know much Black history. So she had me digging out all this stuff. And she would go in the living room, make me go in the kitchen. It's a decent sized house! And I would have to do my speech from the kitchen so that she could hear me. Oh, she was a taskmistress! But it actually ended up teaching the teacher something. So that's the kind of experience that I had. It was always that they were encouraging me to keep moving forward.

Somewhere in my sixth-grade year, as I was looking forward to being one of the patrol people on the corner—that was really one of my goals!—Mother decided that there was a place that I should go other than McKinley. Apparently, my father's boss's children went to University High School,[15] and that sounded really good to her. Plus, the tuition was the same as you were paying at the U. And I enrolled there ultimately, the only Black kid in the school of seventh through twelfth graders for at least four years and probably the first one to go from sixth grade to twelfth and graduate. I think tuition was like $35 a quarter. I mean, what could you lose?

The Hollow[16] was where I learned to skate. And I was good! If you were at my house, I would show you my medals and trophies from speed skating. Anyway, my dad had started me skating as a very young child, and had

First Black in the Midway Speed Skating Club, 1951

taken me up to the Hollow to skate. And as I got a little bit older, it turned out that I was pretty good. The Hollow was about a half a block from my house, and I won a little race up there, and then the next level of that particular competition was held at Phalen.[17] In that particular race, I used my father's speed skates, which we stuffed with paper so my feet would fit! And I won that! That would be about 1943.

The Midway Speed Skating Club was the big club in Saint Paul. It was basically the only club that sponsored speed skating and coached. None of these clubs had Black kids in them. When Shop Pond gang decided they wanted to establish a speed skating club, they had a competition for kids who were not in Midway, and I won! And they were all excited until they found out I was Black. And then that was it. They never invited me into the club.

Now a year or two later, Mrs. Christoferson, who was the mother of the Midway Speed Skating Club, finally managed to get them to accept me into the club. By now, this is high school. At that time, there were no other Black kids involved. And this is talking about nationally. As a result of my getting involved, there were some other Black kids who came behind me and started doing some speed skating.

Hallie Q. Brown was part of my family's life. My mother worked there, I worked there, and later was chairperson of the board of directors. Because my mother worked at Hallie at the very beginning, I was there a lot and exposed to many things earlier than some of the children. We had an exceptional opportunity, both with Hallie and St. Philip's.[18] One of those things that was at Hallie was the Forum Council. Folks like A. Philip Randolph,[19] Thurgood Marshall,[20] and Judge William Hastie[21] at one time governor of the Virgin Islands, amazing people, who spoke to those gathered at the Forum Council session at Hallie.

Aunt Becky and her friends were the inspiration for the formation of a group called the Boys and Girls of Yesteryear. My mother was instrumental in establishing the program. She had recognized a need among older folks for social outings and gatherings, and had worked with Miss Carden, the executive director of Hallie Q. Brown, to see that it was formed. This was a precursor to Golden Agers,[22] and to the best of my knowledge was the first such group in the region if not the country.

The only live music that I remember as a kid was at Hallie. And that would have been during World War II.[23] Percy Hughes[24] was stationed out at Wold Chamberlain,[25] in that area, and he used to bring his little band in every now and then and they would play at the old gym at Hallie. And since my mother worked there, I could get to go! But I was really too young to be there. Didn't faze me. It was great fun. Great fun. But the majority of activities that we had were—we had records. Old vinyl.

Hallie had the teen dances. I'm talking now later on, when I was in the teen years. They'd have dances really quite regularly, maybe every week, every two weeks. It was one of the activities that they used to keep kids out of the street, keep them active. And they were great fun. Great fun. At these dances it was pretty much a DJ type thing. Somebody would be playing records and changing them. There really wasn't the money for live music, and so we used what we had, which was the records.

From the beginning, 1929, Hallie had a history of being involved with music. People like the late Deputy Chief Jimmy Griffin's brother, Billy Griffin. Mother used to constantly extol Billy. Billy was so clever and he was so brilliant and was such a genius and he did choreography and directed shows and he did musicals and he designed the costumes. Actually, for a while I used to get sick and tired of hearing about Billy, but it's true that from early on the interesting music in the community had a place where it could reside and that was Hallie.

Billy Griffin, Hazel Butler, and John M. Whitaker were all involved in the music program at Hallie Q. Brown. They are pictured here in front of the old Hallie Q. Brown building in the 1930s.

And one person after another who came in there—John Whitaker. I'm gonna miss some names, too, and it's going to be really bad. John Whitaker was one of the big names. He did *The Frog Prince* with kids. And I think we were around ten to twelve years old at that time. It was my first appearance in an operetta was as *The Frog Prince*. I played the king! I don't remember much about what I had to do, but I remember one of dear friends who was one of the Eight Debs could not sing. She still can't sing. She couldn't carry a tune. And she really didn't have that much sense of rhythm. So this was her little phrase that she was supposed to sing: [sings]

The cast of *The Frog Prince*: Kathryn Coram as the King, Delbert Crushshon as the Frog Prince, Barbara "Petey" Vassar as the Queen, and Constance Brown as the Princess

"Bonjour, mon amie from lovely France to thee. See me dress all dainty. It came from gay Paree. France has made the fashions for all the world to see. Bonjour, mon amie from lovely France to thee." Now that's what her song was. Here's how she did it, since she couldn't sing it. They were going to just play behind her? She went, bonjourmonameefromlovelyFrancetothee-seemydressall-dainty . . ." That's how she did it! I like to kid her about it still today, but it was hysterical. That was my first really big experience, and John worked with us, had us singing in choruses all the time. In terms of perpetuating music there he has several choral groups going on. Many of his groups were young adults, eighteen to twenty-five, something like that. It was a variety, a wide variety of music from traditional choral music to classical that he did with us. He was really quite an inspiration there at Hallie.

One more thing John Whitaker did when he was at Hallie, he had what they call Sunday Evening Salon. This was an effort to provide us with some culture, okay, but he had people—Marian Anderson never came to sing there, but he had people like that come, and you learned how to sit in a chair. I mean, this would be people of all ages, little kids. I had to go because my mother worked there and I loved it. But you learn to sit still until intermission or until the end of the program, to listen, to be at least moderately appreciative, and applaud. The Sunday Evening Salons were wonderful.

Leah Mae Minor, she preceded him there and was dealing with the music. There were tap dance classes. So we had all kinds of music going on.

Usually folks like the Harding Madrigal Singers came over and sang for us, and I remember that very clearly, because one girl in the Harding Madrigal Singers had red nappy hair. She was White, but her hair was nappier than mine will ever be, and I kept thinking, "Um, I know the hairdresser she should be going to."

In front of Hallie at 553 Aurora: Beatrice Vassar, Veronica Curruthers, Barbara "Petey" Vassar, Dorothea Hill, Rosie Mae Johnson, Beverly Carroll, Kathryn Coram, Constance Brown, Patty Brown; boy in back unknown

I was baptized at St. Philip's. It's been my church all my life. When I hit twelve and was confirmed at church, Father Williams said, "You-you-you will be in the choir." So you know, it wasn't a question of do you want to. I was in the choir from the age of twelve.

At St. Philip's Church, we used to have these dances in the undercroft. Now I don't know why they call it that unless they were trying to make it sound like it wasn't really a basement. But most Episcopal churches talk about undercrofts. Anyway, this was more like a basement! This was the old church. It stood on the same corner, but it basically faced the other way. Creaky! Had great big steel cables I'm sure were there to hold the walls up. It must have been limestone slabs that created the foundation. We had dances when Father Williams was there. Father Williams used to stutter. We had dances there, and we had blue lights and red lights. You know, sorta keep the lights down and the kids would get over in the corner and get dancin' all close! Well, one of the parents came down there one evening while we had this party going on. Now we had chaperons, mind you, and they were scattered throughout the room. He came down there. He wanted his daughters out of there! What were we doing down there with all this light dimmed down? Where were his girls? He was looking around, and Father Williams, who I said stuttered, went over there and said, "You-you-you-you just gooo on home. I'm in charge here!" Sent him packing. We had a wonderful time down there. And the kids from all the different churches would come and participate in those dances. They were really great!

For dances that were legit, those were basically held either at Hallie or at our church. Hallie used to have dances almost monthly it seemed. Oh, I used to have jumps at my house. You know what jump is? It's like an open house dance kind of thing. It's where you let people know there's a jump at my house at such-and-such a time, and then almost anybody who wanted to come could come. And it was usually your friends. Kids would come by after the dances at church and you'd do the same thing. You'd sort of dim the lights and put the records on, and kids would dance. It was fun. Didn't cost a penny. They were not really dressy-dressy. They were casually dress-up. It was always some nice little dress, little skirt, something like that. And the guys, they'd put on some of their best.

The Eight Debs at the Columbia Chalet: Kathryn Coram, Mary Lue Sizemore, LaDoris Foster, Constance Brown, Constance Hill, Yvonne Crushshon, Earline Neil, Joyce Vassar

We had a group called the Eight Debs.[26] We were not Debs, and it was a combination of Oatmeal Hill[27] and Cornmeal Valley[28] folk as far as that's concerned, but there were eight of us who had been friends for—let's see, now we're all seventy. We've been friends for at least sixty years. Anyway, the eight of us decided, since the druggist's daughter had a coming-out party, a debutante ball. We were pretty good kids, so why can't we have one? We got together and decided, okay, if each of our parents can come up with $25, that's eight people with $25 each. Out of that, we will rent the Columbia Chalet.[29] We will get a some snacks to serve, some punch. We had dresses made, and some of us had our own material. My material was antique lace. We could each choose what color we wanted. And the dresses were all made on the identical pattern. Sent out invitations, and the eight of us had a ball. Then they came back to my house and we had a sleepover after that. It was just great fun!

I finished Mount Holyoke[30] with a B.A. in geography. Yeah, geography! It was easy. I loved it! I spent most of my time at college in dance, but I had a major in geography, a minor in geology, art, and education. Then finding a job had its challenges until Alice Onque, who was head of Hallie at the time, knew that I had been raised through Hallie. Said, "Why don't you come over here and be the junior girls' director?" Whatever they called it, I was working with the younger kids, setting up programs for them. When I was there I choreographed a piece for a duet—I don't even know if I have a name for it. It was my style to write beat-type poetry, and it used the music of one of the TV shows. I went over there and I stayed there a couple years, and then I ended up working as a social worker at Jewish Family Service.[31] What I was doing was basically intuitive. What Alice had hired me for was the dance, athletics, theater, all that other stuff. Anyway, I was there for about a year, and Max Fassler [who] was the executive director suggested that I go get my master's in social work. I had fought this for a while because my mother had been a social worker, and you don't just go do what your mother does! And while I was at Hallie, I got a master's in theater from the U. So I had the two master's, and as of several years ago, I got certified in educational administration so that I could be a principal. I was supposed to be getting a Ph.D., and I got as far as through the prelims. But we had great discussions about what I was going to do my dissertation on. They and I could not agree. So I'm ABD—All But Dissertation!

The thing that most people look for to identify individuals is skin color. And because my skin is very light, they just passed me by. You know, because I would fit in. I'd been fitting in all my life. Not intentionally. It's not like "passing," which a lot of kids did in those days. Not so much the younger kids, but as the girls got to the point where they wanted employment. You couldn't work at the Emporium,[32] you couldn't work at the Golden Rule[33] if you were Black unless you were willing to work as the janitor or the matron or something of that nature. You were not permitted to be a clerk. Now I knew one girl who was Black and Mexican, Peggy Aparicio, who was working there. And there were two girls, one of whom goes to my church right now, who eventually got jobs as clerks, and we would avoid them because we didn't want to blow their cover. You know, they had got the job. We understood what the situation was. That's how it was in those days.

That's the part of being Black which is the chameleon aspect. If most of my friends who are successful, what they need to know is you have three or four different languages you speak. You speak school. You speak Mama-Daddy. You speak maybe church. You speak friends. They're all different languages. And so when you're in school, you speak that language. When you're with your friends, you speak another. And this is something that most of the Black kids I know are skilled at.

We talked about music in the community. I think music is an expression of the soul of the community. It has the capability of unifying, it has capability of soothing, it has the capability of providing solace. I think it's important for every community. I think it's an important piece of life that we all deal with basic rhythms and we hear music all the time, whether we recognize it or not. I think one of the things that the music actually allowed us to do was to have a focus when gathering together and a reason for gathering. No matter what the age group, no matter what income level, no matter what the educational level, that there was an opportunity for people to share and to be one. People will go to these churches just to hear a sermon, and when they do go hear the sermon it's because the sermon is music. If you listen to some of the Southern Baptist preachers, they don't talk, they don't orate, they sing their service. And so you may not feel like going to church, but you can have church come to you through the opportunity to sing and to listen to music.

There was vibrancy in Rondo, there was a community, there was a sense of—you know, they talk this stuff about a village raising kids. That's what it was. We didn't call it that. It was just that you knew that if you were a part of that community there were people who cared about you. They cared whether you acted like you had sense. If you acted like you didn't have sense, you will be dealt with, you will be corrected and you better not say anything back. Don't sass anybody. That was not acceptable.

A lot of that has been lost, and I think in part because of the way the community itself was physically disrupted. It was a warm, accepting place. It was a place with contrasts. There were people there who were on welfare and people who were considered professionals. It was a place where you felt really and truly safe.

Kathryn with Billy Taylor (now a retired air force colonel) at the oak tree in front of the Coram home, 495 St. Anthony, c. 1937

KATHRYN CORAM GAGNON, the single parent for twenty-five years of Lori, Philippe, and Angelique, was a lifelong member of St. Philip's Episcopal Church. Besides growing up at Hallie Q. Brown Community Center, Inc., she went on to be chairperson of its board. She was the first Black person to graduate from University High School. Receiving a four-year scholarship, she attended Mount Holyoke College and then earned a master's in theater, a master's in social work, and was ABD in educational administration from the University of Minnesota. After thirty years in the Saint Paul Public Schools, Kathryn retired, having served as the assistant principal of five schools. She was a Bush Leadership fellow and was involved with the Humphrey Institute of Public Affairs for Leadership Effective Schools. An accomplished singer, and a member of Actors Equity, she appeared in front of audiences all over the country from Massachusetts to Texas to Minnesota at Orchestra Hall and the Ordway. Kathryn was a lifelong respected and beloved community leader.

♦ NOTES

1. Kathryn Rebecca Coram Gagnon was born July 11, 1933, and passed December 20, 2004.

2. Awerta Mae Phillips Coram was born October 26, 1898, and passed November 10, 1982.

3. The National Association for the Advancement of Colored People (NAACP) was founded in New York City in 1909 by a multiracial group of activists. The NAACP believes that all men and women are created equal. Attorney Fredrick McGhee of the Rondo corridor was invited by W. E. B. Du Bois to attend the second meeting of the Niagara Movement. When he returned to Saint Paul, he organized the Twin City Protection League, which become the Twin Cities Branch of the NAACP in 1912.

4. Hallie Q. Brown Community Center, Inc., was opened in the Union Hall at Aurora and Kent Streets in 1929 as a community center specifically to serve the Black community when the Black YWCA closed in 1928. Hallie Q., as it is affectionately known, has served all ages through child care, youth and senior

clubs, athletics, music, and social events. In 1972, Hallie relocated in the Martin Luther King Building at 270 Kent Street at Iglehart in Saint Paul. The center's namesake was an educator who pioneered the movement of Black women's clubs in the late 1800s.

5. Ulysses Grant "Duke" Coram was born August 15, 1898, and passed May 30, 1976.

6. Ford Motor Company is located at 966 Mississippi River Boulevard at Ford Parkway.

7. Warren Given was located at 905–909 Grand Avenue.

8. John Dillinger, a well-known bank robber in the early 1930s, often spent time in Saint Paul as the Saint Paul Police Department ignored his presence.

9. Hetfield Queenan was located at 1037 University Avenue at Oxford.

10. Lincoln Food Market was at 499 Rondo in the northeast corner of Rondo and Mackubin.

11. WPA: The Works Progress (later Work Projects) Administration was a relief measure established in 1935. The WPA provided work through programs in highway construction, building construction, slum clearance, reforestation, rural rehabilitation, the Federal Writers' Project, the Federal Arts Project, and the Federal Theatre Project. Its average employment was 2,300,000. The WPA employed more than 8,500,000 different persons on 1,410,000 individual projects until it was officially terminated June 30, 1943.

12. McKinley School was located at 481 Carroll Avenue, between Mackubin, Arundel, and Rondo from 1903 to1966. Fire destroyed the building in 1977.

13. Yolande Enid Coram Holley Jackson Sims was born February 19, 1923, and passed October 4, 1959.

14. George Washington Carver (1864?–1943) was born a slave and went on to receive a college degree. At Tuskegee Institute he gained an international reputation as director of the agriculture research department. His efforts improved the economy of the South and position of all Black Americans.

15. University High School, located at 159 Pillsbury Drive Southeast in Minneapolis, had an outstanding reputation and was on the campus of the University of Minnesota. It was a place for University students to do their student teaching and for faculty and students from the University to explore teaching methods. The building now is Peik Hall.

16. The Hollow was an open space located in the square block between

Kent, Mackubin, St. Anthony, and Central. It had four playing fields, horseshoe beds, and in the winter, an ice-skating rink. It was used by families, churches, and schools in the area (see Evelyn Fairbanks, *The Days of Rondo,* Minnesota Historical Society Press, 1990).

17. Phalen Park is located between Frost Avenue, Maryland Avenue, Arcade, and East Shore Drive, and was first planned by the Saint Paul City Council in 1872. The city acquired the land in 1899 at a cost of $22,000, and it was opened to the public soon afterward. The park was named after early settler Edward Phalen, who staked one of the first claims to the land around Phalen Creek. Today there are 3.2 miles of trails around Lake Phalen, a playground, beach, golf course and clubhouse, and an amphitheater.

18. St. Philip's Episcopal Church was formed as a mission church in 1894, meeting in a home on Carroll Avenue. Later they rented a store on Rice Street, and in 1900 purchased a white frame building at Aurora and Mackubin. When this was torn down in the early 1950s, the altar was salvaged and placed in the structure built on the same northwest corner.

19. A. Philip Randolph (1889–1979) was a labor and civil rights leader. He was known for his organizing work for the Brotherhood of Sleeping Car Porters in 1925, the first union of predominantly Black workers to be granted a charter by the American Federation of Labor. In 1957 he was elected a vice president of the AFL-CIO.

20. Thurgood Marshall (1908–1993) became the United States' first Black Supreme Court justice. He was a staff lawyer for the NAACP, and for more than twenty years he served as chief council for their Legal Defense and Education Fund, wining twenty-nine of the thirty-two cases he argued before the Supreme Court. His most important victory came in 1954 with *Brown v. Board of Education.* He was confirmed to the Supreme Court in 1967 and retired in 1991.

21. William Hastic (1904–1976) was an attorney, judge/magistrate, and state government official/executive. He was governor of the Virgin Islands from 1946 to 1949 before his appointment to the Third U.S. Circuit Court of Appeals.

22. Golden Agers is a senior citizens' social group that began in the 1940s and continues to meet as a women's club at Hallie Q. Brown Community Center. At times, Golden Agers has served men and women. Before Golden Agers, Hallie Q. Brown's senior club for men and women was known as the Boys and Girls of Yesteryear.

23. World War II was fought between the Allied powers (England, the Soviet Union, the United States) and the Axis powers (Germany, Italy, Japan) from 1939 to 1945.The United States entered the war in 1941 following the bombing of Pearl Harbor by the Japanese.

24. Percy Hughes broke the "color line" for Black bands in Minnesota as a pioneer jazz "big band" leader after World War II. He continues as an active musician and band leader in the Twin Cities.

25. Wold Chamberlain Field is the airfield that became the Minneapolis-Saint Paul Airport. The first flight from the airfield took place in 1919. The field was renamed after the first two pilots, Cyrus Chamberlain and Ernest Wold, who were killed in 1918 in World War I. Fort Snelling, which is adjacent to Wold Chamberlain Field, was an active military base for inductions during World War II. While men were temporarily stationed there waiting for their assignment, they attended dances, and women from the community were transported to the base to help keep up military morale.

26. The Eight Debs are Connee Brown Freeman, Earline Neil Estes, Ladoris Foster, Connie Hill Walker, Yvonne Crushshon Robinson Harrington, Mary Lue Sizemore McCoy, Joyce Vassar Smith Clark, and Kathryn Coram Gagnon.

27. Oatmeal Hill was a term referring to Rondo west of Dale Street toward Lexington, sometimes known as Upper Rondo. More affluent residents tended to move into this area, giving the impression the residents had a higher social standing. This middle-class neighborhood consisted of predominantly single-family homes.

28. Cornmeal Valley, also known as Lower Rondo or Deep Rondo, was east of Dale Street. This was a lower-middle-class residential neighborhood with predominantly single-family homes. From the 1930s, this part of the community struggled with growing poverty.

29. Columbia Chalet was located at 3300 Central Avenue Northeast in Minneapolis.

30. Mount Holyoke College began in 1839 in South Hadley, Massachusetts. From its inception, Mount Holyoke has led the way in women's education.

31. Jewish Family Service was located at 355 Washington, Room 300, in 1955.

32. The Emporium Department Store was located downtown on Seventh Street at Robert Street.

33. The Golden Rule was originally established as a department store in Saint Paul in 1886, and moved into a three-story building at Old Seventh Street between Robert and Jackson in 1891. In 1961, the store merged with Donaldson's and became Donaldson's Golden Rule. In later years, the name of the store was shortened to just Donaldson's and remained at this location until 1980, when the business moved into the Town Square complex at Seventh, Minnesota, and Cedar Streets.

GLORIA YVONNE PRESLEY MASSEY

The community took care of everyone.

I AM GLORIA PRESLEY MASSEY.[1] Hallie Q. Brown[2] brought us all together. Hallie was at 553 Aurora. I was more into the community at Hallie Q. Brown than I was at my church. From the time I was little, because when my mother[3] worked, I had to go over to Hallie Q. Brown for their day-care center. That was fine because she knew I would be okay at the day-care center. I was there actually from about the age of nine because my mother had worked.

At about ten, eleven, or twelve, I remember being a Girl Scout.[4] I was beginning to get active in the community as a whole. I was in Troop 52. Miss Hazel Butler. She was our troop leader. I remember we had our little green uniform and my little cap. I liked that.

Then I started with the gymnasium, playing sports and playing basketball and softball. We would have equipment and take it over to the Hollow Playground,[5] and we played softball in the Hollow Playground. The Hollow Playground almost covered an entire block. It was on Central and St. Anthony. It was located between Kent and Mackubin. Now, there were four entranceways into that playground, two on Central and two on St. Anthony. There was a lot of activity for the teenagers to go into that Hollow Playground.

I was with modern dance. I was on the newspaper at Hallie. I was in different clubs. As I got older, I was in Teen Debs. At that time I must have been

Bill Dickerson's Teenage Club in 1952 with Robert Hickman and Gloria Presley planning a program. The Teenage Club was a vital part of the program at Hallie Q.

thirteen or fourteen. It was for girls and I guess we would make plans for dances for the teenagers. As a group we would make some kind of arrangement so that we could sell tickets and have a little dance amongst the teenagers.

I was at Hallie Q. Brown's five days a week. I had chores to do around the house when I came home from school—make sure the dishes were clean, maybe sweep up or whatever, take the trash out. I had my little duties I had to do, and once I did them, then I could be free to go over to Hallie. Of course, I had to do homework, too. I don't know how I managed to do it, but I managed to do all of that so I could get over there. I had an activity every day of the week. I was on the newspaper. I think maybe Monday or Wednesday may have been practice for our team. Tuesday could have been a club night. Thursday would have been modern dance. Friday, maybe that would have been the dance that we had planned or whatever. So there was something to do five days a week. I lived at Hallie Q. Brown.

Being a teenager, my mother did not let me have a boyfriend at fourteen, fifteen, sixteen, and yet there were some girls that had boyfriends that could come by their house and pick them up. I would have a boyfriend, but if he wanted to walk me home, he had to stop about a block away. So anyway, how I got to be given permission to date actually was when I was seventeen and I was running for the contest of Hallie Q. Brown. Miss Hallie Q. Brown. It was in 1952, and I had to have an escort. So that was the first time that I was given permission. Mother knew then that I was going to need an escort, and that meant someone was going to have to come and pick me up. So that was my first chance to have a boyfriend legally.

At Hallie the community embraced everyone and took care of everyone. We loved our city, Saint Paul. My parents and my grandparents believed in raising a family and they wanted the best for them. They taught us to try to appreciate and do the right thing. My parents were separated. I did live mainly with my mother, but I was able to go down to my dad's[6] house every day, so I really had my dad in my life every day.

My sister[7] also lived in the community on Carroll and Chatsworth, so when I was at home and I was living with my mother on Dale and St. Anthony, I'd walk over one block to Rondo, and then I would walk out to my sister's house to Chatsworth on Rondo. And it was a community where everybody knew everybody. At that time, as I was walking out to my sister's house. That was about seven or eight blocks that I had to walk out there, with traffic. I knew this person, or that person would honk a horn or I'd be waving to that person. You know, that's how it was.

At that time it was so beautiful because you knew everybody. It was so different back then. You knew everybody and people I knew that were in a car would have been willing to give me a lift and that would have been fine, but that was my way of just going out to my sister's house. I would always walk west out there on Rondo.

Or I would walk east to my dad's house. As I walked I knew different families along both sides of the street. There were kids my age, older kids, their older brothers or sisters who might have been friends to my brothers, so I just knew everybody. As I would be on my way to my dad's

Sister Jerry on Rondo between Dale and St. Albans

house I could stop and talk to a few people. I'd probably get to my dad's house after an hour or two, just from visiting along the way.

As a teenager we walked everywhere we would walk. There was no place that we didn't think of that we couldn't get there. A couple of us would get together and we'd walk. Then while you're talking and carrying on, you'd be wherever you were going. You didn't think about being cold or anything because you dressed for the weather and it was fine. We ventured out, too. We

Nephew Donald Doty in front
of Field's Drug Store

would go out to the Dairy Queen,[8] which is still there on Lexington at Fuller, just south of University. We used to go to Phalen Lake.[9] Hop onto the Dale and Como bus and go out to Phalen. Go swimming, and I used to love to do that. Couldn't swim, never learned. I've been the kind of person that wherever the crowd went, I'd be right along, okay?

Mr. Field had a real nice drugstore.[10] Mr. Field was a pharmacist. Lafayette Field's Pharmacy was a teenage hangout. He had a soda fountain and everything. Every Sunday, like after church, everybody had to go there to congregate. He moved locations several times, but wherever Mr. Field went, all the kids went.

On Rondo we all watched out for each other. Being the youngest in my family my brothers always watched over me, and their friends did, too. Right now today, I feel safe. I feel safe when I am out and I run into people that I knew at Hallie or from the old neighborhood. We would all do for each other if someone needed something. That's my whole story to you is that the community was just involved, embraced, and took care of everyone.

Intersection of Rondo and Arundel Street
Photo reprinted with permission of the
Minnesota Historical Society

GLORIA YVONNE PRESLEY MASSEY loves her family and is thankful for the good life with which she has been blessed. From the strength of her mother's wisdom and teachings, she was able to raise a family of her own. Her older brothers—Dan, Leon, Kenneth, and Ray ("Red")—taught, supported, and protected her. Mrs. Massey's sister, Jerlyn ("Jerry"), was fifteen years older and therefore Jerry's son, Donald, was like another brother. She is proud of her secretarial work in every branch of the civil service; she retired from Ramsey Hospital after sixteen years in 1996. Mrs. Massey is very proud of the talents and accomplishments of her children: Craig, who lives in Kansas City, Missouri, and works as a security guard, and Ellen, who works with Viking Drill and Tool, Inc., in Saint Paul. She is blessed to have her children, whose first interest is looking out for her.

♦ NOTES

1. Gloria Yvonne Presley Massey was born July 30, 1934.

2. Hallie Q. Brown Community Center, Inc., was opened in the Union Hall at Aurora and Kent Streets in 1929 as a community center specifically to serve the Black community when the Black YWCA closed in 1928. Hallie Q., as it is affectionately known, has served all ages through child care, youth and senior clubs, athletics, music, and social events. In 1972, Hallie relocated in the Martin Luther King Building at 270 Kent Street at Iglehart in Saint Paul. The center's namesake was an educator who pioneered the movement of Black women's clubs in the late 1800s.

3. Mother Lucile M. Presley was born July 18, 1900, and passed September 8, 1973.

4. The Girl Scouts are an international organization founded in 1912 in Georgia by Juliette Gordon Low. From the beginning Girl Scouts has been a multiracial organization dedicated to helping girls build character and gain life skills. The Girls Scouts of Saint Paul began in 1922.

5. The Hollow was an open space located in the square block between Kent, Mackubin, St. Anthony and Central. It had four playing fields, horseshoe beds, and in the winter, an ice-skating rink. It was used by families, churches,

and schools in the area (see Evelyn Fairbanks, *The Days of Rondo*, Minnesota Historical Society Press, 1990).

6. Father Dan J. Presley was born January 9, 1890, and passed January 22, 1963.

7. Sister Jerlyn "Jerry" Presley Doty Gooden was born March 19, 1920, and passed April 6, 2004.

8. A Dairy Queen soft serve ice cream stand is still located at 450 North Lexington Parkway at University Avenue.

9. Phalen Park is located between Frost Avenue, Maryland Avenue, Arcade, and East Shore Drive, and was first planned by the Saint Paul City Council in 1872. The city acquired the land in 1899 at a cost of $22,000, and it was opened to the public soon afterward. The park was named after early settler Edward Phalen, who staked one of the first claims to the land around Phalen Creek. Today there are 3.2 miles of trails around Lake Phalen, a playground, beach, golf course and clubhouse, and an amphitheater.

10. Lafayette Field's Pharmacy/Majestic Drugs was located at 626 Rondo at Dale. Later it relocated to 542 Rondo, between Mackubin and Kent.

FLOYD GEORGE SMALLER JUNIOR

You had strong Black individuals in the community that held the other people together.

I AM FLOYD G. SMALLER JR.[1] In my latter high school years, and a few years after I graduated, I was in the Gopher Elks Drum and Bugle Corps.[2] This was 1953. Growing up as kids, we all wanted to be a part of it. We'd see these people beating these drums and blowing these bugles and the majorettes and everybody on the street watching them, and that was just another show that everybody wanted to be in. I don't care what age you were. I mean, we'd get sticks off of trees and we'd be beating on mailboxes and marching in the street, beating tin cans. If you weren't a member of the Elks, you weren't anybody, okay. So this was the application you made in your mind: "I want to be a member of that drum and bugle corps before I die." So most of my friends, me and Marvin Roger Anderson and Joe Lewis and Donald Powers and Eugene Price and Pudgy Thurston, we were all in the Elks. At one point they voted me commander of the Elks.

I was commander for about two years. Being commander means you're in control of all the people, except the big honcho, who is the major. These are older men. These men were fifty-five, sixty years old. I know one was named Harold Walker and Willie Burrell.

They used to sign us up for the parades in Blue Earth,[3] Owatonna,[4] and Rochester.[5] We marched all over the state. They would have corn celebration.

They'd have the tractor race celebration. You know, all these little towns had all these little kind of things they celebrate during the summer and we would show up for these parades and celebrations.

The Minneapolis Elks was our rival. A lot of the parades, we'd say, "You know Minneapolis is gonna be there." So everybody gotta put on his best show because now you got these two Black bands that shows up in these White communities that's located out of the Twin Cities. It's showtime, baby, it's showtime! They'd show up, we'd show up, we'd do our regular parade thing.

After the parade was over, here comes the beer and whatever else you wanted and all these old drunks would be in the street and they'd be celebrating. "Hey, boys, you want a drink? You want a this?" So we'd march in and out of these liquor establishments. Like, if there was a beer joint in Owatonna and the front door was open, we'd march right through the front

Gopher Elks: Duane Perteet, Eugene Watts,
Marvin Roger Anderson, Wally Pettiford, Elroy Haraway

door and out the back door, and all these people would be sitting in there drinking and the noise would be loud. We'd be beating these drums and these people would be having just one heck of a time. We'd march out of that joint, go across the street and march through another joint, come back and march through another joint. And we'd do this and have two, three parades every week.

That's how we spent our summers, doing these type of events. And you're talking about fun. I mean, it was like *Saturday Evening Post* days. It was like everything was great. We'd have the full moon coming home on the bus and people would be singing and laughing and just having a jolly old time. Then our girlfriends would be waiting for us when we got home, no matter what time it was, if their folks would let them stay up, 'cause sometimes we wouldn't get home till 3:00 in the morning from our parade trips.

It was boys and girls. Now, girls didn't play the drums or the bugles, but the girls were the majorettes. So we had probably twelve, thirteen majorettes. Big fun. Big fun! We had about thirty-two people. The ages varied, but you really had to be a teenager to go because we'd go out of town, and a lot of time there was alcohol and stuff, so most of the kids was seventeen, eighteen, nineteen, twenty, twenty-one, you know, twenty-two.

We were all in school during the year, so on Saturdays we'd go up to the Elks during the winter and we'd practice indoors, upstairs, and beat the drums and get ready for our summer escapades. That was fun, too. We didn't have nothing to do, so we'd go up there and beat the drums and then some of the girls would come up and sit around or they'd go in another room and practice their steps while we were doing that. It gave us something to do.

And we'd march in the Winter Carnival.[6] We marched in the Aquatennial.[7] We did this every year. We wore the army khakis and the spats and little army hats. It was a cute outfit. In fact, we sponsored ourselves. We'd go out and buy our own uniform. But see, all we needed, we needed the white belt. We had the white spats and we had the khaki cap, khaki shirts, khaki pants, and either brown or black shoes and we shined them. We looked real good.

Peters Meats,[8] they probably started sponsoring them after I'd retired and I think I was in college and out then. And Peters got some old used stuff. That stuff was so ugly. I think Lee Ballard was commander then, and that's when Peters Meats was sponsoring them. They had these old gray uniforms

Crazy 8 Friends: Donald Powers, Joe Lewis, Wally Pettiford, Floyd Smaller, Harry Fullford, Marvin Roger Anderson, Jackie Ellis

and they marched in the Aquatennial. They almost looked like Confederate[9] uniforms or something. Gray wool, itchy, you know.

On our practice days, all the people in town would line up on the sidewalks between 5:30 and 8:30 in the evening to watch us practice, and by the time it got dusk, dark, and the lights were not yet on, people behind us would turn their car lights on. So the lights would be glancing off the drums and the sticks and the bugles would be shining, and it was just one heck of a picture to see. Everybody would follow us around the community. We'd march around Hallie Q. Brown[10] and Field's Drug Store[11] and by the Elks and down by a few of the old liquor establishments, and people would be just out there yelling. It was like they'd never seen us and they'd just seen us the day before. All the little kids would be running behind us, "I want to be like him! I want to be like him!"

I think Rondo was unique in that you had strong Black individuals in the community that held most of the other people in the community together. The Elks was one of the places that provided this bond and leadership. The Elks was a fun positive situation and gave me an opportunity to learn to be a leader. I was able to learn to work out some problems in my peer group, within the rules and values of the organization. The Elks helped me and others build our personal strengths and our character. It was about fun, it was memories, it was traveling, and learn about other people from other places other than Rondo, and it was a positive experience.

◆ ◆ ◆

FLOYD GEORGE SMALLER JR., son of Floyd Sr. and Esther Lee, and grandson of Sadie, Alf, and Henry, is proud of what he was able to give his family. He is also proud of being an athlete and a college graduate, working in the communities in which he lived, and in particular developing the recreation program in Lake View, Arkansas. Mr. Smaller retired from Central High School after twenty-six years as a teacher, coach, and administrator. He was inducted into the Minnesota State High School League Hall of Fame. Mr. Smaller has eight siblings: Shirley, Robert, Betty Jean, Richard, Sheri Ann, Carolyn, Alfonso, and Roosevelt. He and his wife of forty-six years have four children, Brian, Trent, Floyd II, and Gayle, and grandchildren including Gayle Jr., Malcom, Angel, Amena, Blue, Yasmin, and Jordan. Floyd is a cofounder of Rondo Days.

◆ NOTES

1. Floyd George Smaller was born November 24, 1936.

2. The Gopher Elks Drum and Bugle Corps was sponsored by the Gopher Elks Lodge, which was located at 559 Carroll. In 1955, the Lodge moved to 803 St. Anthony between St. Albans and Grotto. The Improved Benevolent Protective Order of the Elks of the World (IBPOEW), the Black Elks fraternal organization, was formed in 1898 when two Pullman Porters were denied membership in the all-White order in Cincinnati, Ohio. IBPOEW followed the same commitments to youth as the BPOE (White Elks) through artistic endeavors, athletics, scholarships, and camps.

3. Blue Earth is 135 miles southwest of Saint Paul near the Iowa border.

4. Owatonna is seventy miles south of Saint Paul.

5. Rochester is eighty miles southeast of Saint Paul.

6. The Winter Carnival was founded in 1886 to contest a claim that Saint Paul was uninhabitable during the winter. The carnival is a celebration of Minnesota

winters over a ten-day period that includes the crowning of King Boreas and Queen of the Snows, day and evening parades, a medallion hunt, and other activities. Occasionally, elaborate ice castles are built.

7. The Minneapolis Aquatennial began in 1941. This summer festival celebrating the lakes of Minneapolis includes a daytime and torchlight parades, as well as many summer activities, including aqua follies and milk carton boat races. The Aquatennial is always held the third week in July.

8. Peters Meat Products, Inc., was located at 940 Beech and 350 East Sixth Street.

9. In the early days of the American Civil War (1861–1865), the uniforms worn by soldiers of the Confederacy (the eleven Southern states that had seceded from the Union) were for the most part gray.

10. Hallie Q. Brown Community Center, Inc., was opened in the Union Hall at Aurora and Kent Streets in 1929 as a community center specifically to serve the Black community when the Black YWCA closed in 1928. Hallie Q., as it is affectionately known, has served all ages through child care, youth and senior clubs, athletics, music, and social events. In 1972, Hallie relocated in the Martin Luther King Building at 270 Kent Street at Iglehart in Saint Paul. The center's namesake was an educator who pioneered the movement of Black women's clubs in the late 1800s.

11. Lafayette Field's Pharmacy was located at Dale and Rondo. Later it relocated to 542 Rondo, between Mackubin and Kent.

MARVIN ROGER ANDERSON

A person could be a shoeshine man during the day, but he could be Mr. President at night.

MY FULL NAME IS MARVIN ROGER ANDERSON.[1] I define my life as the two major divisions— Saint Paul, which taught me so many things, and then after going away to school, acquiring an education which has kept me going for the rest of my life. And it's funny how when you look back on your life and you say what were the major influences in your life, growing up in Saint Paul, growing up in the Rondo neighborhood, probably is as strong to me as going away to Morehouse College[2] in Atlanta, Georgia. Both of them provided me with the best education that a person could get.

Rondo and Saint Paul taught me that it is possible and indeed, one is capable of constructing a life, of contributing value to your community, of living a certain way, without having to have an education. Most of the people who influenced me, my father[3] and my mother and my father's friends, did not have a college degree. They were intelligent men and women. They were deprived of the opportunity to go to college for any number of reasons. Mostly they had to work. A lot of them were railroad men or men in service industries. From these individuals, I learned that it's not so much what you do in life that counts, it's how you choose to live your life. That's the thing that matters. These men were waiters on the railroad. They were Pullman Porters.[4] They worked in the packinghouse. They were shoeshine men.

They were delivery men. They were in the service industry. As butlers or cooks, they would go to work in uniforms that befitted a service industry. They wore waiter uniforms, Pullman caps, maid's aprons. The men that worked at the packinghouse would wear these long aprons that had rubber things. However, no matter what they wore at work, I was always amazed how they came home and they took a shower, took a bath and cleaned up and emerged later as kings, princes, and queens, because that's the life they chose to lead in their community.

They would read about it. They would adopt the habits of the people that they worked with. They were well read. Saint Paul had a tremendous amount of social clubs[5] and institutions that required them to be presidents, vice presidents, chairs, secretaries, and board members. These institutions that are still in existence, some for over eighty years, like the Sterling Club.[6] And when they were in the Sterling Club mode, when they were in that part of their life, they would call each other Mister. They gave each other a great deal of respect. A person could be a shoeshine man during the day, but he could be Mr. President at night.

I grew up watching those individuals come through my home or come to the apartment buildings that my father and five other men, who were railroad men, built. They came together as a group, they formed a corporation, and obtained what they call the largest Negro loan ever given to anybody in Minnesota for $247,000. They constructed twelve exquisitely made apartment buildings[7] in Saint Paul.

We lived in one of them at 989 Rondo Avenue, Apartment D. We moved there in 1947. We stayed there until they were taken by the State of Minnesota under eminent domain for the freeway. And throughout the course of the time that we lived there, a lot of families came through Saint Paul and they lived in my father's apartment building.

And I would see people in meetings. They would conduct meetings in their apartments, because they were like townhouses but aligned together, so that we could be sitting in one area and we could see people coming into someone else's home and conducting meetings and they would be served tea. It was just an incredible, fascinating way to watch people grow up, and I was always impressed by that.

At Rondo and Chatsworth there were six units on each side separated by a green area. Rondo ran east and west. The apartments ran south and north.

There were two apartments that faced on Rondo, and six of them went back towards the alley.

When they decided to route the freeway, those apartments were designated for removal. At first, my father and his partners (Ira Rawls, Lionel Newman, Mr. Gilmore, and Mr. Henderson) weren't too upset about losing the apartments. Mr. Rawls, who was my godfather, and my father, Lucius Anderson, decided that they were going to take any profit that they would make, and they would put that profit and purchase another parcel of land. On this parcel of land, they had plans drawn up which would allow them to construct a shopping center. And that shopping center was designated for the corner of University and Lexington, because by this time the Coliseum[8] had gone and Lexington Ball Park.[9] And I saw plans at around seventeen years old, and they had a shopping center, they had a drug store, they had a grocery store, they had office buildings. I had never seen my father and Mr. Rawls so excited about a concept. These are two guys with just a high school education created this corporation.

They would have their meetings at the house. My sister used to keep their books for them, the minute books. They had resolutions. It was all done just very appropriately, as I later found out. Then they were told that the

Rangh Court advertisement

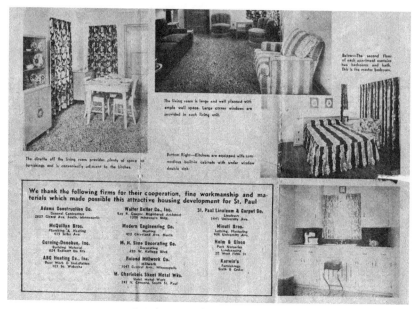

Rangh Court advertisement, cont.

apartments were inferiorly constructed, and the amount that they were looking for would not be realized. They challenged it and they went to court and
every hearing along they way, the valuation never changed. I could sit in my
home, and next door could be—the music would be as loud as it could get,
and I never heard one thing. They really built these things, quality-wise.

Ultimately they ran out of funds and they decided that, "Well, it's over."
They dissolved the corporation. I remember that day. I was getting ready
to go away to college, and my father and Mr. Rawls came by the house and
they dissolved the corporation, and it was a very, very sad day.

It got worse after they had transferred title to the apartments to the state.
They weren't immediately destroyed. I thought they would be destroyed.
When I went away to school, and I would write back and say, "Have they
torn the houses down yet?" They said, "No, they're still standing." And then
one day when I was away at school, I got a letter and I was told that these
so-called inferior constructed apartments that would not allow a proper
valuation to be made were sawed into smaller units. They were sawed in
twos, threes, and in four parts, placed on trucks and they were transferred

throughout the City of Saint Paul. They're still standing to this day, almost fifty years later.

When I heard that this had happened and they waited until the time to appeal had passed, I got so angry. And that's when I decided I was going to become a lawyer. That is what gave me my focus. I realized at that moment that you can have all you can get. They can call you Mister, they can call you this, but unless you have some way to protect your rights legally, going to court and to argue and to fight and to understand what they were fighting for, it would never be protected. I made the decision in college at that time that I would become a lawyer. Saint Paul influenced my life for the next forty years.

My father was a waiter and Mr. Rawls was a cook for the Northern Pacific.[10] My father was unofficially given the designation of number one waiter. What that meant was whenever the president of the Northern Pacific Railroad had to leave town, do an inspection of the rails, have an out-of-state meeting, he would choose one waiter and one cook to prepare the president's meal, work the president's private car. All waiters and all cooks are on a very rigid rotation. Five days in, five days out. However, whenever the president wanted to go anywhere, the president had the authority to take somebody out of that rotation and put him on his private car. The private car could go out anywhere from one day, two days, to two weeks. Every year, the private car would go out to Yellowstone, and the private car would pick up dignitaries along the line. They would go out and they would stop at some of the wonderful national parks, and they would sightsee and they would come back to the private car.

Mr. Rawls and my dad would prepare their food for them. When Mr. Rawls retired, my father took over the job of cook and waiter. They were given quite a bit of respect by the railroad, because they were the president's number one. I used to go with my father when he would prepare the train for number one, down at the commissary.

The majority of my father's income came from tips. My father would only get like $7,000 in actual pay. To make ends meet my father was also a caterer, and for many, many years he was the caterer for very wealthy Minnesota families. My brother and I had the job of taking these white napkins that were in the bottom of his suitcase. And we would untie these—one napkin would have fifty-cent pieces in them, another would have quarters, another dimes, and another nickels. And he'd say, "You keep the pennies." We would add this up, and soon we were able to save enough money to build the apartments.

The life of a waiter was very hard. When I became of age, I went down to the railroad and applied for a job, a summer job. And when I told them my name, the man who was in charge of it called me aside and he said, "Son, there's no way that you're going to be hired by the Northern Pacific Railroad. Your father wouldn't allow it." And I was very upset with my father, because I figured he was trying to influence me and my life. Because I had the idea that it was lucrative. I didn't realize at the time, but later I realized why my father instructed the NP personnel not to hire me when I applied for a job. It is a cruel job that drove grown men to drink.

During the time that my father was on the railroad, and this is why the union was so important, five grown men had to work inside of a space about the size of a closet. They had to maneuver, carry their trays, maneuver in such a way that they couldn't impede each other. They worked from 4:30 in the morning to maybe 10:00, 10:30 at night. There was always, always something to do. They had three calls for breakfast, three calls for lunch, and three calls for dinner. When that was over, they had to make sure all the silverware was washed. They had to tear down. They had to set up. They had to make sure that everything was completely spotless. They had to go through that three times at breakfast, three times at lunch, three times at dinner. The first indignity was here you have this procedure with five men on a packed railroad car.

And there would be a White steward who would have to come over and take the order. For some reason, the waiter couldn't take the order from the patron at the table. He had to describe the food, he had to tell them what was on the menu, but then he had to nod his head or make a wave of the hand so the steward could come over and take the order, write it up. And then give it to the waiter to take back, as if the waiter wasn't capable of doing that act himself. Then when it was over, you had to call the steward over who would calculate the bill, then give you your bill. The waiter couldn't. Either they didn't trust the waiters or they didn't think they were capable of performing this algebraic calculation.

The quarters where the waiters slept, it was an unheated boxcar with wooden platforms for beds that was next to the engine. So the roar of the engine, the breeze from the elements, all were a part—and the heat from the engine would be the heat that would heat the waiter's car. Now these are the conditions in which they had to work from sunup, basically, to sundown for forty years.

From the time I was young I noticed that the first night they get back home, they're exhausted. They come in at about 9:30 at night after they cleaned the train up and finally get home 10:30, 11:00 at night. We're usually in bed. When you wake up the next morning, you'd see your dad. He's tired, so you go off to school. When you come back home that afternoon, your dad is up and he's moving around. The second day, your dad is up before you. He's probably making breakfast for the kids. He's getting out to do all the chores that need to be done around the house. My father was the one who paid all of the bills. He would get ready. He would write his checks out. He would get dressed up. He'd go downtown, and he'd take care of all of the bills. The third and fourth days they were in town would be devoted to their social activity or business activity. In my father's case, it was either being in a social club, working on the construction of the apartments. But they always took care of business.

The fourth day is when everything changed. On that fourth day, they started drinking. For many years, my father drank. A lot of my friends whose dads worked on the railroads noticed this, too. They would take a little drink the first, second, and third day, but by that fourth day the drinking got heavy. I came to realize later on in my life that the fact that the next day they had to go back into that life again led a lot of these guys to drink. And they would wake up on the fifth day with a tremendous hangover, and somebody would come and pick them up and they'd go down to the railroad and then off they go for another five days.

This five days on and five days off rotation, it would create panic in the home because we all knew it was coming. We all knew that on that fourth day, Daddy was going to get—something was going to go wrong. And I always thought it was just something innate about my dad. But then I realized that the idea of that work, the idea of being in those conditions, the idea of sleeping on those platforms, the idea of not having any heat in your car.

The final indignity my father endured occurred at the time the Northern Pacific decided to integrate the dining car stewards' positions. They were going to integrate the stewards, and for the first time the steward was going to be a non-Caucasian. A lot of waiters who would come by the house just knew that my father was going to be the first Negro steward, having been number

Local 516's offices

one waiter all those years. When the time came to select a steward, they selected one of my father's best friends, a man who could almost pass for White, to be the number one steward, to put on the face of, "Look what we're doing." And I don't know how it affected my dad. He never said anything about it at all. But I always felt this was a big disappointment for him. He had a lot of disappointment in his life, and he kept a lot of the things inside of him.

That's why I think my father fought so hard for the union.[11] He started off at fifty cents an hour. When my father retired in 1964, his income was something like $9,000 a year. The rest was in tips. It was a brutal life. The young guys, the college guys glamorized it. They were only there for the summer. You make good money on tips. But the men who had to live this condition for thirty, forty years, many times were broken men by the time their railroading days were over. And that was just the waiters. The Pullman Porters had it even worse, in certain regards.

As much as he put his life in there, my dad had no great love for the railroad. He could have been a businessman. He could

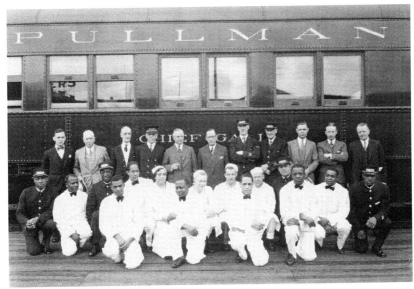

Northern Pacific Railroad Train Crew, including waiters, cooks, Pullman Porters, conductors, stewards, and nurse. Father Archie Anderson is fourth from the left in front, c. 1930

have been a lawyer. He could have been a professor. I don't know. And what makes it sad is my belief that the lives of most of the railroad men had similar reactions to the railroad, to the conditions, the five in and five out, and the tremendous damage that did in marriages.

The family gets used to your father or your breadwinner being gone five days out, you can tolerate that individual for five days. The women became very independent, because they had to do things during those—I mean, in those days, there weren't snowblowers, so snow was there, the women had to get out and clean it, or they would get their kids out to clean it. Then all of a sudden a person retires, and they have to turn around now and say, "You're in my way. I put the paper towels on this way. You put 'em on the other way." Men would always have to reassert themselves within the home and that caused frictions, and I was gone when that happened in our home.

My father retired and was dead within two years of retiring. It was one of those things that the railroad and the Rondo thing had severely affected him. They had a great impact on me. I would imagine that they had a tremendous impact on my dad.

My mother, Ora Lee Jones Anderson, raised herself from age fourteen years old. By eighteen she was working and met my father, who had transferred here from Seattle, Washington, his hometown, to work on the Northern Pacific Railroad. She was an independent, strong person that had to carve out her own personality because of the circumstances in which she lived.

All of her life she has been realistic and blunt. She plays by the rules and expects everyone else to do the same, irrespective of whom or what you think you are. I'll tell you this, my mother never had a job that paid more than the minimum wage, and to this day she has more money than all of us put together. I have no idea how she does it!

One story crystallizes what my mother is like. My mother ran an elevator at a place called Newman's Department Store,[12] which had three or four floors. After school, we often had to go downtown and get directions from my mother, especially if my father was out on the road. We were told to come downtown to the department store, get on that elevator, and she'd have a list of things for my brother and I to do. "Go home. Do this. Go to the store. Buy this. You go home. Do your books." My mother was just a real independent woman, running the house. And as we would go up and down the elevator, on the fourth floor there was the cage where you would pay your bills.

One of her best friends was a teller at the cage, and they would chat and chat until the bell rang and my mother would just close the door, go downstairs, and when she would come back up, they would continue their conversation right exactly where they had stopped. I was on the elevator with her one time, when she was talking to her friend and the bell rang. That day the store manager came from around the around the other corner. And he said, "Ora! When you hear that bell ring, I don't care what you are doing! You shut that door and you go downstairs and get that customer. I am so tired of the two of you having conversations. That bell rings and people are downstairs waiting! Do you understand what I'm saying?" My mother looked at him and said, "'Course I do."

I didn't know what to say. This guy really jumped on my mother. Maybe two or three weeks later, I was back downtown on the elevator, and we were on the fourth floor and it was right around 4:30. Through the mirror she could see the manager running to catch this elevator. And as soon as he started running, she heard the bell go off, and she waited until the last moment and shut the door in his face and went down. I said, "Mama! What are you doing?" She said, "You heard him say, 'No matter what happens, when you hear that bell ring, you shut that door and you go down.'" When she came back up again, he was standing there. He was so mad! But he couldn't say anything to my mother, as she had done exactly what he told her to do. She waited until the perfect moment. She had planned this. And maybe not just for me, but she knew that there was going to be a time when she was going to catch that guy and from that moment on, he never said anything like that to my mother again.

My mother is down-to-earth with a lot of common sense. She's the type of person that just believes a bird in the hand is worth two in the bush. Never spend money you don't have. Don't spend your money before you get it. Save a nickel for a rainy day. Put something away. Never owe anybody any money. Always take care of yourself. If you don't have but two things to wear make sure they are clean. Learn how to press your clothes, shine your shoes. Very, very basic things that she's acquired over the years that have just sustained her. And being the youngest, I learned all of these basic things. Never be late! Always be five minutes early if you can. Never go any-place late, because if the person is late, the train's gonna be gone. She's got a saying for everything.

My father was almost six feet tall. My mother was barely five feet. However, she never backed down from my father at all. She would say, "I'm tellin' ya something. I've been on my own since I was fourteen years old, and you or nobody else is gonna tell me what to do!" And that's been my in-fluence. My mother and my father have been the two greatest influences in my life, because of the way they taught me to be independent, to be strong, to be proud.

My parents had a great impact on me. For that reason, I came back here to try to do what I could to revive that memory and relive the community and try to give some dignity to these stories of how they lived, how they so-cialized, how they worked, how this community was created, sustained and grew. It had a tremendous amount of things to offer those who grew up here and absorbed this magnificent history.

◆ ◆ ◆

MARVIN ROGER ANDERSON, JD was born in Saint Paul to Lucius ("Archie") and Ora Lee ("Coopie") Anderson. He graduated from Central High School in

1958 and earned a degree from Morehouse College, a J.D. from Hastings College of the Law in San Francisco, and an M.A. from the University of Minnesota. Mr. Anderson was Minnesota State Law Librarian for twenty-two years. In 1996, he established the Everybody Wins Power Lunch Reading Program at the Benjamin E. Mays Magnet School. It has been an outstanding success, pairing elementary school students with some of the most important figures in state and federal judicial branches. Mr. Anderson was named a recipient of the KARE-11 Eleven Who Care Award in 2000. In March 2004, Marvin R. Anderson was named executive director of Everybody Wins!–Minnesota. He and his wife, Gloria Anderson, have three children and two grandchildren. Roger is a cofounder of Rondo Days.

♦ NOTES

1. Marvin Roger Anderson was born March 5, 1940.

2. Morehouse College, founded in 1867, is the largest liberal arts college in the nation for Black males. Morehouse has conferred bachelor's degrees on more Black men than any other institution in the world. The college is located in the west end of Atlanta, Georgia.

3. Father Lucius Archibald "Archie" Anderson (1909–1966).

4. Pullman Porters worked for the Pullman Company and carried baggage only for Pullman sleeping car passengers. The Pullman sleeping cars were transferred between railroads and traveled nationwide.

5. Social clubs were formed out of necessity since recreation and entertainment facilities for Black people were limited in the 1920s and 30s. None of the better restaurants served them, nor did the major hotels rent rooms to them. By 1935 there were two dozen clubs of various kinds in the Twin Cities. By the 1940s the hotels began to rent party rooms to these social clubs.

6. The Sterling Club was founded in 1918 and incorporated in 1919. The club built and owned its club home at 315 North Dale Street at Rondo. In 1958 it built a new home at 300 North St. Albans at Carroll. This private club was formed to give prestigious Black men, who were not allowed in White facilities, a place to meet and network.

7. Rangh Court was a townhouse development located at 989–991 Rondo. Developers were the Twin Cities Negro Development Company made up of

Misters Rawls (a cook on the Northern Pacific Railroad), Anderson, Newman, Gilmore, and Henderson (waiters on the Northern Pacific Railroad). The Anderson, Gilmore, and Henderson families lived in the apartments. Construction was completed in 1947 with a loan of $247,000, the largest loan made to a Black organization at that point in time.

8. The Coliseum Pavilion, located at 449 Lexington and University, was built just east of the Lexington Ball Park, originally as a dance hall and later as a roller-skating rink.

9. The Lexington Baseball Park, at Lexington and University, was the home of the Saint Paul Saints baseball team from 1897 until 1956. The original stadium was rebuilt in 1916, and a dance hall was added just east of the baseball stadium.

10. Northern Pacific Railroad's home offices were in Saint Paul. J. J. Hill, Saint Paul's early railroad empire builder, acquired this line in 1880. The Northern Pacific merged with the Great Northern and other railroads to create the Burlington Northern Railroad. A Northern Pacific office was located at 175 East Fifth Street.

11. Local 516—The International Brotherhood of Waiters and Sleeping Car Porters, a predominantly Black American labor union, was located at 441 Rondo Avenue. In 1955 it relocated to 525 Rondo Avenue, and later to 976 Rondo.

12. Newman Cloak and Suit Company was located at 25–31 East Seventh Street.

ORA LEE O'NEAL PATTERSON

Pullman Porters and the unions were the unrecognized leaders.

I'M ORA LEE PATTERSON.[1] MY MAIDEN NAME WAS O'NEAL. My father[2] was a Pullman Porter.[3] He was gone a lot, but he had a short run. He ran up to Brainerd, Minnesota,[4] and so they were short runs that Daddy went on. The railroad was the reason why many Black men came here to Minnesota. They were good-paying jobs up North, where they could come and make a living for their family. The porters made good money back then. When I say good money, I remember looking at one of my dad's checks, way back when I was a little girl, that he brought home. And it was $58. Can you imagine that? This would have been 1947 or 1948.

My dad didn't talk about his work as a porter much. I remember hearing him and my mother[5] talk, and he said, "Ora." My mother's name was Ora, also. He came home and he was always so tired and he would always say, "Got to go back now. Got to get ready. I gotta get some sleep, Ora, so I can deal with these White people out there. They drive me crazy." He would say, "I get so sick and tired of being called 'boy.' How old do you have to get before people respect you and say, 'Yes, sir,' or just call you by your name. They say, 'Hey, boy, would you bring me this? Hey, boy, would you bring me that?'" And of course, my dad, being a very proud man, couldn't take that.

But he did, because it was his job and that was the only job that he had to support his family and the only job that he could do.

Growing up in that era, the men of the house didn't sit down and share things with their children. It was always the wife who they would sit and talk to about things. If you heard something, you heard it, but they didn't intentionally just tell you about how life was. Because of course, the kids, they had to look at their parents as being perfect and nothing was wrong. But I did overhear him when he told my mother he had to get sleep because he had to go out there and deal with those prejudiced White people on that run. He said, "They're rich people. They're rich people. They go up to Brainerd and up to those cabins."

There was one man out there that took the run regularly that was very nice to my father. Daddy referred to him as the Blue Man. I have a picture of him with the Blue Man. He was a White gentleman, but he had some condition to his skin where his skin was kind of a light blue. He was a very wealthy man, and he was very good to my father. As a matter of fact, that's where I got my love of classical music, through the Blue Man, that's all I knew his name was—the Blue Man.

John O'Neal in his Pullman Porter uniform with the Blue Man

He never came to our house, but the Blue Man used to give my dad records for the Victrola. They were classical records, and that was the only music that we had. We had one of those old Victrolas where you put the needle on to play records, but we didn't have any records.

We had a huge house. In the evenings we'd sit in the front room all together and Daddy would turn on the Victrola and play the record, and of course the first time we heard it, it would be nice, but we didn't know who it was. We had to play the guessing game. "Who is this? What artist is this playing

O'Neal Family picture
Front row: Cousin Barbara, Harriet, Mother Ora, Gloria, Ora Lee
Back Row: Donald, Johnny, Father John, Fred, Ronald

this song? And what is the name of it?" So that was a game for us. We got used to listening to all this classical music, and it sounded pretty good to us.

And one of the records he brought home was Marian Anderson,[6] and on that was Marian Anderson's "Ave Maria." And I used to sit, when Daddy wasn't home, and put that record on and listen to it. I would sit there and I would cry. The woman in me! The tears would come out and I would think of many things when I was crying, listening to her sing "Ave Maria." It was so pretty. So then my girlfriend, Penny—Penny Martin, now. Her name was Penny Johnson at the time. We graduated together. She was a pianist. She's attended Juilliard, and she loved classical music, and I loved classical music. It was nice, because now I had a friend that liked classical music as well as me.

When I was in high school, it was rough having a father who was a Pullman Porter, because the Pullman Porters' Association, the Brotherhood of Sleeping Car Porters,[7] was really under fire with A. Philip Randolph[8] heading it. And Frank Boyd, who was like the general chairperson of the Pullman Porters' Association, worked out of his house, at 443 Mackubin, because the union did not have any money.

I remember one Christmas, I had the nicest Christmas present. It was an Olympia typewriter, kind of gold and yellow with gold on it. I thought, "Oh, this is so nice!" I says, "Now I can practice my typing at home and everything." So my dad let me know that he had bought that typewriter for me because my oldest sister, Gloria, had left, going to Washington. And he wanted me to do work for the Pullman Porters' Association! I thought it was a gift!

So a lot of the work, addressing envelopes, I did. That's where I think I picked up my spirit of volunteerism. Just doing that volunteer work with Frank Boyd and the Pullman Porters' Association. And doing their papers. Daddy would bring them home for me and I would type them and he would take them back to Frank Boyd. By using me to do the typing, that helped them to get by because they couldn't pay anyone to do it.

What was so hard was watching my dad. The Brotherhood of Sleeping Car Porters under A. Philip Randolph, they were taking a lot of heat. I don't really understand right now to this day the whole story about it, but all I know was what took place in the churches. And the Pullman Porters' Association was accused of being Communist, because of A. Philip Randolph and some of the tactics that he used.

Union logo: Brotherhood of Sleeping Car Porters

I attended Pilgrim Baptist Church[9] all of my life, and my dad's uncle, Mr. Jordan, was one of the old pillars of the church. He and my dad at one time were at odds because of the Pullman Porters' Association. Some of the Pullman Porters stopped going to church. They'd send their families to church, but they didn't go. When I was young and doing work, you don't think enough to ask these questions. But now I'm asking myself, "What was all of the riff? What was it?" It just couldn't be because they accused him of being a Communist. What was it that made them stay away, at least some of them, and just send their families to the church?

And I think what you had then, just like you have right now, are those house-grown Negroes and in-the-field Negroes. And so Randolph was definitely a field Negro. He wasn't a house. He was fighting for the rights, and people that were the "established quo" could not deal with his tactics. That's what I believe. That's the picture I'm seeing as I'm older. Mr. Jordan didn't want to rock the boat. And my dad, on the other hand, he was always a rebel.

I'll never forget when I got highly involved in politics and I got involved during the McCarthy[10] campaign. I ended up moving over then to support Hubert Humphrey,[11] and my dad was so happy. He said to me, with tears in his eyes, he said, "You know, in 1948, I was selected to be a delegate to the convention." And he said, "They did not want us to be delegates to the convention, especially those involved with the Pullman Porter Association. So what they did with me . . . I was on the run going up to Brainerd and they planted watches on me and said that I was taking watches and selling them and bringing them back from Canada. That's where it was. Nothing was further from the truth. So I got my delegate seat taken away from me. Because of that. Because I was a member of the Brotherhood of Sleeping Car Porters. That's the reason."

I said, "Well, why didn't you fight it, Daddy?" He said, "You couldn't fight the system at the time. And the union wasn't strong enough even under A. Philip Randolph. It just wasn't. I am so happy that you are involved with politics. I am so happy." And every poster I would bring home of Hubert Humphrey, he had it in his room. When he died in 1968, he had big picture of Hubert Humphrey on his wall. All the pictures I brought home from the convention, he had hanging in his room and he was so proud, just proud to the fact that I had gotten involved and to make a change. And you know, "One person can't make changes, but just think, my daughter is involved in politics. Something that was taken from me. And she's involved to the extent that she's doing all of these things. I'm so proud of you. I'm just so proud of you." So that was good.

I also figure that I'm this extension of what my father was. All he was, was just an activist. And not a popular activist and he was not well known. Those people who were well-known people were of course the doctors, the lawyers, people like that, who got recognition. If you were a police chief, deputy police chief, or if you were one of the first Black firefighters, you were in that camp. But Pullman Porters and the unions were the unrecognized leaders.

ORA LEE O'NEAL PATTERSON, widow of Robert M. Patterson, is the proud mother of Dawn Joyce, Andre, Michelle, Denise, and Roberta. She has been active in the community, serving as chair and vice chair of her Senate District, on the Steering Committee of the Women for Humphrey Campaign, on the DFL State and Fourth District Central Committees, as chair of the Debbie Montgomery for City Council Campaign, and as a delegate to Democratic National Conventions. She also was vice president, secretary, and political action chair of the Saint Paul NAACP and cofounder of the Limited Thirty Black Women's Network. She is a Founding Feminist Award winner, Barbara Jordan Award winner, and NAACP Rosa Parks Woman of the Year, and longtime active member of Pilgrim Baptist Church. She has worked in Senate Majority Research, as the administrative assistant to Mayor George Latimer, and for six years was chair of the Saint Paul Human Rights Commission and executive director of the Summit University Education Consortium. Ora Lee is respected for her extensive work in the Black community and Saint Paul.

◆ NOTES

1. Ora Lee O'Neal Patterson was born October 16, 1940.

2. Father John O'Neal was born November 3, 1896, and passed September 6, 1987.

3. Pullman Porters worked for the Pullman Company and carried baggage only for Pullman sleeping car passengers. The Pullman sleeping cars were transferred between railroads and traveled nationwide.

4. Brainerd, Minnesota, is 140 miles north of Saint Paul.

5. Mother Ora Lee Bates O'Neal was born August 24, 1900, and passed January 13, 1977.

6. Marian Anderson (1897–1993) was a strong Black woman with a soul-filled contralto operatic voice. She broke many racial barriers including being the first Black to sing at the Metropolitan Opera. In 1939, when she was denied a concert at Constitution Hall, Eleanor Roosevelt arranged for her to sing at the Lincoln Memorial. Seventy-five thousand people attended this historic concert.

7. The Brotherhood of Sleeping Car Porters was the union of Pullman Porters located in Frank Boyd's home at 443 Mackubin.

8. A. Philip Randolph (1889–1979) was a labor and civil rights leader. In 1925, he organized the Brotherhood of Sleeping Car Porters, the first union of predominantly Black workers to be granted a charter by the American Federation of Labor. In 1957, he was elected vice president of the AFL-CIO.

9. Pilgrim Baptist Church was first organized as a prayer group before 1863, and formally organized as a church November 15, 1866. Their first house of worship was constructed in 1870 at Twelfth and Cedar Streets in Saint Paul, and it moved in 1918 to the current location at 732 West Central Avenue, Saint Paul.

10. Eugene McCarthy (born 1916) grew up in Watkins, Minnesota, and graduated from St. John's University in Collegeville and the University of Minnesota. He served in the U.S. House of Representatives and Senate from 1949 to 1971. McCarthy was an unsuccessful candidate for the Democratic nomination for president in 1968 and 1972, and he was a leading spokesperson in raising anti–Vietnam War awareness in the late sixties and seventies.

11. Hubert H. Humphrey (1911–1978) served as mayor of Minneapolis, 1945–1949, Minnesota U.S. Senator, 1949–1964, and the thirty-eighth vice president, with Lyndon Johnson, 1965–1969. In 1968, Humphrey's main competitor for the nomination as the Democratic Party's presidential candidate was Minnesota Senator Eugene McCarthy.

MARY KALLEEN MURRAY BOYD

There was education everywhere, all around me.

MY NAME IS MARY KALLEEN MURRAY BOYD.[1] My grandparents' past experiences helped me to really understand the necessity for education. In my grandmother's[2] case, she came from Mississippi and she was threatened. She was told that she could not leave because she was the nanny for the landowner's children. He was trying to hold her hostage, as they did a lot of other Black people, because the landowner owned the general store and said that she owed him money. Sharecroppers that lived on that land would get whatever goods they needed from his general company store, and he kept a tab. But my grandmother could read. I think she had gone to eighth grade, so she had kept all of the records of payment and owing. So that education gave her the information, gave her the confidence that she could confront him with the truth. So that was a very powerful understanding for me of why it is necessary to come out of ignorance and to move into enlightenment, and that's what education is.

The approach to education in my community as I was growing up was that there was education everywhere all around me. In the Rondo community that I grew up in it was like you breathe, you learn. You learn, you breathe. You breathe, you learn. It's all education. And all of us kids were to go as high as we could, and to go beyond where our parents had gone, beyond their education,

Grandmother Callie Murray, in front holding
Mary Kalleen's hand, c. 1945

where they stopped in terms of formal education. It was even beyond the community. It was even beyond where we could dream at that time. Always be open to the dreams because education can carry you there.

Education was something that had been valued by our people way before my time, my parents' time, and was of value to our community. Because education was really about not only the survival of our people, it was about the history of our people. And so many of the contributions that have been made that we were not to lose sight of, and we were to leave our contributions. So it was really about the community and furthering our people and about the survival of our people and not just the Rondo community.

There was a lot of storytelling in our community through sharing of family history, like my grandmother's. We had books and our parents promoted our education through the books they read to us and later had us read. The Bible was used a lot, especially in our younger years and during Sunday school. I remember a Bible, a child's version of the Bible. It's all stories. I still have this edition that is probably close to a hundred years old that is a set of five books. And the reading of the newspaper. I'm dating myself, but sitting down around the radio with my grandparents, the big Philco radio, listening to the news which was educating us. That's the way a lot of adults got their education, and reading the newspaper.

And it was keeping the community informed from the pulpit. Our minister educated his congregation about policy, about politics, about situations that would impact and affect our community. Always there was talk. We'd come home from church. Dinner would be started before church and simmering on the stove. Well, you never knew how long church was going to be. You'd come home from church, and of course we had meals together. Families sat down and had meals together. And there was talk about what was said in the pulpit from church and Sunday school.

People in the community were always in our corner, encouraging and pushing. I have to go back even to preschool, where in Sunday school we were given these little pieces or speaking parts. "Can you say your little piece?" At Easter, you'd have to recite a little poem, you know:

> *I love Mommy and I love Daddy,*
> *And Jesus Christ loves us all.*

And everybody would clap. As I look back on it, it was so wonderful that they gave us such encouragement, because we probably cried and stumbled through stuff, but that's the way you give kids a start. So that started in preschool and in Sunday school, and continued as time went on, junior high and high school.

Parents taught through questioning. "So what did you talk about in Sunday school?" "What did you learn in school today?" Or some of the other activities that we were involved in. They always asked the questions. And I think a way that they educated us by asking the questions and having us report to them was to then kind of correct our perspective or our take on whatever it is we were reporting and our opinion about it. So that's the way teaching and learning went on in the home, too.

Our parents wanted to address the way that we treated people, I think! If somebody made you mad or upset if you didn't agree, the comment that "So-and-so just made me so mad" would be an educational opportunity. We would be taught about what to do with that, that so-called being mad—how to make peace with that, to go beyond that, and to learn the truth and not have to just sit with being mad.

I can recall in my home and among a lot of our friends, when we had experience of discrimination we were really taught to rise above it and feel sorry for those that were the perpetrators of that. I can't remember exactly being taught to turn the other cheek, because I don't think my family really believed in turning the other cheek. But they didn't really preach an eye-for-an-eye, either. They really did teach us that you rise above that, and it's almost as if you are feeling sorry for those who have the ignorance and demonstrate the ignorance to go so far as to be that disrespectful and to show discrimination.

There were opportunities that came my way that my parents weren't always the originators of, but they were good at recognizing that this was an opportunity for guiding and coaching and supporting me. Such as, I remember the director of the Red Cross[3] called my mother.[4] They used to have these little groups when I was at Hill School,[5] these activities, and Junior Red Cross was one of them. And I guess nowadays they might call it character education. Somehow I got to be president of the Saint Paul Junior Red Cross, and I was in elementary school. I think I was maybe sixth grade. So my mother, she'd never been in anything like that, but she encouraged me and she supported me as both of us were being taught about what that meant, what my duties were.

Sometimes they would create the opportunities within the community, such as the Three Fours Club that started in late elementary. We would meet on a regular basis at different homes. We had formal dining with tablecloths and a number of pieces of silverware so that we could learn how to eat in formal settings. We had instructions on the proper way to make a bed, with square corners on the sheet. We would go out to restaurants and then we would practice how to act. We were exposed to the arts. So they did things with us in groups and in the homes, and they would look for things for us to do outside of the homes.

And these mothers all looked out after each other's children. I can remember one time when my mother was working at the telephone company. I had a dental appointment, and my mother couldn't take me. Well, Aunt Ruby took me. My friend's mother, she took me to the dentist. So that's why I guess to this day, of the mothers that are alive, we call them our aunties. But the Three Fours Club, I think that was kind of what I would call the village finishing school.

Music was very important to my parents. First of all, I think it was mostly my mother that believed that every child should have some training in the arts, and so it was piano for me. I don't know how I came about accompanying my father[6] when I was twelve. Even though I had the ability, I didn't really have the interest in playing the piano. It had to have some purpose for me, and accompanying him gave me purpose. It was real sly the way they did it, actually! Then when I found out I could make some money, it became even more appealing.

When I was in junior high school. I was kind of the official piano player for funerals at Brooks Funeral Home.[7] Maybe there was a small family or they didn't have a church affiliation or didn't know an organist. Then I would be called and asked if I could play for the funeral. And so my mother would write a note. I'd get excused from school and go play for the funeral and then go back to school.

Hill School was a place that there were some opportunities that I wasn't going to miss out on. I did go to religious training. We were excused every Thursday to go to the nearest church, or I guess for some of the Jewish kids, synagogue. And I remember one of the teachers found out that I played the piano and wanted me to come in to the class and play piano for the class. So even there I was given the opportunity to kind of explore my talent.

Many people thought I was going to major in music. I'm an appreciator of music, but I'm more of an audience person. And I am an accompanist. I find that there's a lot about accompanying that has given strength to my chosen career, and that is a supportive role. And if you don't have the supportive roles, then those that think they're out in front don't look so good unless they've got good support!

I was president of the youth branch of the NAACP.[8] The youth branch of the NAACP was very strong then. We had people that were mentoring us and teaching us. You know Robert's Rules of Order, and how to run caucuses, amendments and proposals, and all that. The political process. Then also there was the social side of that, but the greater cause was that which was about the NAACP nationally, and so as the president of the youth branch, I was involved on the national level as well as the local level, which was an education in itself. There was education everywhere all around me.

With the adult chapter of the NAACP we did demonstrations, and that was in sympathy with the South when they were trying to get served at the

St. Paul Pioneer Press newspaper picture with caption: "NAACP activists picket a downtown Woolworth store in 1960 because of discrimination at the stores in the South." Mary K. second from left

Woolworth's counters in the South. And we had a Woolworth's[9] store here, so our NAACP was boycotting, and so we marched and we boycotted and we actually had a picket line, and we walked the picket line. I didn't know. At the time, I guess I thought we were really showing support for our brothers and sisters in the South, not realizing at the time, until that experience how much discrimination and how much prejudice was in the hearts of some of the people here. Because there were White people who drove by, threw bottles at us, spit on us, called us names, threw other things at us. And then there was some Black people that walked through the picket line. That was the most hurtful thing! But I was in charge of organizing and getting the youth, and then we did it along with the adult chapter.

My parents looked back years later and they said, "We shouldn't have let you do so much." Simply because years later, they realized that my health had probably suffered because I had sinus trouble and asthma. I was involved in so many things—and I don't know how to do it any other way. Because if an opportunity came along, they encouraged me, "If this is what you want to do . . ." We'd sit down and talk about it. "Well, if this is something you want to do." But I am an experiential learner, and I've learned from these experiences that I go into the experience and don't have to know everything about it, but along the way, I become informed and then I search out more information. Sometimes the experience precedes the understanding of the theory behind it, and that's how I learned about my way of learning, I guess!

My father was an ambassador through his music. His musical career took him to many places that he probably would not have gone otherwise, and it also allowed him the privilege to cross many barriers because of his singing, many cultural lines, many boundaries. I think it was his ministry, his avocation, and it's what sustained him.

James T. Murray

He was very talented when he went to Central High School,[10] and when he went back to Mississippi, to attend college, Alcorn College.[11] He had this gift of singing. When he was younger he sang in choirs, and even after he and my mother married, he sang in glee clubs and here in Saint Paul. He had a magnificent voice. When he came back from serving in the U.S. Army, he used the GI Bill to further his training in music. He attended MacPhail School of Music,[12] and he trained under an excellent vocal coach, Madame Mady Metzger Zeigler. She was from Germany. She was such an extraordinary coach that later on, in the early Fifties, she ended up being the vocal coach for the *Porgy and Bess* company.

There wasn't really a way to make a living and be a family person. Not in Saint Paul. So he worked to support his family. There were a lot of people who were college educated that were running on the railroad as well. A lot of the Black people found their stability and taking care of their families by working for railroads, packinghouses, places like the government, and the post office, as he did. He worked at the post office, and he kind of sang on the side.

His talent was recognized at a variety of places. He sang for church. He sang for funerals. And then there were White organizations that would want him to sing. And the postal service. Postmaster General Bertelsen[13] brought him in to the national conferences as the national soloist, so that way he was exposed to a much more national group of people, even though he was still working for the post office as a mail carrier. He was the national soloist for the post office. He had a lot of different opportunities that gave him this outlet for singing and for bringing joy to other people, but it wasn't bringing a lot of money to the family. He still was taking care of his family through his other job.

I remember when he would get calls sometimes and my mother would say, "Tell them what you charge." That was kind of a little rub between them, because she wanted to really be his business agent, and she wanted to charge. And sometimes they would tell them what they had. "Would he sing for that amount or that's what was in the budget or the part that he was going to play. It was salaried at such-and-such an amount." And there were other times that he would tell them that there was a fee for him and also for his accompanist. So it varied. There was no set scale. But it was always very fulfilling. Very fulfilling.

His music was the connector. It helped to bridge many differences. He often spoke of music as a universal language. He believed that music was a universal language and he built bridges between cultures, gender, age groups, with the renditions of his music. In reviewing some of his clippings and programs, I see that he sang for just about everybody: Jewish veterans' group, Presbyterians, Catholics, Baptists, Red Cross. It didn't make any difference. And so I think in that way he was an ambassador of goodwill.

The invitations probably came more often in the Sixties and Seventies and from more of a variety of groups. He was becoming better known, but the culture was changing. I started accompanying him in the Fifties, and I continued to accompany him until soon after I was married and had children. In the Fifties sometimes he faced prejudice and then there was also resentment among people of his own race. The prejudice that he faced came when he was in shows of mostly White casts. One instance I remembered reading about. The cast was rehearsing. I think it was either the Opera Workshop or some opera group. I think it was *Carmen*. They were rehearsing at Central High School. And as is written, because he was playing the lead part of Escamillo, and there was a female lead who was White. And the principal of the school, having the fear that this Black man was going to embrace or kiss this White woman on stage, re-neged on the agreement for the group to practice at Central, so they had to find someplace else. And then there's some other instances where that he was to perform on stage with another White lead, and this person was refusing to go on stage as long as my dad was going to be a part of the show. In that instance, I don't really know what happened. His voice usually overrode whatever. I mean he was pretty much in demand and he was backed probably by the directors, so however it was resolved, I have a sense that it was resolved.

There were people in his own race that thought he was singing songs that were too much in the past, and that devalued and shamed Black people that were Negroes and Coloreds at the time. Because he loved singing spirituals and he loved singing songs of emotion that were cre-ated by his people.

He liked to sing "Sometimes I Feel Like a Motherless Child," and there's a story about that. It's called Hannah's story, and he used to tell that story. I'll do the best I can to recall this. Hannah was a slave woman who had lost a child. Her husband was ill. She was walking down the road on her way to pick cot-ton and she heard this moaning and there was a shack door that was open. She went inside and there was an old woman sitting in a rocking chair, smok-ing a corncob pipe, and a child in the corner that was weeping, and a still fig-ure. And Hannah asked, "What's wrong?" And the woman that was rocking, the old woman, said, "She's dead. Her mom is dead." And she looked over and she tried to comfort the child, but not being able to comfort the child and having to go on to the fields to pick cotton. And she started down the road and she began to feel that sometimes she, too, felt like a motherless child. So she began to hum and to sing, to make up these words: "Sometimes I feel like a motherless child." And when she got to the fields, she was humming and another slave man asked, "What's that you're hummin', Hannah? What's the words that you're singin'?" And she shared what she had begun to create from her own heartfelt, emotional sadness, and he picked up the tune and others in the field began to add words to that song:

Sometimes I feel like a motherless child
Sometimes I feel like a motherless child
Sometimes I feel like a motherless child
Long way from my home

Sometimes I wish I could fly
Like a bird up in the sky
Oh, sometimes I wish I could fly
Fly like a bird up in the sky
Sometimes I wish I could fly
Like a bird up in the sky
Closer to my home

Motherless children have a hard time
Motherless children have-a such a hard time
Motherless children have such a really hard time
A long way from home

Sometimes I feel like freedom is near
Sometimes I feel like freedom is here
Sometimes I feel like freedom is so near
But we're so far from home

That was one story that he would tell. And the spirituals were very dear to him, because they were history and a way to relate that history. And a way to try to get an understanding of that history and of our people was through his rendering of those spirituals. So that was just one example.

There were some people who believed that we should move forward and not look at the past, did not want to know anything, did not want to bring forth anything about history. And probably rightfully so. Many who had lived that life didn't want to recall it. But then there were others who may not have lived that life, who were not born in the South but had some disdain for the Black Southerners and felt that we were moving up into the middle class. We were starting to assimilate and therefore we should not look back, but we should look forward and try to be as much like the majority culture as possible.

I think my father had a ministry that was so deep in his soul that he just didn't let discrimination stop him. He was bothered at times, I know that. He would talk to my mother about comments sometimes that were made, but then there was so much appreciation for the music that he brought. I think quite often in the community, even though it was called upon, it was more or less taken for granted. But he rose above that. He looked beyond that. And as I said, he had a ministry. He had something to do. He didn't feel that that voice had been given to him to just use for personal gain.

I remember going into some of those affairs as his accompanist, and we would be ushered in the back door, or after the meal was over, we would be asked to come and only perform for that particular time that we were on the program and then it was over for us. And I remember the resentment. I remember feeling the anger. "How dare they?" But my dad always had this calmness. It was almost like, "Okay, get over it." He was doing something that he knew we as a people would get beyond. And I don't think he could have articulated that at the time, but he would feel the joy in singing. And that joy of singing, as long as someone wanted to listen, it overrode everything else. And I think that going with him to these places, experiencing this myself, and having to work through and talk with him sometimes—it was a wonderful father-daughter time and experience, because we would have to talk through this on the way back home. Although they applauded him, they enjoyed his music, they did not accept the person, and that I did not like.

My dad traveled with *Porgy and Bess* and in 1954 and '55. Before he auditioned, he had been asked to sing as a replacement the part of Joe with the *Showboat* cast in Detroit. This *Showboat* cast later did *Porgy and Bess*. So when *Porgy and Bess* came to Saint Paul, the man whose place my dad had taken as a sub soloist wanted to meet my dad, because he'd heard about this great voice. And he and my father hit it off, and he took my dad to where *Porgy and Bess* was rehearsing here. The director auditioned my dad right there, and then it just kind of snowballed out of the blue. He wasn't even looking for it. He got a call some months later asking if he could report in five days for the international tour. And they were very gracious in asking if he would confer with his wife, and I remember that my mother was very supportive of him going. Five days was not very

Parents Lavinia and James Murray with fourteen-to fifteen-year-old Mary K. after she accompanied her father at a concert

much time to get ready. His voice was so appreciated that he had no problem getting the time off from the government, because they considered him an ambassador of goodwill from the United States of America. For ten months in 1954 and '55 he was a fisherman in the cast, and then the understudy for Porgy. And he did get to do a fill-in for the original Porgy.

For me it was exciting that I had a father that was way on the other side of the world, because at that time, it was quite an experience to make a phone call across the ocean and it sounded like somebody that was in a tin can. But my mother, I think, missed him more. During that time my mom was working at the hospital. But after ten months to a year, they realized that it was too costly because in those days the members of the cast were responsible for their own expenses out of what they were paid. So it had a lot of experience and acclaim and opportunity to meet great people. I mean, he brought back autographs for me that were autographed by Humphrey Bogart and Lauren Bacall, Judy Garland and people like that. And he spent time with Satchmo[14] and that was all very good experience, but it didn't send any money home.

My father use to say, "Education is so important because it is something no one can ever take away from you." I just can't stress enough that education is all about life. You wake up in the morning, it's a new day and there are new lessons, there are new classrooms. They're all around you, and it's all in the way that you perceive it and you just owe it to yourself, you owe it to your people, you owe it to it the future, you owe it to our past. We have to continue to learn, we have to continue to grow. We are standing on the Black history others built before us. We have a responsibility to continue to build on that history.

◆ ◆ ◆

DR. MARY KALLEEN MURRAY BOYD, born to Lavinia and James T. Murray, is proud of the challenges overcome by each generation and the uphill road she walks for which her family laid the foundation. First a volunteer, after more than thirty-five years she retired as area superintendent of the Saint Paul Public Schools. She received an honorary doctorate from Concordia College. Mary K. helps children seek the question in everything. Besides being a respected elder in the community, she is member of Alpha Kappa Alpha Sorority, on the Board of Trustees of Hamline University and the Board of Saint Paul Children's Collaborative, and manages her own business—MKB and Associates Consultants. She pursues her interests in Tai Chi, Pilates, traditional African healing, and music. Mary K. is very proud of her son, Jeffrey, his wife, Racara, grandson, James (three), and daughter, Laureen.

◆ NOTES

1. Dr. Mary Kalleen Murray Boyd was born June 29, 1942.

2. Grandmother Callie O. Sanders Murray was born July 9, 1897, and passed January 19, 1967.

3. The Junior Red Cross was formed in 1917 with very active membership during wartime. In nonwar years, it concentrated on international service and domestic programs, provided public assistance, and in the process nurtured good citizenship. When the programs moved from in-school to after-school and volunteer leadership by teachers weakened, active membership significantly declined.

4. Mother Lavinia Stone Murray was born August 1, 1917.

5. J. J. Hill School was originally built in 1905 at Selby, Hague, Chatsworth, and Oxford. The school housed kindergarten through eighth grade. This building was torn down and a new building built in 1974 for J. J. Hill Elementary School. Currently, the building serves as Montessori School for four-year-olds through sixth grade.

6. Father James T. Murray was born September 2, 1918, in Shuqualak, Mississippi, to Luchious and Callie Murray. He passed in Saint Paul, on October 9, 1995.

7. Brooks Funeral Home was originally located at 697 Rondo Avenue. It moved to 862 Concordia (Old Rondo) in 1960.

8. The National Association for the Advancement of Colored People (NAACP) was founded in New York City in 1909 by a multiracial group of activists. The NAACP believes that all men and women are created equal. Attorney Fredrick McGhee of the Rondo corridor was invited by W. E. B. Du Bois to attend the second meeting of the Niagara Movement. When he returned to Saint Paul, he organized the Twin City Protection League, which became the Twin Cities Branch of the NAACP in 1912.

9. F. W. Woolworth & Company had several locations in the 1940s and 1950s that included 81 East Seventh Street, 438 Wabasha, 1088–1090 University Avenue, 1624 White Bear Avenue, and 969–971 Payne Avenue.

10. Central High School began in 1866 and consisted of two rooms in the Franklin Building in downtown Saint Paul. By 1872 it was known as Saint Paul High School and moved to Seventh and Jackson. In 1883, a twenty-seven-room building on Minnesota Street in downtown Saint Paul was completed and the school was named Saint Paul Central High. Because of space needs, a new school was built at 275 Lexington Avenue in 1912. In 1977, the building was reduced to its structural form, then rebuilt into the current building.

11. Alcorn Agriculture and Mechanical College at Alcorn State, Mississippi—between Vicksburg and Natchez, Mississippi—was renamed Alcorn State University in 1974. This was a traditional Black college.

12. MacPhail Center for the Arts was founded in 1907 and located at 1128 LaSalle Avenue in downtown Minneapolis. In the late 1950s into the 1960s, it was the music school for the University of Minnesota.

13. Sigurd Arnold Bertelsen worked for the Northern Pacific Railroad for forty years before he was appointed postmaster general in Saint Paul by President Dwight D. Eisenhower. He retired from the post office in 1974.

14. Louis "Satchmo" Armstrong (1900–1971) was a Black cornet and trumpet player, jazz singer, bandleader, and entertainer. Born in New Orleans, he began leading his own band in 1925, recording with some of the most renowned blues singers of the time. He preformed all over the world as an unofficial ambassador for the United States. He won a Grammy award in 1964 for "Hello Dolly." Queens College, in the New York City borough of Queens, maintains a museum in his honor.

NATHANIEL ABDUL KHALIQ

Raised in the Rondo community as **Nick Davis**

I'm just thankful God has chosen me to be part of this.

I AM NATHANIEL ABDUL KHALIQ,[1] formerly Nathaniel Raymond Davis, also known as Nick Davis. My closest friends and relatives still call me Nick. I was born and raised at 304 Rondo, and I remember our house was probably a quarter of a way off of the cross street of Farrington. I remember Love's Cleaners[2] being next door to us. I remember a couple of grocery stores on the corner. I remember a guy named Sterling had a big, beautiful house, probably the nicest house on the block, next door to us. And then my cousins lived down the street. Melvin Carter Sr., they lived across the street from us, and I have a lot of fond memories some of my friends and my cousins. Growing up, I didn't have any brothers or sisters. I was raised by my grandparents, and so my cousins, the Ransoms who lived down the street from us, were just like brothers and sisters to me.

We had a ton of fun. You know, no drama. I just had so much fun growing up, and I guess the only trouble in my life back then was I didn't see my mother[3] that much, and not knowing who my father was. But because of the extended family, the cousins and stuff, they filled that void and I had friends.

I remember my grandfather,[4] Reverend George Davis, who was a wonderful man and he was a minister, and he would be out in the yard and these people would come by with liquor and cussing and raising hell. And they would see him and hide the liquor, and the cussing would cease. And they would greet him, "Howya doin', Reverend Davis?" and go on about their business and go on their way and continue on with their unacceptable behavior.

Another fond memory I have of Rondo was the respect that people had for my grandfather. He was a reverend but he didn't have a church. The house had a sign on it: Union Gospel Mission. And so he would have little church services and maybe one or two neighbors would come besides the family. And he lived by very strong principles. I didn't find out until later that he used to be a drunkard. And I found out later about his history that he was the son of a former slave master, that he spoke Spanish fluently and spoke other languages, and he was from Texas. He was a child of the slave master, but he was one of the few slaves that was able to go to school and stuff. He was a tremendous individual. I remember his station wagon, his bib overalls, and every now and then he would put on a suit and a derby hat and go on about his business.

I was going to get involved in the Ober Boys Club,[5] against my grandfather's wishes. He didn't like us to participate in sports and stuff. He said, "You'll end up getting hurt." So I used to sneak and go to the Ober Boys Club, and sure enough, I got hurt. My big toe got knocked off once, off the bone. Somebody jumped on the mat that I was under. And later on I was playing football up there and fell and cut my knee on the rock because it was a rough field. The third thing that happened to me up there was I was

Grandmother Bertha Miller Davis

playing baseball and we lost the game and I was walking across the street and I got hit by a car at Western and St. Anthony. My grandfather knew a little bit about what he was talking about!

My grandmother[6] was blind and was the most spiritual and religious person I've ever met in my life. She never ever complained about anything. Every day all she talked about was God. At that young age I just couldn't figure it out. She's blind and she doesn't get to hardly do anything, just around the house doing all these things. But she never complained. So I had a very strong spiritual upbringing and foundation. My grandfather and grandmother were outstanding role models for me as far as being rooted in spirituality.

He would talk about other Blacks during that time, about they're so smart and everything, but they still can't get the same respect as White men get because segregation in the South was running rampant, and even up here we had de facto segregation. That's something that he talked about. In Saint Paul our de facto segregation was that certain places you just knew you didn't go—Rice Street, even Grand Avenue. Later on when I started going to Marshall Junior High School,[7] and we had some White girlfriends that lived on the other side of Selby, we would go over there and once we got tired, we would have to sneak back across Selby into our area. And I remember one guy got jumped on up there. Some White guys jumped on him, and so after that people said enough is enough. Blacks started sort of going up there and acting like, "What are you going to do about it?"

I was talking about my grandfather. The story goes his real name wasn't Davis. I believe it was Stewart. And like I said, he was raised on a plantation and was the child of a Black woman and a White man, and he was mixed with all kinds of different things. Beautiful man— golden brown skin, white hair, and a beautiful mustache and everything. And so he came up here. He had had a conflict down there and supposedly killed a White man, and they got him out of town and he ended up here in Saint Paul. When he first came here he was in a boardinghouse a little while. Then he met my grandmother, who came up here with a couple of her brothers and sisters from Memphis, Tennessee. So she got hooked up with that no good scoundrel, as he was at that time, and he evolved and turned himself around and they stayed here. They had, I believe, eleven or twelve kids.

Well, one of the things that stands out in my mind is he was a man of enormous courage, and I think it's difficult to have courage unless you have faith. And I would just watch him interact with some of these mean people on the streets, and he demanded respect, whether it was from the police— he was looking and watching the police question a Black man and so forth. He would stand there and observe things. And just talking about the injustices of the day and none of it really sunk in. I didn't just grab it at a young age and say I'm going to get here and get involved. I didn't really come to my senses until later in life. But as I would reflect on how courageous he was and how he had a sense of justice and demanding justice and respect, it's just something that sort of stuck with me later in life.

He felt very passionately that with the freeway coming in he should not lose his home. For some reason I wasn't aware that we were really the last house on Rondo. People were moving out and I knew they wanted to do the freeway and everything, but I wasn't really aware of the deep controversy, even though I watched his demeanor and attitude change, and he got a little more embittered. Something I noticed later on when this whole thing about them taking the house—he expressed a bitterness towards White people that I had never heard him express before, because he was part White himself. He kept saying over and over again how he wasn't giving up his house. He couldn't understand why all these other people that were a lot smarter and had money to get attorneys and do all this other stuff, why they would just give up without a fight. He wasn't going to do that.

And my grandmother, she would just sit there and listen. And he made it clear that he would draw the line in the sand, and I knew he had a shotgun, but he wasn't going anywhere. If they came in there to take him out of his home someone was going to get hurt, and he was willing to give his life because he felt that was his, that he was old and he'd probably never own any land, and land was important to him.

So one day I went to school, and when I came home, these White dudes were tearing the house up with sledgehammers and axes. Not knocking it down, but later I realized they were just making it unlivable. I'm walking around looking, no Grandma, no Grandpa or anything, and I'm wondering, "What's going on?" And I started crying, and I don't know if it was a highway patrolman or a police officer, but someone came up and I told them who I was and stuff, and they said, "We'll take you to your grandma and your grandpa."

What they had done, they threw all this stuff in the back of the truck and moved us from 304 Rondo off to a house up on the hill on East University past Regions Hospital,[8] it's where Valley Apartments[9] is now. It had to be thirty or forty steps from street level to get up to the house. And they dumped all her stuff in there.

So when they dropped me off and I walked in there my grandpa was just—they just beat him down. I mean not physically of course, but he just didn't have it. He just lost it. I mean not screaming and hollering, but he was just a shell of a man after that. My grandparents stayed there awhile and then I eventually moved in with my mom and they ended up moving onto Central Avenue. Shortly after that, I'd say maybe a year or two after that, he passed.

It just tore him up. I don't know if he lost faith. I know my grandmother didn't, but I don't know if he lost faith or what. He was never the same. Our interactions and stuff, when I would go by and visit him—he just never got over it, how they could do that to him. Nobody—I mean no organizations, nobody—did anything about anything, about his situation and how they treated him.

And the thing that stuck in my mind over the years was how long and hard the White neighborhood along I-35 fought to prevent that from even being built, and eventually they ended up building and calling it a parkway with reduced speed for lower noise for the neighborhood, but with a minimum amount of problems for the neighbors. And so that left sort of a bitter pill in my mouth about a lot of things, about doing the right thing, about faith to a certain extent. Here's a man that worshipped God, and my grandmother—you know, what did they do?

I've said this before, that even though I know the Urban League[10] and the NAACP,[11] and there were Black ministers back then and so forth, there wasn't anybody. And not so much to just fight for my grandpa, but to fight for the other older people there that were losing their life's homes. I mean this was a place that was his, and so whatever they gave them would have been insufficient to go and purchase something else.

When they came through with the freeway and did what they did, it was more than just tearing down a physical building. They destroyed many lives. It destroyed relationships between family, within the extended family, and just a sense of peace and camaraderie that I've never been able to enjoy or find joy in moving in other neighborhoods.

I was so young back then, but I just think that somehow the way they presented that thing, it sort of caught people off guard and people didn't get a chance to react and respond to it. As they started one by one knocking down these houses, this cocoon that many of us had been blessed to be a part of started falling apart. One minute we're living in this community where there's

St. Paul Dispatch

HOUSING MOVE—

Pastor Threatens Cops, Then Agrees To Eviction

Sheriff's deputies, city policemen and police-women, and housing authorities had to make their way today into the home of Rev. and Mrs. George Davis, Rondo and Farrington, and remove them to new living quarters at 233 E. Fifteenth.

The elderly self-ordained cleric first told the officers that "if you force your way in here, it will be the last time you force anything."

There was some sparing for time, because some of those who had talked with Mr. Davis previously felt that he might use some form of violence. Finally, after authorities emerged through the rear service door, Mr. Davis admitted the officers over the protests of his wife.

Mrs. Davis, partially blind, said she had not been out of the house for more than 25 years. She was holding a small grandchild.

Officials of the housing authority, who had already deposited $3000 for Mr. Davis as the condemnation award for the property, said they had provided a five-room lower duplex in the eastern redevelopment area.

After the members of the family had been escorted to a police car at the curb, Mr. Davis began to show in-

Police officer Walter Freiberger evicting Reverend Davis from his home. Reverend Davis held the police at bay with a shotgun until he was finally convinced to vacate his home.
Minnesota Historical Society. St. Paul Pioneer Press 9/28/56.

terest in the new home. The authorities said demolition of the condemned property, the last property on Rondo between Rice and Western, will follow quickly.

Transferred to the new living quarters with Mr. and Mrs. Davis was their daughter Josephine and a small grandchild. The housing officials said a total of about 650 families have been moved from the Western area.

Black businesses and people getting along and everything is just wonderful, you can sleep on the porch. All these insulators were there to protect us, by the grace of God, and then all of a sudden, you're losing this family, and you're losing that family. And people wonder what is going to happen, where are these people going to go? There wasn't any comprehensive plan to say, "Well, we're going to bring a freeway through here, and then we're going to relocate people if they want to relocate in this particular area or that particular area." It was like they dropped a bomb and pieces of the cocoon went scattering all over never to be put back together.

It was a really difficult time, and I think it broke a lot of hearts, not just my grandfather. In fact, I think a lot of people was hurt that they didn't stand up. Back then they said, "Well, that old man is crazy." But then later on—I used to enjoy talking to Tiger Jack, because he would always say—and my heart would just pound and swell up—he would always say, "Your grandfather was a *man*! He stood up." And that would make my day.

Some of those older folks. I don't think their heart ever mended from that. You know, a lot of relationships that people had established—"How ya doin', Mr. So-and-So?"—over the years, talking to people over the fence, on the sidewalk. That was gone. And being transplanted somewhere else where you pretty much had to start all over.

My grandmother's faith carried her through the day. I never heard her complain until the time she passed—she probably passed some fifteen, twenty years later—she never spoke a bitter word about it. She got through it. She managed.

My grandparents' faith was always an inspiration to me. I think first of all, we are all children of Adam and Eve, and of Abraham. My new faith, Islam, is just an extension of my earlier experience with my grandmother and grandfather, even though they were Christians. We're trying to reach the same destination. I'm trying to get the same moral strength that they gathered from faith—without putting a title on it—and for whatever reason, God has decided to give me a little different understanding. I may not say the Father and the Son and the Holy Ghost. I say Allah, but it's just a different name. It's the same entity. And so as I got older, I began to appreciate and understand why he and my grandma were so strong. Because if you're out here in this mad world and don't, as we say, hold on to the rope of God and have some faith, you're going to get into a little bit of trouble. You will end up succumbing to all the different things out here.

That's not to say that I've led a perfect life. I can't even come close to that. But because of that spiritualness, and that foundation from my grandparents, it set some limits in my madness. That early experience with my grandfolks would bring me back to reality. I've said I'm sorry a lot of times in my sixty years, and have pleaded and begged for forgiveness. I'm sure I would have my grandfather's blessings. Even though it's not of the same faith, it's the same road, and we're just using different means to get to our destination.

So now, God willing, when I go on this Hajj,[12] one of the first things we will do is discard all our garments, and we all put on the same two-piece wardrobe, covering your top part and your bottom, so when you look around you don't see a king, you don't see someone with diamonds. You don't know who you're standing next to. That's that transformation, and I'm just thankful and blessed that God has chosen me to be a part of this.

◆ ◆ ◆

NATHANIEL ABDUL KHALIQ was raised by his grandparents, Rev. George Davis and Bertha Miller Davis. He was born to Annie Davis Sanders who married John Sanders, and he has three sisters: Mary, Bertha, and Anita. Mr. Khaliq has been married to Victoria A. Alexander Davis for almost thirty years, and he is the proud father of Malik, Mikal, Peridot, Nathaniel II, Kimberly, Natalie, and Nicole; and grandfather of Gabrielle, Mia, DeDe, Mekhi, Brandy, Kaion, and Little Mikal. He is influenced by his grandmother's faith, Ora Lee's unyielding commitment to justice and her contagious laugh, Katie McWatt's character and dignity, Mary Brokman's love and encouragement, Sister Anisah Dawan's motherliness, and his wife's dedication to family and community. Mr. Khaliq started N. R. Davis Construction Company and owns the Malcolm Shabbaz Apartments. He is committed to his faith in Islam, making his first Hajj in 2004.

◆ NOTES

1. Nathaniel Raymond Davis was born September 11, 1943.

2. Love Tailor Shop was located at 306 Rondo. Morris Love, a Black proprietor, later added dry cleaning to his business.

3. Mother Annie Davis Sanders was born August 29, 1922, and passed June 3, 1995.

4. Grandfather Reverend George Davis was born June 15, 1875, and passed September 29, 1957.

5. Ober Boys Club, at 375 St. Anthony at Western, was founded during World War II by the Union Gospel Mission. It was named for Edgar Ober of 3M and provided recreational activities and taught Christian values. Boys who participated also attended Snail Lake Children's Camp. There was a Girls Club located at Welcome Hall. Sometime after 1960, the club became part of The Boys and

Girls Clubs of America. However, the building is still owned by Union Gospel Mission.

6. Grandmother Bertha Miller Davis was born May 30, 1895, and passed September 19, 1972.

7. Marshall School was built in 1925 at Grotto, Holly, Ashland, and St. Albans. It was Marshall Junior High from 1926 to 1937. In 1937, tenth grade was added; in 1938, eleventh grade; and in 1939, twelfth grade was added, with graduating classes from 1940 to 1953. It returned to junior high only in 1954. Webster Elementary School was built on the same site in 1926. The two buildings were connected in 1975 and become Webster Magnet Elementary School.

8. Regions Hospital is located at 640 Jackson Street.

9. Valley Apartments is located at 261 East University Avenue.

10. The Urban League has served the Black community since 1923 as a human service advocacy organization. The Urban League addresses issues of quality employment, housing, education, and health care. The Saint Paul and Minneapolis agencies were combined until 1938. Saint Paul offices were initially located in various buildings downtown until the late 1960s, when they moved into their own building at 401 Selby Avenue, four blocks south of the Rondo corridor.

11. The National Association for the Advancement of Colored People (NAACP) was founded in New York City in 1909 by a multiracial group of activists. The NAACP believes that all men and women are created equal. Attorney Fredrick McGhee of the Rondo corridor was invited by W. E. B. Du Bois to attend the second meeting of the Niagara Movement. When he returned to Saint Paul, he organized the Twin City Protection League, which become the Twin Cities Branch of the NAACP in 1912.

12. Hajj is a pilgrimage to Mecca in Saudi Arabia that every adult who follows Islamic traditions makes once in a lifetime.

The Three Fours was our village finishing school.

VANNE: I'm Vanne Owens Hayes.[1]
LINDA: Linda Griffin Garrett.[2]
MARY K.: Mary K. Murray Boyd.[3]
PAULA: Paula Thomason Mitchell.[4]
CAROL: Carol Dawson.[5]
(pictured here left to right)

PAULA: There were two Paulas in our friendship group: Paula Wood, and I was always known as *Paula T*. Paula and I decided we wanted a club, and we asked our mothers[6, 7] who were visiting at the time. They thought it sounded okay. They would help us. We gathered people from our neighborhood, church friends, and began the club. We were ages eight, nine, and ten. Linda was eight, Vanne nine, and the rest were ten. So that would have been 1952 when we began.

CAROL: Every month the meeting was at a different house.

PAULA: The mother whose home it was at was primarily responsible, but other parents would come in as needed. The mothers had a club and the girls had Three Fours. And as a group the Three Fours would make suggestions and then we would give these suggestions to the mothers' group and they would get those things organized. I think the mothers met three times a year, and they kind of mapped out some ideas.

We met twice a month, once for a business meeting and once for an activity meeting. I don't remember exactly who was there. At the beginning I know we had some people who did not stay long.

VANNE: These are the people we remember being involved. I'll just read our maiden names. Linda Griffin, Paula Thomason, Mary K. Murray, Carol Dawson, Paula Wood, Adrienne Coleman, Carol Mills, who's deceased, Leora Myers, Joyce Sims, Annabelle Foster. And also names that we're not sure, Marcia Stewart or Alma Stewart, Lucille Everson, Doris Shannon. Sherrill Slorby was a member, we believe.

LINDA: From our informal list, there were probably about eight or nine people who were in the Three Fours the entire time and then some people that kind of moved in and out. We always had twelve in the club. So we would have rare vacancies and have nominations and elections of new members.

Linda Griffin, Carol Dawson, Paula Thomason, c. 1955

MARY K.: What I remember about Three Fours is what I later called a village finishing school, because we learned how to conduct meetings, we learned how to make beds, we learned how to eat properly when you have more than one fork and spoon. We learned!

PAULA: Each meeting began with, "The meeting of the Three Fours Club will come to order. We will stand and sing our club song."

MARY K.: So let's stand and sing. We're all standing.

ALL: *Three Fours is our club's name, a riddle and a game, with fun and frolic, work and play our aim. We call ourselves Three Fours and as we do our chores, we laugh, we cry, we dance, we sing the same. So three plus three plus three plus three is twelve, you see, and twelve happy growing girls are we. Three Fours is our club name, a riddle and a game, so three plus three plus three plus three we be.*

Paula Thomason, c. 1956

PAULA: Adrienne's mother, Beatrice Coleman, played the piano and she wrote the song. My mother worked and Bea was home. We would go to Adrienne's house for lunch sometimes, and her mother would play the piano and Adrienne and I would march around and then we'd march out the door.

MARY K.: I remember we named it ourselves. I remember recommending that name.

LINDA: One of the things that I recall about Three Fours is that it was run like it was a real organization, with officers and dues, because I remember once I was the treasurer and I think our dues were five cents a meeting or ten cents at the most. We didn't have a whole lot, but I remember writing down the names and I remember one time we were angry with someone because they owed their back dues and we had some big discussion in the meeting about what to do about people who owed back dues.

Linda Griffin, 1956

And we had an annual meeting. And I remember one time it was at the Wood home. We had tables set up and we dressed up. It was an evening dinner, and Paula Wood's dad was a waiter on the railroad and he put on his uniform and he carried out the food and served us.

ALL: I remember that.

LINDA: And was that the time that Paula stood up—was she the president that year? And she stood up to give the speech and the chair fell and she fell. Trying to be so grown up and the chair collapsed.

VANNE: I remember a lot of the activities. I remember us going to Frances Hughes's[8] for a scavenger hunt.

Frances Hughes

PAULA: Frances Hughes's station wagon that had the real wood sides on it. Frances lived in Maplewood[9] on County Road B and Hazelwood, but at that time that was the country. Ten acres of land, and for us city kids it was an adventure. Frances had fruit trees, angora rabbits, wild asparagus, and Frances could hunt, fish. She was very adventuresome. Those things that she enjoyed, she was able to share with us because we didn't really know women who did the kinds of things that Frances did.

VANNE: I remember that, and being at Paula T.'s house making ice cream as an activity. And I remember us going to the Forum[10] in Minneapolis and practicing our manners and going through the cafeteria line. The Forum was a formal cafeteria.

LINDA: The Forum was a big thing, going to this cafeteria, because we didn't go out to restaurants to eat. I don't know whether it was because there wasn't a lot of choice in our community or whether our parents didn't have money to take us out to eat. Going out to eat for me was to go over to the Thomasons' or the Thomasons come over to our home to eat. So that going to the Forum, that was a big thing.

VANNE: It was a big thing. One because it was in Minneapolis and going from Saint Paul to Minneapolis was a big thing. But our community was pretty segregated in the sense of social activities, which were pretty much concentrated in the community. And our activities, if they weren't at St. James[11] or Pilgrim,[12] Hallie Q. Brown,[13] they were at the Sterling Club.[14] You know, birthday parties. It wasn't possible just to decide, like we can now, to take the kids to a restaurant, because all restaurants weren't receptive. It was a time of testing, to see if they were receptive to Black people, and we were Negro then, coming to restaurants.

Mary K. Murray

MARY K.: I think our parents protected us. There was a lot of entertainment. Our parents entertained in the homes. Because of their social clubs, they would meet in each other's homes. But I think a lot of it was because of protection and they knew what was out there. They wanted us to have the best training so we'd be prepared. That was their way of preparing us in a very protective way for when the world would become more open to Blacks.

VANNE: I want to support that and also add that our parents knew the community very well. Mary K.'s dad[15] was a postman, Linda's father[16] a police officer, Paula T.'s dad[17] was a firefighter, Paula Wood's dad[18] worked on the railroad, Carol's dad[19] did a variety of things. My father,[20] who I think had died somewhere in the first year my being in the club, was the executive director of the Saint Paul Urban League.[21] And we were all kind of connected through church, in terms of where everybody got together and did the church's social activities. I would bet money that was the protectiveness so that we would have the freedoms they thought we should have and they were very aware of what was waiting out there.

PAULA: Much of what we learned has served us well throughout our lives. Learning Robert's Rules of Order and as we went through life and we joined different organizations and were a part of the broader community, we were able to use those skills to our advantage.

VANNE: Our parents tried to identify every which way they could, skills we lacked and needed to work on or at least expose us to so we could make choices. We got exposed to a lot and that was a positive thing.

PAULA: Besides the mothers, Frances Hughes was very active with our group. Frances Hughes was a librarian with the State of Minnesota and at

Gillette Hospital. One of the things that Frances was very interested in us doing was looking beyond ourselves and doing good deeds for others. And I can remember her taking us to Crispus Attucks Home[22] for the Elderly. We would have been to Frances's house and picked wild plums or something and then we'd take them over to the old folks home so that they could make jelly. So I think things like that that we learned in Three Fours have continued throughout our lives. One of the things that I remember about your dad, Carol, was when the Three Fours had a meeting at your house and your dad and mother worked together and they helped us fix a little shoe-shine kit.

CAROL: Oh, my goodness, I don't remember that.

PAULA: And we had like a washcloth. We did that blanket stitch all the way around that washcloth so you could use that for your shining classes, and your father gave us these real specific directions on how to shine your shoes correctly. We all had our little cloths and we were just shining away. Because those were before the days when everybody was wearing tennis shoes. We were wearing leather shoes.

CAROL: I'm glad you shared that.

MARY K.: So that's where I learned how to buff and shine. I remember the how to set a table properly and how to make a bed properly at Paula Wood's house. That's where I learned to make a bed properly, you know, to make the square corners before we had fitted sheets.

VANNE: We had to have it so you could bounce a quarter on it, and it had those square corners. I still make a bed that way.

CAROL: I do, too. Yes indeed!

MARY K.: We were taught how to sit, how to back up to a chair and let the chair touch the back of your knees. You lowered yourself onto a chair, you just didn't plop.

VANNE: And cross your legs at the ankles.

PAULA: Also getting in and out of a car. And do you remember the bra fitting? When we were developing, they showed us all about how to put on a bra, how to get the proper fit, and how to lean forward.

Mary K. spoke earlier of our little charm or finishing school, and what people had. I don't know how well known it is among the general population that when African Americans worked in homes of wealthy people, they learned a lot. They were observing. And when they had the money they did the same things. And so as Vanne was speaking about the silver service, the linens, the table linens, the way meals were put together, we know how to do it.

MARY K.: We didn't go to the finish.

Carol Dawson, c. 1952

CAROL: That's right. We're not quite finished. I do recall so well when my father worked at the Minnesota Club,[23] I got introduced to a lot of different kinds of foods, because he'd bring home leftover food and oftentimes those leftovers were our meal.

MARY K.: I remember eating at your house.

CAROL: So, I got introduced to French pastries and a number of things. I think he even brought some pheasant home one time.

VANNE: I don't know who it was that went hunting, but I remember at Paula T.'s house having venison and having duck or quail. I think it was, duck or quail.

PAULA: Partridge.

VANNE: And then Mary K.'s dad was able to go to Europe singing, and so I think he brought us back some viewpoints of what was going on in Europe. We had that, too. And then we had piano playing. Nobody has talked about the piano playing, which all of us didn't stick with.

MARY K.: How many of us learned? I started taking music before I was in Three Fours. Adrienne, myself, and Paula, you could play very well by the time you were twelve, so you must have started when you were—

PAULA: I think I started when I was about seven.

CAROL: One of my very valued memories is going over to Mary K.'s and listening as she would accompany her father during rehearsals. Mary K. got a lot of practice and she accompanied him publicly. Mother[24] gave me a choice and I chose climbing trees, because I think she had put it that way, "You can climb trees or you can take piano lessons." And I said I'd rather climb trees.

PAULA: Mary K. was very advanced. The rest of us went to Mrs. Howland's house on Iglehart for piano lessons. And some of us were not very good.

VANNE: I remember going to Mrs. Howland's and she would always cook something in the kitchen while she gave lessons and you'd be sitting there and she'd be out of the room and you'd be playing the piano. I was less interested than most people, so I didn't stick with it that long, but she would correct you from that kitchen. And then periodically as a favor to you, she'd bring you out to taste what she was cooking. Her greens, her soup, her whatever.

LINDA: She had to have that dinner ready for her husband, right?

CAROL: Right.

LINDA: The moms had dinner ready.

PAULA: And we were taking piano lessons after school, so that was time for her to cook her dinner.

LINDA: I brought these photos that I found in this old album, and one of the things that's really striking to me is that we had dresses on for the meetings. Remember that was before you didn't wear pants very often. Pants weren't allowed at school yet.

VANNE: You could only wear pants when it was cold and you took them off and put them in your locker. And tennis shoes were gym shoes and you didn't wear them for everyday. You had three pairs of shoes: school shoes and church shoes, and tennis shoes were for gym—when you got them.

LINDA: I remember making hats as an Easter activity and we made hats out of paper plates and crepe paper. It was at my house and we decorated them. I have a photo from 1955.

Standing: Sherrill Slorby, Carol Mills, Leora Myers, Paula Thomason, Linda Griffin
In front: Carol Dawson, c. 1955

VANNE: I remember some campouts, because I think we spent the night in a tent in Paula T's backyard. We had a cooking group activity in Paula T's kitchen. We learned how to do measurements for cooking. We made ice cream and learned how to make taffy, and then we spent the night in the backyard. Another time we made ice cream with snow. That was when you could make ice cream from the snow. You'd go outside and get the snow and put it in. Now, you know, you'd die if you did that because of the pollution.

PAULA: We did a lot of artsy-craftsy kind of things. We also did a lot of games. And I don't know if kids nowadays do those kinds of things. They were mental games. You know the kind where you'd have the anagrams. You'd have three fours or some letters, and you had to come up with a country for each one of those letters. They had us doing a lot of thoughtful activities.

CAROL: I was remembering our Christmas caroling. There was a sense of community among ourselves that began with the Three Fours. I think that sense of community had been instilled in us when on Christmas Eve we would get together and we'd go caroling. Sometimes I think we would go to a public place to do some caroling, and sometimes we'd go home to home and then spend a little time at each person's home. The benefit of a group of lifelong friends that I've had is something that has enriched my life just tremendously.

VANNE: Also, as I said earlier, my father died in 1952. I don't remember much about him being around, but when I was fourteen my mother[25] died and all these parents continued to parent me and guide me. So when I was making choices to go to college, when we actually were debutantes and had to make those choices, when I got married, they were all there. I remember Paula T.'s mother telling me all the things I had to do and remembering the people I'd forgotten about and maybe had lost some importance to me because I hadn't interacted with them that much. The parents always kept us involved.

Vanne Owens Hayes

I think it was very important in the group that we learned values and the values of friendship and loyalty. When I think about our growing up, we stayed loyal to each other even when we were not close, in terms of interacting.

And we also learned public speaking, the importance of your self-presentation and all the things that you needed to do so that you could walk in any circle of life. That was one of the things that our parents wanted us to be able to do is go anywhere.

MARY K.: Also, our parents taught us how to look after each other's children. And I can remember when I had a dental appointment and my mother[26] was working and she wasn't able to take me to the dentist and Aunt Ruby, Paula Wood's mother, took me to the dentist. And we've continued things like that. In our extended family network, we call each other's parent Aunt or Uncle. You know, we were like an extended family.

PAULA: And as we've been talking, I noticed how much we've been talking about our parents. We were all very fortunate we had parents who were very accomplished. Of course, at the time when they were our age and when they were parents, they were not always able to fulfill the life that they had prepared for. But they had hopes that we would be able to live that life, that we would be prepared and we would be able to have job opportunities, social opportunities, and living opportunities that they felt they had prepared for, but the world wasn't ready for them.

VANNE: As you said that I was reminded that in their time, women, regardless of what their education and training was, were to stay at home and the husbands were the breadwinners. So it was. I think they made sure that we knew how to be independent women, to prepare us to stand on our own, not that they weren't independent women. They were savvy, but they made sure that we got all the benefits that society had to offer and that we gained the tools so we could use the tools and take it a step further than they were able to go.

PAULA: Our mothers were not always stay-at-home mothers. For periods in their life they may have been at home, but they had jobs. Many of them were college educated. They were readers. They were writers. I remember Mary K.'s parents learning about different religions and teaching us those kind of things. So they were very accomplished people. They were very intelligent, very accomplished in their own right.

CAROL: When I spoke earlier about the sense of community, and you probably aren't aware of this, but my own sister and I have come to realize that we credit our associations with our friends as being the motivating factors for our having gone to college. I didn't know this growing up, but I realize looking back that I think my family perhaps struggled a little bit more in terms economically than some others. So they were so focused on that survival mode that they never had any expectations or never pushed us toward doing something outside of finishing high school. And I realize that the only reason why I was motivated to go to college was because it seemed the thing to do, because my friends did it. My sister also has made the same comment. She believes that was what inspired her as well. I was an adult before I realized how many of your parents actually had some college education. My own father went to business school, but my mother I don't think finished high school. So yes, your parents as role models made a huge difference in my life.

LINDA: I remember Doris Shannon was a tomboy. She was real active and after about two meetings she got up and walked out with a "Sheesh." You know, these business meetings were not for her and she quit because we weren't active enough for her.

We were talking about all these really positive things, but I remember we were still kids. We were at Mary K.'s house for a meeting and we had a vacancy and we were nominating people. You had to be nominated and voted on. I mean this was a real organization and someone nominated someone. There were several nominations and when we had the vote it turned out one person didn't get any votes. And Mary K.'s mom said, "Now, this is strange. Who nominated So-and-So?" And I said, "I did." "But you didn't vote for them?" "No." "Why did you nominate them?" "Because my mother[27] told me I had to nominate her, but she didn't say I had to vote for her." So we were still kids and that person never became a member of the Three Fours club.

PAULA: I think the ground foundation was laid for Vanne to be a lawyer in Three Fours. Vanne was the secretary at one point, and by this time we had accumulated several secretary books that Vanne was in charge of. So one day Vanne came to the meeting, and when it was time for the secretary report Vanne stood up and said, "I have misplaced the minutes. I have not lost them."

MARY K.: Miss Diplomacy—that's what she was then, that's what she is now. As you mentioned, some of these times were a little bit tense. There were some times of conflict and tension. But we learned how to work through those because our parents helped to guide us, which was a good beginning for the conflicts that we've had to deal with in our jobs, I'm sure. When I think about how we always resolved whatever it was in that meeting. If it was the business meeting, we were guided.

VANNE: The Three Fours Club began to dissipate because we were becoming active in our own church youth fellowships, and we each had activities and a schedule. I think those things began to replace some of the activities that we were doing through Three Fours. It ended when we were around twelve or thirteen years of age. My memory is that we dissipated after we had this sort of powwow picnic where we all cooked things and we invited boys to come and it was a mixed bag, but I think that was kind of the beginning of the end, if not the end.

PAULA: I think it was junior high, because in junior high was when we began developing other friendships. We were at a larger school, and we started developing other friendships.

LINDA: One of the things that Three Fours did for me was I got to be around older girls because I was the youngest. I was exposed to a whole lot of things that I might not have otherwise. My dad was working two, three jobs all the time—he was a police officer, traveled a lot with his sports refereeing. My mom went to college but was raised in the country. The Three Fours exposed me to a lot of things that maybe my mom wouldn't have known of. Paula's mother, Aunt Shirlee, just had all these ideas. The Thomasons and the Three Fours really exposed me to a lot of different things that I might not have otherwise experienced at that point in time.

VANNE: It's hard to say whether it was the Three Fours or the times that we grew up in, but I know that my feeling that "I can do it" is in part due to Three Fours. The expectation of what you needed to do to go out there and do it—how to talk and walk, I guess, to be in society. I know that when we were growing up there was a language that you used at school, at church and around adults. Slang and other things you could use a little bit when you were among yourselves, but there were lines you couldn't cross and it was definitely something we paid close attention to. There were rules and values, that there was no doubt about it. We had to live by them and anybody at our church, definitely any parent, would correct us.

And they supported us as a village. If it's true that it takes a village to raise a child, we had our village through Three Fours and it lasted. It's lasted. I think that all the parents that continued to be around have been there for us, have celebrated with us, have supported us, have done whatever they could and that's been ongoing.

MARY K.: It helped to solidify a very good foundation even though there are those of us around the table that don't see each other all the time, but there's that connection. You know, it's like family. So it feels good to know that you are a part of an extended family. Something that's bigger, motivates you and also gives solace when it's needed. And we are so proud when one of us accomplishes something.

All of our parents had different gifts, and they contributed those gifts to us and we're doing the same.

CAROL: I know the Three Fours was pivotal for my development, although during the years I experienced it, I didn't think that way. I took it for granted.

My friends keep me involved in things and I know if it wasn't for that that I would soon dry up because I have to have that variety. And when I look back on it and I think about all the things that we've done and the variety that has existed within the group, because we're all remarkably different individuals. But we have come to really value one another.

And another thing that—I know Mary K., Vanne, and I have talked about this. I learned as an adult that oftentimes young women, girls, in growing up, would have these tremendous conflicts having to do with their boyfriend. And I was appalled when I heard about that because that was something that was never even an issue. If one of us had a relationship with somebody, that was their relationship and we respected it and we never had any of that kind of nitpicking. I think it was very unusual. And I am still awed by the value of it in my life.

VANNE: I also want to add that we were taught to do what was important. Whatever we achieved it wasn't about status. It was about achieving a goal. We're good people. We come from loving families, and that is really where our importance is. Not in these other kinds of things like whatever position you had or however much money you got. That's something to celebrate, but it's not something to envy or to feel less than or more than. It's just something that happened, but the central core of who we are is based around those values we learned at that time with Three Fours.

And, remember we ended the meeting with:

ALL: *And a good time was had by all!*

❖ ❖ ❖

MARY KALLEEN MURRAY BOYD's biographical note can be found on page 218.

CAROL DAWSON moved with her parents in 1947 to Rondo's exceptional Black community. She credits her family and community for instilling in her integrity, humanity, and generosity. She retired from the Saint Paul Public School District after thirty years teaching grades 3–6 in nontraditional and traditional settings. She was a member of a curriculum development and management leadership team, and an African American Curriculum Specialist at the District's Multicultural Resource Center. In 2003 she traveled to South Africa and is proud of her faculty presentation at the University of Pretoria. In 2004 she participated in the Healing the Heart of Diversity Leadership Education Study Tour of West Africa.

LINDA GRIFFIN GARRETT, born to James and Edna, is the proud mother of Christopher (Farida) and James Jr., and grandmother of Austin Garrett. In memory of her husband of thirty-one years, James Garrett Sr., she established the James Garrett Sr. Memorial Scholarship Fund at Michigan State University. She was a Saint Paul Public School teacher and administrator for thirty-six years, and has served as a volunteer with Big Brothers Big Sisters, at St. Philip's in the food shelf and as a lay reader, with Loaves and Fishes, on the Arlington High School Site Council, and as a Chosen to Achieve mentor. She is a board member of the Vianne L. Griffin Memorial Scholarship Fund.

VANNE OWENS HAYES, JD is thankful for the "village" that raised her into adulthood. After graduation from law school she became assistant dean at the University of Minnesota, and later the director of the Minneapolis Department of Civil Rights. Vanne is a founder of the Minnesota Association of Black Lawyers, member of Alpha Kappa Alpha Sorority, member of St. Philip's Episcopal Church, and serves on numerous boards. Vanne was married to Kirk Hayes for twenty-six years and is the very proud mother and grandmother of April; Christopher and his wife, Betty; Darren and his wife, Dana, and their children Mikayla and Jadyn; and Christian. She continues to feel blessed with the love and support of many people, particularly Ward Bell.

PAULA THOMASON MITCHELL is proud of her family, proud that everyone is doing well and are good people. She has been married to M. Frederick Mitchell since 1965. He retired from environmental health, and she retired from the Saint Paul Public Schools. Their son, Philip, is married to Rebecca Blaesing and is working as an auto technician. Her daughter, Maria Mitchell, graduated from the University of Minnesota Law School and practices family law. Mrs. Mitchell is the proud grandmother of Bre, Philip, and Caleb. She remains active in St. Philip's Church, and she and Linda Garrett have started their own business as sales consultants for Tastefully Simple Gourmet Foods.

1. Vanne Hazel Owens Hayes was born October 27, 1943.

2. Linda Ruby Griffin Garrett was born November 13, 1944.

3. Mary Kalleen Murray Boyd was born June 29, 1942.

4. Paula Patricia Thomason Mitchell was born August 25, 1942.

5. Carol Jean Dawson was born June 2, 1943.

6. Mother Shirlee Patricia Harris Thomason was born in Saint Paul, Minnesota, June 5, 1918. She was a National Honor Society member and a thespian at Central High School. Shirlee attended the University of Minnesota, but was forced to quit for financial reasons. After taking classes at the business school, she accepted employment with the State of Minnesota and became a research analyst in the Revenue Department. Her avocation was writing poetry, prose, and humorous skits. The Thomasons entertained extensively— family, friends, neighbors, and out-of-town guests all enjoyed their hospitality. Shirlee passed March 5, 1979.

7. Ruby Wood was born May 29, 1919.

8. Frances Elizabeth Brown Hughes was born in the college town of Wilberforce, Ohio, March 12, 1908. As the niece of the famous orator Hallie Q. Brown, Frances was raised in a community that afforded her many intellectual and cultural experiences. She moved to Minnesota in the early 1940s and married James Hughes. Her career was as a librarian for the State of Minnesota. Mrs. Hughes lived in Maplewood and had several acres of land.

9. Maplewood is located seven miles east of Saint Paul.

10. The Forum was a formal cafeteria located at 36 South Seventh Street in Minneapolis.

11. Saint James AME (African Methodist Episcopal) Church existed as a prayer group as early as 1870. Formally organized in 1878, they purchased a permanent home in 1881. The current church was built in 1926 at 624 West Central Avenue at Dale.

12. Pilgrim Baptist Church was first organized as a prayer group before 1863, and formally organized as a church November 15, 1866. Their first house of worship was constructed in 1870 at Twelfth and Cedar Streets in Saint Paul, and it moved in 1918 to the current location at 732 West Central Avenue in Saint Paul.

13. Hallie Q. Brown Community Center, Inc., was opened in the Union Hall

at Aurora and Kent Streets in 1929 as a community center specifically to serve the Black community when the Black YWCA closed in 1928. Hallie Q., as it is affectionately known, has served all ages through child care, youth and senior clubs, athletics, music, and social events. In 1972, Hallie relocated in the Martin Luther King Building at 270 Kent Street at Iglehart in Saint Paul. The center's namesake was an educator who pioneered the movement of Black women's clubs in the late 1800s.

14. The Sterling Club was a social club founded in 1918 and incorporated in 1919. It was located at 315 North Dale Street at Rondo. In 1958 it built a new home at 300 North St. Albans at Carroll. This private club was formed to give prestigious Black men, who were not allowed in White facilities, a place to meet and network.

15. Father James Thomas Murray was born September 2, 1918, in Shugualak, Mississippi. He graduated from Central High School in Omaha, Nebraska, and attended Alcorn College in Mississippi. He moved to Saint Paul in 1937. After his marriage to Lavinia Stone, he served in the U.S. Army. Upon return to civilian life, Jim, as he was known, worked in the packinghouses for a brief stint while attending MacPhail School of Music. He then joined the U.S. Post Office, where he worked as a mail carrier until retirement. Jim had a second career as a singer that was carried on from high school until his passing in 1995. He was the soloist for the National Alliance of Letter Carriers; traveled throughout the United States, Europe, and parts of Africa as a member of the cast of *Porgy and Bess*; traveled to the Scandinavian countries as a soloist with the Minnesota Gospel Choir; and performed as a soloist and member of many choral groups, including the Metropolitan Male Chorus.

16. Father James Stafford Griffin was born July 6, 1917, and passed November 23, 2002. His major career was as a police officer with the Saint Paul Police Department, beginning as a patrolman and retiring forty-two years later as deputy chief. Simultaneously he worked as a high school and small college football and basketball referee in the Twin Cities, greater Minnesota, Wisconsin, and Michigan. A lesser known seasonal job was as a waiter on the railroad. He used his vacation days from the police department to do this.

17. Father Paul William King Thomason is a retired City of Saint Paul firefighter. He was born January 17, 1914, in Fort Scott, Kansas. At the age of fifteen, he began playing the piano in Kansas and Missouri nightclubs. After graduating from high school, he traveled with various bands. He came to Minnesota

in 1936 and formed his own band; although he disbanded the group when he joined the fire department, he continued to play pickup, private parties, and for the enjoyment of family and friends. He passed June 2005.

18. Father Paul Wood.

19. Father Percy Dawson was born May 2, 1912, and passed April 12, 2004. He worked as a waiter with the railroad, a clerical worker at the Saint Paul Courthouse and Ramsey County Welfare Department, and, finally, as a purchasing agent for Ancker/Ramsey/Regions Hospital.

20. Father Sterling Vincent Owens was born in 1909, and passed October 1, 1952. He was a member of Alpha Phi Alpha Fraternity and a graduate of the University of Kansas and the New York School of Social Work. In 1942 he came to Minnesota to serve as executive director of the Saint Paul Urban League. He served on the Governor's Interracial Commission and the Governor's Advisory Council on Children and Youth. When Mr. Owens passed, Governor C. Elmer Anderson issued a statement acknowledging that his untimely death was a significant loss to the state.

21. The Urban League has served the Black community since 1923 as a human service advocacy organization. The Urban League addresses issues of quality employment, housing, education, and health care. The Saint Paul and Minneapolis agencies were combined until 1938. Saint Paul offices were initially located in various buildings downtown until the late 1960s, when they moved into their own building at 401 Selby Avenue, four blocks south of the Rondo corridor.

22. Crispus Attucks Home was founded in 1906 by the city's Industrial Mission Church. The original home was located in 1910 at Randolph and Brimhall Streets and had a sign that said, "Colored Orphanage and Old Folks Home." It was supported for sixty years by the Twin Cities Black congregations. Later it was located at 469 Collins. Crispus Attucks (1723–1770) was the first Black man killed in the American Revolution.

23. The Minnesota Club incorporated 1884 as a place for White Saint Paul residents to share literary and social culture. Initially the club was at Fourth and Cedar Street and later built at Fourth and Washington.

24. Mother Loretta C. Dawson was born February 2, 1922, and passed August 30, 1999. Loretta was primarily a homemaker during the first few years of her marriage. Her out-of-home experiences included working as a waitress at Black-owned Road Buddy's diner; an elevator operator at Newman's Store in downtown Saint Paul; a nursery school helper at Hallie Q. Brown Community

Center; a dietary aide at Charles T. Miller Hospital; and a teacher's aide with the Saint Paul Public Schools.

25. Mother Wanda M. Piper Owens was born in 1911 in Salina, Kansas, and passed April 4, 1958. A high school valedictorian, she graduated Phi Beta Kappa from Kansas State University with a major in Romance languages and was a member of Alpha Kappa Alpha Sorority, Inc. She received an M.A. in education from the University of Minnesota and taught at Hill Elementary School in Saint Paul.

26. Mother Lavinia A. Stone Murray was born August 1, 1917, in Spencer County, Kentucky, the fourth of six children born to Robert H. and Mary Stone. She graduated from Lincoln Ridge High School, a boarding school, and attended Kentucky State College. She moved to Saint Paul in 1940 where she met and married James Murray. She was a stay-at-home mom who volunteered and worked for short periods outside the home at Schuneman's Department Store, Bethesda Hospital, Saint Paul Public Schools, and the airport. She and her husband were foster parents for fifteen years.

27. Mother Edna Smoot Griffin was born May 28, 1916. Most of her time was spent as a homemaker caring for her three children and volunteering in the community at Maxfield Elementary School and St. Philip's Episcopal Church. She worked seasonally for 13 years at the Minnesota Department of Revenue, handling the annual crush of tax returns.

MELVIN THOMAS HENDERSON

We thought we were something.

I AM MEL HENDERSON.[1] My parents migrated from Kansas. I think they came for employment purposes. My dad was a Pullman Porter,[2] and my mother, basically, was a housekeeper.

I lived for quite a few years at 450 St. Anthony Avenue. My mother had a way of disciplining us if we were doing something we weren't supposed to. She just said, "Go out and get your switch." And you'd go get the smallest one you could find and then she'd look at you and say, "No, that won't work." And you'd go back and get one, or she would just pick up a brush and paddle your little behind if you were not doing what you were supposed to do. So in respect to her and reflecting back on her, I am very thankful that she did because I was a kid into everything, you know, and so I think I got a spanking about every other day. I would take apart things like radios and clocks and stuff and never get 'em back together again, and so it was always something I would get punished for.

I was fortunate enough to have a grandfather and grandmother who lived on a farm in Hugo, Minnesota,[3] so in the summers I got a chance to go out and work on the farm. I lived in the Cities, but also got a chance to be on the farm in the summertime. He had the regular cows, chickens, and he raised wheat, cucumbers, and so forth. It was kind of a nice experience.

Sister Marcelene, friend, sister Beverly, Melvin,
Aunt Hazel Fulbright

I had three aunts and then these three uncles. We had some cousins in the area. And for a while there, we lived in one of the apartment buildings that my uncle owned. So that was kind of interesting, having family in one big apartment building, right there on St. Anthony Avenue, between Mackubin and Rondo. It was good because everybody watched out for each other in the family, and it was a close-knit family living together like that.

I would say my relatives, particularly the women, were very assertive. Not overbearing, really, of that nature, but pretty much they were take-charge women. And so that was okay.

I went to St. Peter Claver Catholic School[4] here in Saint Paul. I could do something wrong a couple blocks from the school, and I had close to about a mile to get home, and by the time I got home, my mother knew about it. Yeah, yeah, you had to be on your p's and q's. You were almost in that kind of a fishbowl, in a sense, as a kid, because you could be stealing apples or throwing rocks at cars and the next-door neighbor would know about it. They would call your parents.

Not only was the community or people pretty much concerned about kids, but also the police in those days were, too. They did walk the beats, they rode the beats, and so we got a chance to at least know that they were concerned about us. I remember this one cop by the name of Skally.[5] I remember one time we were hiding behind these cars throwing rocks at cars, and he happened to catch us and so he sat us down and talked to us for, oh, close to about an hour. We didn't throw any rocks at cars after that, but he was just very good with kids, yeah.

So it was a very interesting time, and plus my neighborhood was kind of interesting because it just wasn't all African American in my block per se. There were Caucasian families. There was, I think, even an Oriental family that lived there, and so it was kind of an interesting mixture in my whole block. And so when I went out of my area and I saw just people that were all African American or all White, it looked a little strange because I felt that it should be more of a mixture of people in the community.

Holidays were pretty festive. Everybody had the different kinds of foods in their own little apartment and you'd go from place to place eating, whatever, and everyone had their decorations up. It was pretty festive even though we didn't have a lot of money. But we ate good, though, so that was enjoyable. My mom and dad, they were pretty good about making sure that we had plenty of food to eat because they were pretty good shoppers and they would know where to go to get the best deals on food and stuff like that. We ate good—fried chicken, most of the time. And there was always plenty of cornbread and plenty of the various types of greens. One of the things I used to like quite a bit was a pork chop and then there were times when we would have steak, but I never did like it as a kid. And there were always plenty of sweet potatoes and then white potatoes, and we also ate plenty of oatmeal, you know. For some reason we'd always had more food than most of the people in the neighborhood. I would invite my buddies over, and we'd have cookies or pies and stuff like that. My parents would catch me bringing my buddies over, and then I would usually get it for bringing my buddies over to eat. But that's the way I was. I was very generous.

Going back to my early days, the times that my mother used to read to me were the best. I think I really enjoyed her reading to me and just her time she spent helping me. I liked books. I think I liked primarily things like *Tom's Cabin*[6] for some reason. I really didn't totally understand it at the time, but as I grew older, I understood that whenever someone calls someone "Uncle Tom,"[7] they sometimes would take offense. But I don't think they really understood that Uncle Tom did what he had to do to survive in those days for himself and for his family. So I think people many times are misguided or misunderstand what that really is. And in those days, I think, there were many African American folks in their early times, whether it's slavery, whatever, that did certain things in terms of compromising themselves so that they would live for another day or be able to survive for another day. And so that connotation Uncle Tom really didn't mean much to me.

I was with a family—grandfather, grandmother, uncles, cousins—that had a sense of pride in themselves and what they did, and I got a sense as to how they worked the system. Like my uncles, they served in World War II, but they never went over to Europe. They never went to the South Sea Islands. What they did was, they built the barracks for the soldiers, and so when they left the army, they knew how to build houses and build homes. They built their own homes, owned land, and they were able to do that. And so I saw that. I said, "You know, that's what you have to do. You have to learn something to be able to use it and work the system to help yourself."

And my grandmother, Carrie Fulbright, was an individual who was very, very strong-willed and she was about business in terms of, she would tell you what she wanted to tell you, no matter who you were and what you were, what position you had, and so she didn't care. She said, "Hey, this is me and I'm a little Black woman who has nothin' to lose." I watched and observed her. So I was a kid who observed these things, and so I said, "I have to take the things that they did that were good and basically begin to pull them into myself."

I went to the Ober Boys Club,[8] too, and that's where I've learned how to play football and learned how to box and play basketball. They taught us if you're gonna play football, then be good at it. That was something that they did.

If I wasn't at the Ober Boys Club, I was in school. So I was down there quite a bit. It was mainly boys. We didn't allow girls in there in those days.

I remember that we had a game, stupidest game in the world. It was called Pom Pom Pullaway. But we did it a little different from most people did because you pick up a football and then you'd run as long as you could, and people would be trying to tackle you and take the ball from you. And when you got tired, you'd throw it up and then somebody else would take it.

We got into a lot of fights down there. If somebody took your basketball away from you and they didn't give it back to you, you'd fight about it. But they did have a unique thing down at the Ober Boys Club, because if you were fighting too much, they would have Friday night fights. What they would do is they had a ring and you put on the boxing gloves and then whoever you were fighting with that week, you got a chance to do it in more of a formal way. There were a lot of Friday night fights.

I had one friend pretty much that we played together a lot of times as young kids and, I mean, we would be all over Saint Paul, just about, on our bicycles. I remember one time, there's a street—well, Dale Street the way it is now is a little different than those days. But we used to go across Dale Street on our bicycles balancing on our handlebars doing flips, whatever, across this busy street. But we always knew where the cars were coming and so forth. And people always used to say, "These kids are going to kill themselves," you know. But our bicycles were our transportation all over the Saint Paul area.

Then, later on, there were at least three other guys that I grew up with in junior high and high school, Marshall Junior High School[9] and Central High School.[10] We stayed together for many years and we created a singing group, and we used to sing in night clubs and stuff like that when we were in high school. We called ourselves the Emeralds,[11] and we had mint green jackets and the whole bit. They weren't expensive. They were kind of a mint green and they were something we bought together as a group, so we got a discount on them. We had the cummerbunds and the bow ties and the whole bit. So we thought we were something.

About once every two weeks we sang at a place called the Red Feather.[12] It was a nightclub. I don't know how we got in there as high school kids, but we got in there. We would sing the regular rock-and-roll

HENDERSON, MELVIN
"Bluto"
Jr. Class President
Homecoming King
Student Council, Ex. Council
Soph. Class Rep.
Omega Hi-Y
Soph. & Jr. Medal
Boys' State
'A' Football
Varsity Track
'A' Choir, vice pres.
Stage Force
"Emeralds"

WRIGHT, RICHARD
"Dick"
'A' Football
'B' Football
Gymnastics
Jr. and Sr. Varsity Track
'A' Band
Omega Hi-Y
Math Club
Chemistry Club
Pep Band
Jr. Red Cross Rep.
"Emeralds"
Philosophy Club

DENT, CHARLES
"Chach"
Sr. Varsity Track
'A' Football
Jr. Varsity Track
Gymnastics
Speech Club
Choir
"Emeralds"

SIMMS, JAMES
"Bobo"
'A' Football
'B' Football
Sr. Varsity Track
Jr. Varsity Track
Gymnastics
Speech Club
Pep Club
Choir
Chemistry Club
"Emeralds"

The Emeralds' senior pictures from the 1962
CEHISEAN, Central High School yearbook

Central High School

songs of the time. We didn't get paid much, but we enjoyed just doing it. And then we would sing at some of the high school dances and we would sing at some of the community centers and that was our recreation. It was basically some of the slower music, but also we did some fast things, too. And we did some of the songs by the Flamingos, the Spinners, the Four Tops. Stuff like that. And I think we did a few of Sam Cook's stuff, you know.

We pretty much did a lot of our singing at Saint Paul Central, and we did it at some of the community centers and at the Ys, we sang at Temple of Aaron's[13] youth group, but we would be up on the stage and we would do our thing, we got our money, we were gone. We didn't need to socialize.

We were also athletes. We played football, ran track together. The athletics kept us out of trouble because you had to work out and you had to do certain things and stay in shape, but then also we wanted to do some other things that were recreational. So for our cases, the athletics and the singing kept us kinda on the straight and narrow for the most part.

We were very cocky. We were very proud and, I'll be honest, we didn't take any stuff from anybody, so it didn't bother us. But you know, there is a certain persona that you put on sometimes that people just kinda are taken back. This was never so apparent as when I was in the South. I was in Chattanooga, Tennessee, one time and so I went up to the person who was behind the counter and as soon as she heard me speak, she was taken back. And then I realized that she knew I wasn't from there, and she treated me differently than the other people there. So I realized when I was around twelve or thirteen that you have to put on a certain persona, you have to speak a certain way, and then that somehow transcends those barriers for people.

Oh, it was fun. Because we dated a lot of girls. We dated and we may have had several special girls, but you dated who you wanted to. And there was no restriction, in a sense. At least, not for me anyways. I was probably one of the better athletes in the City of Saint Paul and so I played football, ran track. Matter of fact, I have a plaque that says, "The City of Saint Paul, One of the Better Athletes of the Last One Hundred Years." I got to be homecoming king and all those kinds of things.

There was attitude about interracial dating, but I guess my group of guys, we didn't care. You know, we dated who we wanted to date. We just felt if there was a good-looking girl and we wanted to date her, we did. She could be African American. She could be Jewish. She could be Chinese. She could be whatever. We dated them. Our parents were not exactly fine with it. They just felt that society wasn't ready for that at the time, back in the 1950s and '60s. They were basically old school, and they just thought that we were going to get into trouble and stuff like that. We just said, "No, we're not. We're fine." Matter of fact, nothing ever happened to me.

Later on someone had mentioned to me that when I was homecoming king and the queen was not African Ameri-

Mel Henderson and Judy Grohs,
Central High School Homecoming, October 14, 1961

can, she was White. Someone had taken and circulated this picture of us in the South and the caption was, "This is what happens to your daughter." And so it was the funniest thing. I remember I had gotten a scholarship offer to go to the University of Kentucky and something said, don't go down to the University of Kentucky, even for an interview. And I didn't, but this was posted all over the South and in that area. My picture with this White woman, 'cause I had the crown on and she had the crown on and nothing happened between us.

My family, and the community through Ober, church, and school, all laid the solid foundation for my achievements as I moved through life.

◆ ◆ ◆

MELVIN THOMAS HENDERSON, son of Melvin and Evelyn, is very proud of his wife of thirty-six years, their daughters, and the work he has had the opportunity to do. Judy Henderson is a social studies teacher at Burnsville High School. Mel has worked at Metropolitan State University for thirty-three years as a faculty member and administrator. He teaches courses in human services and counseling psychology, and is a licensed, independent social worker. He serves on the Dakota County Youth Council and Randolph Heights Elementary School Site Council. Mr. Henderson has been a Steward Board member of St. James AME Church for twenty years. He has instilled in his children the values of trusting God, education and community. He is the proud father of Melanie (real estate); Natalie Stute (human resources), who is married to William Stute and they have four sons; and Karie (sales manager for NIKE).

◆ NOTES

1. Melvin T. Henderson was born June 29, 1944.

2. Pullman Porters worked for the Pullman Company and carried baggage only for Pullman sleeping car passengers. The Pullman sleeping cars would be transferred to different railroads and travel all over the country.

3. Hugo, Minnesota, is located twenty miles north of Saint Paul.

4. St. Peter Claver School was part of the St. Peter Claver Catholic Church Parish, which began in an unstructured way in 1889. A new building was

erected for the segregated Black congregation at Aurora and Farrington Avenue in 1892. After the new school and convent were built, the new church building was completed at 375 Oxford at St. Anthony in 1957.

5. Bill Skally served as a Saint Paul Police patrolman from 1941 to 1973. During his assignment as a beat officer on Rondo, he had a reputation of taking youth to their parents before arresting them. He was well respected for his knowledge of the community and its members.

6. *Uncle Tom's Cabin* was written by Harriet Beecher Stowe (1811–1896) and published in 1852. Stowe wrote the work in reaction to the Fugitive Slave Act of 1850, which made it illegal to assist an escaped slave. In the story, Uncle Tom is bought and sold three times and finally beaten to death by his last owner. Stowe's book is credited with building antislavery sentiment in the North and making slavery a moral issue rather than strictly a political one. *Uncle Tom's Cabin* is considered a major factor in the emotional buildup that led to the outbreak of the Civil War in April 1861.

7. "Uncle Tom" is a derogatory term for a Black man who is perceived as selling out to White authority or eager to win the approval of White people. The term comes from the title character in the novel *Uncle Tom's Cabin*. Uncle Tom is a noble, long-suffering Christian slave who demonstrates patience, grace, and dignity through his beliefs. Many object to Uncle Tom's passive and willing subservience, but others assert that his character has been misunderstood.

8. Ober Boys Club at 375 St. Anthony at Western was started during World War II by the Union Gospel Mission. It was named for Edgar Ober of 3M who was active with the Gospel Mission. This recreation club taught Christian values. Boys who participated also attended Snail Lake Children's Camp. There was a Girls Club located at Welcome Hall. Sometime after 1960 the club became part of Boys and Girls Clubs of America, but the building is still owned by Union Gospel Mission.

9. Marshall School was built in 1925 at Grotto, Holly, Ashland, and St. Albans. It was Marshall Junior High from 1926 to 1937. In 1937, 10th grade was added, in 1938, 11th grade; and in 1939, 12th grade was added, with graduating classes from 1940 to 1953. It returned to junior high only in 1954. Webster Elementary School was built on the same site in 1926. The two buildings were connected in 1975 and become Webster Magnet Elementary School.

10. Central High School began in 1866 and consisted of two rooms in the Franklin Building in downtown Saint Paul. By 1872, it was known as Saint Paul

High School and was moved to Seventh and Jackson. In 1883, a twenty-seven-room building on Minnesota Street in downtown Saint Paul was completed, and the school was named Saint Paul Central High located on Minnesota Street in downtown Saint Paul. Because of space needs, a new school was built at 275 Lexington Avenue in 1912. In 1977, the building was reduced to its structural form, then rebuilt to the current building.

11. The Emeralds were Charles Dent, James Simms, Richard Wright, and Mel Henderson.

12. The Red Feather Restaurant and Bar was located at 665 University Avenue, Saint Paul.

13. Temple of Aaron Congregation has been located at 616 South Mississippi River Boulevard since 1956.

DEBORAH GILBREATH
MONTGOMERY

Do the right thing for the right reason.

MY NAME IS DEBBIE GILBREATH MONTGOMERY.[1] I grew up at 978 St. Anthony, which is on the corner of St. Anthony and Chatsworth. I was born to Gloria Gilbreath Wilson[2] and Antonia Pedro Garcia,[3] who were not married at the time, and I was adopted by my grandparents, Isabella Gertrude Gilbreath,[4] whom I called Mama, and Elbert Gilbreath,[5] whom I called Dad. They came up following the railroad. Dad was the captain of the porters[6] down at the Saint Paul Union Depot,[7] and Mama was the matron in the bathroom at the Saint Paul Union Depot. She cleaned the bathroom, mopped the floors, cleaned the toilets, cleaned the washroom and the sinks, and made sure that there were towels. So I know all of the nooks and crannies of the Saint Paul Union Depot! Dad was the captain of the porters, so when people had to have their bags carried and stuff, he assigned people to go carry people's bags to the train and made sure they got to the appropriate trains in a timely fashion. He was a Redcap.

I was the firstborn of four children. My mother, from what I have been informed, was an alcoholic, and so when I was born, right in the hospital she gave me to Mama and Dad. I came home, and a year later my brother Dwayne[8] was born. He came home with Mama. And a year after that, I had another brother, Daryl. At that time, Dad decided that they weren't going

to take any more children, and they put him up for adoption. I've never met him. I'm told he lives in Minneapolis. Then there are five years between me and my youngest brother, Dale.[9] When he was born, Mama fought with Dad and brought him home. So my brother Dwayne, who's a year younger than me, and Dale, who was five years younger than me, all of us were raised by our grandparents.

We were Episcopalians, so I went to St. Philip's Episcopal Church.[10] I grew up with Father Denzil Carty,[11] who had a great impact upon my life and the civil rights movement that I was involved in. The churches back then were very strong in our community. I think that had a big impact upon the kids. We went to church on Sundays. That was just required. In the summer, we all went to Bible school, and it didn't make any difference if you were Catholic or Lutheran. I went to Pilgrim Baptist Bible Camp[12] in the summer. I went up to the Lutheran Bible Camp. It was just an opportunity to have a week of getting some spiritual guidance, and I don't think anybody was too worried about where you got it from or how you got it, just as long as you had it. It was an organized activity, and with your parents working, it was somewhere that the kids would be able to go.

Back then it was a village. If you did something wrong or said something out of line or didn't respect your elders, boy, you were going to be disciplined. You probably got two or three lickings before you got home, and then when you got home you got another one. So it was a strong village environment, and everybody looked out for each other's family. If you needed something, you could holler across the street. If you needed a couple of eggs, or some milk, everybody kind of shared, Whites and Blacks together. It was a really close-knit community. It was a really loving community. People cared about you. They were concerned about your success.

Oxford Playground[13] was a block away. Back then it was a swamp. Bill Peterson was a twenty-one-year-old Marine who had just got out of the service. He had this little flattop haircut that they wore back then. He came in there looking like a hunk, and he's got this playground that was a swamp. All it had on it was a little old warming house along with a merry-go-round and six swings. Here he's got all these little Black kids and a few White kids and he's sitting down there trying to teach us how to play ball. We learned how to play T-ball and softball and baseball.

I was a jock. I was very athletic and had a lot of energy. I was a little wiry thing. Down at Oxford, you had Dave Winfield[14] and Paul Moliter.[15] Bill Peterson was the baseball coach of the boys Attucks Brooks–Legion[16] All-State baseball team. Paul Moliter and Dave Winfield and all those guys, they all played on those teams, and they all came through Oxford.

Because it was a swamp and the field was not real good, nobody would come out and scrimmage our girls' team. This was in the heart of the African American neighborhood. A lot of the other rec centers wouldn't come and play us in our park because we didn't have a good field, so all of our games were away and a lot of our parents didn't have cars. What would happen was that the girls would scrimmage the boys' Attucks Brooks baseball team. Dave Winfield was the pitcher then and Paul was shortstop, and these guys were all out there. We'd all be down there and we'd be playing ball, and these guys were throwing that ball in there like they were throwing to guys! Anyway, I ended up being one heck of a softball player. I'd hit the ball Dave was pitching, and I'd just cream it! To this day, David'll say, "Boy, she just killed my pitches!"

We were getting used to playing the All-State boys' team. When we played other girls' teams at other parks, we would kill them. I mean, we beat them twenty-five to nothing or something. You're pitching fast and you're running—it's softball and you're running hard. You're sliding like girls wouldn't slide, but with the boys we had to learn how to slide because they'd be throwing that ball in there at us. I broke my best girlfriend Jackie's thumb about four times because I played shortstop and I threw the ball so hard. Nobody else would catch my balls coming in from shortstop. I was a good basketball player and I ran track. I was a speed skater. I was breaking barriers all over the place.

In the wintertime, Bill'd get out

Mama and Debbie at 978 St. Anthony

Mama, Debbie, brother Dwayne, neighbor Roger Tisdale, brother Dale at 978 St. Anthony

there and flood this area that we'd have to skate on. He just kept us engaged and when you got into the warming house—all that it had inside were benches with a square box with a piece of wood dividers in the middle. It was a box that had a board in between and little holes. He had his office and that was it. Then he'd go out and beg, borrow, and steal skates so we all could skate. I must've had the biggest feet, because I ended up getting black speed skates. The other girls had white figure skates and the boys had hockey skates. Bill taught us to play hockey.

For the Winter Carnival,[17] they would always have the races out at Como,[18] and so he'd put all of us in his little red 1954 station wagon and drag us out to Como. We'd get out there, and I didn't know how to speed skate when I first started, so I literally outran people around the ice on these speed skates. Finally, they took an interest in me and saw that I had some potential, and Bill got a couple of guys to work with me, to try to teach me how to stride and how to skate. I became really, really good.

They had two speed skating clubs that were close to us, and that was the Blue Line Speed Skating Club, which was kind of a high-buck private speed skating club on this side of town. And then East Side Shop Pond, which was over on the East Side. Because the Blue Line Club was over here, Bill took me over to try out for the club, but they weren't letting any Black kids in. The East Side Shop Pond would take me in the club, but we didn't have any transportation to get there. I got all kinds of blue ribbon medals from skating at the Winter Carnival. I beat Mary Meyers, who tied for the 1968 silver medal, two out of three heats in the tryouts. To this day, Peterson says, "What could you have done if you had had any kind of training?" I was obviously an athlete before my time.

There were so many things going on back then in the 1960s, that skating wasn't an important deal. I mean, it was important in the sense that it was an opportunity missed for them to have somebody like me to do that, but the sports part was secondary to people getting the right to vote. You know, we didn't get the voting rights bill in until 1965. We didn't get open housing in Saint Paul until 1960. So there were just tons of issues back then, and sports was an outlet for me. It felt good to succeed, but I never dwelled very much on "this is an opportunity missed."

When I was maybe thirteen, Allie May Hampton was a good friend of mine, and when I say friend, she was an older woman that was real active in the NAACP.[19] She was just a gem. She saw I was a rabble rouser and intelligent and articulate, and she got me active in the NAACP. She was getting us involved in the political process, getting us to understand the issues that were going on back then. This was in the late Fifties, early Sixties. She took me to my first NAACP conference. After I came back from the conference, they made me the president of the youth group.

I got all the kids involved in the NAACP youth group. We had 650 kids in it back then, because we had tons of kids and there were a lot of issues going on. I got really involved with the civil rights movement after that first conference and meeting all the kids from the South and the East and the West. Listening to what was going on down South, none of that was going here on like it was in the South. Our schools were integrated.

When the civil rights movement started they had buses going down to Mississippi and Alabama. In Minnesota, we were good for sending White activists down, and I was one of the Black youth that went down there. I remember taking my first bus ride down there.

Mama was scared to death because she was from Starkville, Kentucky, and Dad was from Lubbock, Texas, so they knew about the South. I didn't have a clue about what was going on, other than I knew I was fighting for a cause, and not realizing that people were killing people. I mean, I *did* realize it, but I didn't think it could happen to me.

I went on the bus with a lot of White kids and White adults and a few civil rights folks, and we got down there and we demonstrated and then got on a bus and came back. We were fighting for voting rights.

I became involved in the NAACP youth branch at the national level. We had to go down to Chicago, Atlanta, or Baltimore for conferences. Dad, he'd get me a pass and put me on the train. Dad and Mama never rode the train in their whole life, but because Dad worked with the railroad they could get passes. He'd take me down to the depot. He'd hook me up with a porter, one of his porter friends, and the porter would put me on the train. They'd usually put me in the food car because they could feed me there and make sure I was taken care of. Then when I got to Chicago and had to transfer, they'd take me by the hand and take me to another train and hand me over to another porter and say, "This is Gil's daughter. She's on her way to Baltimore, and she'll be comin' back at such-and-such a time. If you're on the train back, tell 'er where to meet you when you let 'er off. Let 'er know that you'll pick 'er up when she comes back."

I was probably about fifteen then. My parents were just scared to death, but I was just kind of a freewheeling kid. "I gotta go do the right thing for the right reason."

When I was seventeen I was elected to the National Board of Directors for the NAACP. As I said, at fifteen and sixteen, I had gotten really active in national youth movement, so I made friends with Chris Nelson, who was the president of Region I, the West Coast Region, and Andrea McKissick, who was from North Carolina and was in charge of that region.

I was just a rabble-rouser. I had made friends with everybody in the youth group. Floyd McKissick[20]—if you read up on the history, he was one of the big civil rights leaders in North Carolina. And Aaron Henry[21] was a big civil rights leader in Mississippi. Their kids and I were friends. We were all active in the national youth movement, and so they're telling their dads, "Oh, man! She's neat, man. She's smart. She's articulate. She's from Minnesota." They thought Minnesota was off the world.

Chet Lewis was an attorney out of Wichita, Kansas, and he was a Region IV representative to the national board out of our region. He was a big-time attorney and it's those kind of folks that got into those positions. He wasn't out there fighting and rallying and stuff like that. He wasn't inspiring anybody. So the kids got together at the national youth branch and said to me, "We're going to run you for the national board." They got together and they rallied all the kids together, and they got their parents together.

If you look at the NAACP history you'll see that at the age of seventeen, I ran nationally, at large. I got elected to the national board of directors, with Roy Wilkins.[22] I mean, all of the people that you see in there, and here's this little seventeen-year-old girl out of Minnesota that's sitting at the board with all these big shots.

I was on a mission. I was fighting for civil rights. I was speaking up for people. Trying to get voting rights for the people. I mean, these Black folks, they were in the army, they were serving their country and yet they didn't have the right to vote? If you look at the history, Blacks were on the front lines and getting killed in larger numbers, and they didn't have the right to vote. They didn't have the right to own property. They had the poorest jobs.

I look at Mama and Dad and the folks on Rondo. They did not get high-paying jobs, but never once did I feel that we were poor. There was a richness in our house. There was a strong faith in our house. My faith has been the stronghold in my life. I don't look at the downside. I just saw the up, and I wanted to help the next generation move up.

Debbie Gilbreath's
high school graduation picture

On the national board it was interesting to listen to the discussions. I mean, you had lawyers, bankers, politicians. You had lawyers that were talking about legal issues. Thurgood Marshall,[23] how he was going to deal with the legal issues taken to the Supreme Court. What's going on in Missouri? What's going on in Kansas? They had huge issues, and you're sitting there and you're listening to the discussion and listening to how they're going to handle it, who they were going to target. That's when I found out about target voting. "We're going to try to go after these seats, and we're going to try to get somebody in these positions." And trying to get folks registered. Back then, there were poll taxes.[24] Folks in these rural areas had to pay a poll tax to go vote. As you know, they were killing young people that were going down there in cars, similar to what I was doing.

I was kind of blessed. I marched from Selma to Montgomery with Dr. King, and I was in the March on Washington when he gave that "I Have a Dream" speech. You just talk about the mood, how you felt, the energy. People were standing around, 250,000 people, and they're listening to this guy talk and it was just phenomenal. You get a rush and think, "Hey, we've got to fight for our rights. They have to give us the right to vote. We have to be able to buy homes. You know, we need to buy property." Trying to get banking institutions to give loans to people. There were just so many major issues going on back then, I didn't have time to think about little things. My mind was always out here. I'd come home and the adults here were always talking about how bright I was. I wasn't any brighter. I was just kind of active in everything, trying to figure out how you make things work.

◆ ◆ ◆

DEBORAH LOUISE GILBREATH MONTGOMERY received her B.A. from the University of Minnesota, an M.A. from St. Thomas University, and an M.A. from the Humphrey Institute; in addition, she is a graduate of the Senior Police Management Institute at Harvard University. She was the first woman to participate in the same training as men and to become a full Saint Paul police officer. She was also the first Black woman to retire as a senior commander after twenty-eight years in the department. Debbie served as a Minnesota assistant commissioner of Public Safety from 1991 to 1998. She is chair of the YWCA Board of Directors. She was elected the first Black woman to the Saint Paul City Council in 2004. She is an extremely proud mother of three sons and one daughter; she and her husband, Robert, have been married thirty-eight years.

◆ NOTES

1. Deborah Louise Gilbreath Montgomery was born April 17, 1946.

2. Gloria Ellen Gilbreath Wilson was born August 7, 1925.

3. Antonia Pedro Garcia was born June 27, 1921, and passed March 8, 1998.

4. Grandmother Isabella Starks Gilbreath was born in August 11, 1894, and passed January 5, 1981.

5. Grandfather Elbert Gilbreath was born October 18, 1889, and passed January 18, 1961. In World War I he was a corporal in Company 13 of the 366th Infantry, 92nd Division. He was the head Redcap at the Saint Paul Union Depot.

6. Redcap Porters worked at the Saint Paul Union Depot. The uniform included a red cap, so as to be easily identified by passengers. Redcaps' salaries were minimal, and they supported their families mostly through tips. Responsibilities included carrying baggage for travelers, mopping floors, polishing brass, parking cars, and cleaning offices.

7. Saint Paul Union Depot is located at 214 East Fourth Street.

8. Dwayne Cortney Gilbreath was born July 27, 1947.

9. Dale Carlyle Gilbreath was born April 30, 1951, and passed July 17, 1969.

10. St. Philip's Episcopal Church was formed as a mission church in 1894, meeting in a home on Carroll Avenue. Later they rented a store on Rice Street, and in 1900 purchased their current building at Aurora and Mackubin. St. Philip's Episcopal Church was formed as a mission church in 1894, meeting in a home on Carroll Avenue. Later they rented a store on Rice Street, and in 1900 purchased a white frame building at Aurora and Mackubin. When this was torn down in the early 1950s, the altar and reredos were salvaged and placed in the structure built on the same northwest corner.

11. Father Denzil Carty (1904–1975) was born in the British West Indies, educated in New York City, and served Episcopal churches in that city until he came to Saint Paul in 1950 to serve as rector of St. Philip's Episcopal Church. He was an outstanding leader and activist for civil and human rights.

12. Pilgrim Baptist Church was first organized as a prayer group before 1863, and formally organized as a church November 15, 1866. Their first house of worship was constructed in 1870 at Twelfth and Cedar Streets in Saint Paul, and it moved in 1918 to the current location at 732 West Central Avenue, Saint Paul.

13. Oxford Park is located at Oxford, Iglehart, Lexington, and Rondo.

14. David Winfield (born 1951) was selected in four major league drafts in 1973: NFL (football), NBA (basketball), ABA (basketball), and MLB (baseball). He choose baseball and played in twelve All-Star games over a twenty-two-year career.

15. Paul Molitor (born 1956) was All-American shortstop at the University of Minnesota in 1976; he spent fifteen years with the Milwaukee Brewers, then three years each with the Toronto Blue Jays and Minnesota Twins. He was the Most Valuable Player in the 1993 World Series.

16. The American Legion—Attucks Brooks Post 606 was located at 976 Rondo Avenue

17. The Winter Carnival was founded in 1886 to contest a claim that Saint Paul was uninhabitable during the winter. The carnival is a celebration of Minnesota winters over a ten-day period that includes the crowning of King Boreas and Queen of the Snows, day and evening parades, a medallion hunt, and other activities. Occasionally, elaborate ice castles are built.

18. Como Park surrounds Lake Como and is between Lexington , Hoyt, and Como Avenues. It was initially planned in 1872. In 1873, $100,000 was donated to purchase land for a park, and the City acquired 300 acres around Lake Como. The lake was named in 1848 by Charles Perry, who farmed a tract of land on the shore of the lake. Today there are 1.67 miles of paths around the lake, picnic shelters, tennis courts, ball fields, swimming pools, fishing, paddleboats, a conservatory and gardens, a zoo, amusement rides, a golf course, and a historic streetcar station.

19. The National Association for the Advancement of Colored People (NAACP) was founded in New York City in 1909 by a multiracial group of activists. The NAACP believes that all men and women are created equal. Attorney Fredrick McGhee of the Rondo corridor was invited by W. E. B. Du Bois to attend the second meeting of the Niagara Movement. When he returned to Saint Paul, he organized the Twin City Protection League, which become the Twin Cities Branch of the NAACP in 1912.

20. Floyd McKissick (1922–1989) was from North Carolina and graduated from the University of North Carolina Law School. He was national director of CORE, the Congress of Racial Equality, from 1966 to 1968.

21. Aaron Henry (1922–1997) was from Mississippi and graduated from Xavier University in New Orleans. He was active in the formation of the Mississippi Freedom Democratic Party and the Council of Federated Organizations (COFO). He was state president of the NAACP. He lived through recurring death threats and thirty-three stints in jail, as well as Klan violence to his home and family.

22. Roy Wilkins (1901–1981) grew up in Saint Paul and graduated from the University of Minnesota in 1923. He became executive director of the NAACP in 1955. Saint Paul's River Centre complex at 175 Kellogg Boulevard includes the Roy Wilkins Auditorium.

23. Thurgood Marshall (1908–1993) was the first Black Supreme Court Justice in the United States. He worked as a staff lawyer for the NAACP and

for more than twenty years served as chief council for their Legal Defense and Education Fund, winning twenty-nine of the thirty-two cases he argued before the U.S. Supreme Court. His most important victory was *Brown v. Board of Education* in 1954. He was confirmed to the Supreme Court in 1967 and retired in 1991.

24. The payment of a poll tax, also known as a head tax, was sometimes a prerequisite to exercising the right to vote. It was often imposed in Southern states as a means of excluding racial minorities from voting.

DAVID VASSAR TAYLOR

All that we ever needed was within walking distance.

I AM DAVID VASSAR TAYLOR.[1] While growing up in Saint Paul my family lived on several streets, including at 1016 Rondo. I grew up in a large extended family in a supportive community. Although we all have different last names, the family name in the matriarchal sense is Vassar, and so anytime you talked about Black families in Saint Paul, it was the Vassar family and the Vassar sisters. Seven of them, and you could do no wrong if you were part of the Vassar family. You couldn't hide from that because everyone knew who the Vassar sisters were.

David in his mother's arms with brother Clarence in front of 1016 Rondo

Carroll Minges Vassar, my grandfather's uncle, moved to Saint Paul in 1888. He and his wife had sixteen children. My grandfather, Joe Vassar, moved his family to Saint Paul in 1920.

There was a lot of rivalry between the sisters to the point of which it kind of scarred family relationships for all of their lives. As children, we tried to stay out of harm's way by not aligning ourselves with any one of the sisters but having

Standing: Barbara "Petey" Vassar Gray, Eloise Vassar Muldrew, Josephine Vassar Wade,
Vivian "Myrt" Vassar Redd, Eula "Kitty" Vassar Taylor Washington Murphy
Seated: Lola Vassar Finney, stepmother Beatrice Eaton Vassar,
father Joseph Vassar, Beatrice Vassar Coleman, c. 1954

more to do with the cousins. We knew that was their life and we couldn't
change that, but it need not be part of our relationship.

I had more uncles and aunts and cousins, and we relate to one another
today in that vein. They are usually close, very close friends of the family
for which there was no real term, because they were family, but they weren't
blood, so we just knew them as uncle, cousin.

The mother of one of my very good friends, even to this day, is a surro-
gate mother for me and we talk. It just grew out of childhood and when I
couldn't talk to my mother, she would talk to me.

Discipline-wise, my parents would not put a hand on us after the age of
eight. My mother[2] was a housewife, and we had a stepfather who worked at
the Saint Paul Post Office,[3] downtown. My mother didn't want him to dis-
cipline us in a manner that would cause fragmentation in the family. She

was very protective of us, so they would simply take privileges away. If that didn't get your attention, well, you know, your life was like a serf. After a while, you just didn't have a life. You couldn't do this, couldn't do that, and you couldn't do it for months on end. That captured our attention.

Secondly, we were taught to be much more independent because with three boys in the house, it was a lot of cooking, a lot of cleaning, a lot of everything, and she just decided at one point, being the only female in the family, that this was not going to drive her to an early grave. We were taught to wash our own clothes, to iron our own clothes, to clean up after ourselves, take care of our room and then they were insistent that we find employment and that we use our employment to save towards college.

Believe me, my mother was only 5 foot 3 inches. I thought she was 6 foot 7 inches. It wasn't until I was a senior in college when I realized I was taller by a couple inches.

I was a newspaper[4] editor by the time I was thirteen. We had a newspaper that came out once a week and that was usually on Friday. At the end of the school day we would leave school, go home, check in, and then go over to our other friend's house who had an attic that was semifinished. We had typewriters and carbon paper and onionskin paper and we had block prints, and so we would act as reporters. Monday through Wednesday we would go out and gather the news, Thursday and Friday we would type it up, and by Friday evening, early Saturday, we had seventy-five copies and went around to the people that had subscriptions and then sold what was left. We sold advertisements, for a quarter. We had a lot of businesses along University Avenue.

We had friends and we would pool our chemistry sets together and we would create chemicals. When rocketry became a fad, we researched that and created propellants. We could have done violence to ourselves, but only had one rocket blow up on us. We were always experimenting with electricity and, you know, finding ways to—oh, it was just—I mean, circuses! Bored in the summertime, wanting to raise money, we would have a backyard circus with puppetry and all sorts of things that kids could get into. But that was just a creative outlet for us. When everything else failed, there was reading.

We had the first Black or predominantly Black Cub Scout pack, and that was because we couldn't get into any of the White Cub Scout groups. Then there was a need to graduate us to something else, so we formed the first Black

Boy Scout troop. It became a point of contention when we got to big gatherings. We would be the only Black troop and there weren't any Black kids in any of the White troops, although we did have White kids in the Black troop. They couldn't understand what the big deal was when these other White guys would call them out of character for their affiliation with us.

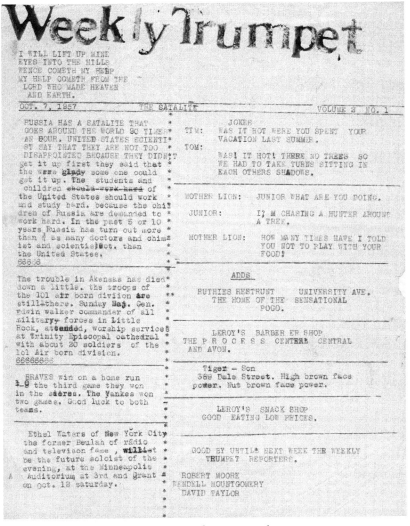

The *Weekly Trumpet*, October 7, 1957, volume 3, no. 1

Mr. Martin's Barbershop,[5] that's where I came into contact with the lives of adult males and I would listen to their conversations and pick up a lot with respect to culture. Of course, when we were there, Mr. Martin wouldn't let them talk in profane ways or get into subject matters that we shouldn't be listening to. They knew that our mothers wouldn't appreciate it. It was a socialization sort of thing. The barbershop was where you needed to go and hear these conversations.

The schools, community center, religious institutions, churches, church school, youth, what have you, playgrounds, all that we ever needed, including a Dairy Queen,[6] was within walking distance. As we got older, we began to chafe under such close proximity to one another and not having enough territory to stretch your wings, so we became more ambitious.

Truthfully, you could not go anywhere without being under the watchful eye of some adult or some caring adult who knew who you were and your family connections. That was tough. Because as a young man who wanted to sow oats! No play whatsoever. By the time we were juniors in high school we were venturing out of the community, but at the same time we had to tell our parents where we were going and report back and that was without cell phones. You just had to stop what you were doing and get to the nearest phone and let them know where you were, because it simply wasn't safe for us.

The conflict where it did arise along racial lines was Selby Avenue and because many of us attended Marshall Junior High,[7] we had to cross Selby Avenue and in doing so, conflict erupted between Blacks and Whites. I can just remember fight after fight. The equivalent of gang fights, but they weren't called gangs, just troubled youth, I guess. Marshall really became a melting pot. We just had differences in racial and socioeconomic backgrounds. By the time we shifted up to Central High School,[8] all of those things had worked out and there was relative harmony.

If we were poor by sociological standards, didn't know it. I didn't know that I was poor and Black until I got to the University of Minnesota and sat in sociology class and read *The American Dilemma* by Gunnar Myrdal, and some of the others who theorized on race in America. I couldn't believe that this was me that they were talking about because it didn't seem to parallel my existence. I didn't feel disenfranchised. I wasn't educationally disenfranchised. I was as bright as any of the other kids I competed against. I came from a two-parent household, albeit my mother was married three times, but we still always had parents. We may not have had a lot of money, but we had what was necessary to do the things that they thought were necessary for us.

I always had role models around me. You know, I lived on Carroll Avenue. I had a district judge living across the street from me, I had lawyers living up the street. I had teachers living down the street. The church I went to was totally middle class for our circumstances, and they drove big cars. If I was poor in the middle of that, then truly, poverty was different.

We were always taught that we should be achieving educationally. And we were always exposed to better things, however you want to define that. Now there was a sporting class[9] and there probably was a lower class. But we weren't allowed to engage those folks and they did not attempt to engage us. Because, you know, they knew of our parents and knew to let us alone, no matter what they were involved in. It would have been a crisis to get these other kids engaged in those sorts of things.

One of the things that would happen to us in junior high and high school is when there was a Black celebrity that would come through town either for a performance or lecture, concert, whatever, the adults in the community would get money together. The NAACP[10] or the Urban League[11] or some organization would get a hold of free complimentary tickets or they would purchase them.

There was a lot of hoopla about Martin Luther King coming to town and speaking at the University. This was in the early 1960s before the March on Washington.[12] It could have been '61, I think, which would have made me a sophomore in high school. I recall getting permission from my parents, being picked up at school and several cars going out to the University to Northrop Memorial Auditorium.[13] We sat and dutifully listened and then at the end of his presentation, we were invited backstage to meet with him personally. They were doing these sorts of things in order to prepare a way for us. It didn't dawn on me until the movement continued to accelerate, what an opportunity that had been.

It's kind of interesting because again the Black Episcopal churches tend to attract, historically, very well educated people, very middle class people. I'm still a member of St. Philip's Episcopal Church[14] to this day. Truly I could look at people and see them doing great things, and they in turn, querying me about what my plans were. People who saw the man in the child and wanted that man to get out and blossom. The church is one of those places where people with honesty, fine intellect, and a keen sense of social justice worked to create in us that sense of fairness, rightness, dedication to cause, and working with other people for a better world.

Coming along in high school and junior high, I was in accelerated programs. I was one of the few Black children that were put into these advanced courses in math and science. In fact, I had Mrs. Ruby Moe, my junior year American history teacher, take me aside after class and tell me that I was one of the brightest students that she had taught in thirty-five years of teaching at Central High School and that I should go on and get a Ph.D. in history at the University. Well, I do have a Ph.D. in history, and I did get it from the University. Throughout my professional career I've had people who recognized that I was a fine teacher, but probably as fine or better administrator and encouraged me, and that's why I ended up in administration.

The youth branch of the NAACP was all-encompassing. You just belonged and that was it. Interestingly with the NAACP, the first racial riot I was in occurred when we had secured space out in Spring Lake Park for our roller-skating extravaganza. It was our understanding that we had rented the entire rink. It was a private party and they had agreed to it. When we showed up to take the rink for the hour-and-a-half that was allotted us, the White students, kids, refused to leave. The management wasn't encouraging them to leave, and then they began to push young women around and otherwise flex their muscle. It got to a real nasty show with, I don't know, it must have been about twelve squad cars and it never reached the newspapers.

Central High School
graduation picture, 1963

When we were seniors in high school and during the summer, we were trusted to go over to someone's house and play cards until 1:00 in the morning. As a group, we would walk home dropping off people, and there was no fear of being molested or preyed upon. The parents would communicate and know that we were on our way home and when to expect us. We were trusted, you know, just being out late at night when it was seventy degrees and feeling like you were an adult because you would stroll home, unescorted. We liked the trust that they put into us, and the expectations that they held us to. Summertime sitting on the porch of our home being left alone to read, going down to the bookmobile when it would come in with my collection of books and turning them in and getting more. Experimenting, I mean, doing the sorts of things I told you, the building and creativity. Having close friends, boys and girls that we could play with and talk to about things. Being able to go over to houses and their parents would take you in and offer you lemonade and sit down and listen to your issues, as it were.

I simply didn't know poverty. I have come to know that there is impoverishment of spirit and poverty. We may not have had a lot, but we were not impoverished in spirit. I think that makes the difference.

$$\bullet \; \bullet \; \bullet$$

DR. DAVID TAYLOR is most proud of being able to assist young people in achieving their educational goals. In 1967, he earned a B.A. from the University of Minnesota, an M.A. in history from the University of Nebraska–Omaha in 1971, and a Ph.D. in history from the University of Minnesota in 1977. For 16 years, Dr. Taylor was dean of the General College at the University of Minnesota. In 2005, he became provost and senior vice president for academic affairs at Morehouse College in Atlanta. He has authored two books and contributed to several others, written numerous articles and book reviews, and written and lectured extensively on the migration and settlement of African Americans in Minnesota. Dr. Taylor and Josephine Reed-Taylor have two children: Tyrone Vassar Reed-Taylor and Kenneth Vassar Reed-Taylor. David Taylor has made significant contributions to many community and professional programs, including St. Philip's Episcopal Church, where he grew up as a youth.

◆ NOTES

1. David Vassar Taylor was born July 13, 1945.
2. Eula "Kitty" Vassar Taylor Washington Murphy was born August 25, 1919.
3. The Saint Paul Post Office Building is located at 141 Fourth Street East.
4. The *Weekly Trumpet*.
5. Martin and Crump Barbers was located at 709 Rondo Avenue, and

Mr. Martin's Barbershop was at 358–362 North Dale and at 709–711 Rondo Avenue.

6. A Dairy Queen soft serve ice cream stand is still located at 450 North Lexington Parkway at University Avenue.

7. Marshall School was built in 1925 at Grotto, Holly, Ashland, and St. Albans. It was Marshall Junior High from 1926 to 1937. In 1937, tenth grade was added; in 1938, eleventh grade; and in 1939, twelfth grade was added, with graduating classes from 1940 to 1953. It returned to junior high only in 1954. Webster Elementary School was built on the same site in 1926. The two buildings were connected in 1975 and become Webster Magnet Elementary School.

8. Central High School began in 1866 and consisted of two rooms in the Franklin Building, downtown Saint Paul. By 1872 it was known as Saint Paul High School, and moved to Seventh and Jackson. In 1883, a 27-room building was completed and the school was named The Saint Paul Central High, and located on Minnesota Street in downtown Saint Paul. Because of space needs, a new school was built at 275 Lexington Avenue in 1912. In 1977, the building was reduced to its structural form, expanded and rebuilt to the current building.

9. A life interested in or connected with sports or pursuits involving betting or gambling.

10. The National Association for the Advancement of Colored People (NAACP) was founded in New York City in 1909 by a multiracial group of activists. The NAACP believes that all men and women are created equal. Attorney Fredrick McGhee of the Rondo corridor was invited by W. E. B. Du Bois to attend the second meeting of the Niagara Movement. When he returned to Saint Paul, he organized the Twin City Protection League, which become the Twin Cities Branch of the NAACP in 1912.

11. The Urban League has served the Black community since 1923 as a human service advocacy organization. The Urban League addresses issues of quality employment, housing, education, and health care. The Saint Paul and Minneapolis agencies were combined until 1938. Saint Paul offices were initially located in various buildings downtown until the late , when they moved into their own building at 401 Selby Avenue, four blocks south of the Rondo corridor.

12. The 1963 March on Washington resulted when leaders of various civil rights organizations decided to organize the "March on Washington for Jobs

and Freedom." The 1963 march is best known for Martin Luther King Jr's "I Have a Dream" speech.

13. Northrop Memorial Auditorium is located on the University of Minnesota campus. It was named after Cyrus Northrop, the University's second and longest-serving president. It was built in 1928.

14. St. Philip's Episcopal Church was formed as a mission church in 1894, meeting in a home on Carroll Avenue. Later they rented a store on Rice Street, and in 1900 purchased a white frame building at Aurora and Mackubin. When this was torn down in the early 1950s, the altar and reredos were salvaged and placed in the structure built on the same northwest corner.

TERESINA "WILLOW" CARTER FRELIX

All we knew was Rondo.

MY GIVEN NAME IS TERESINA CARTER.[1] I married and now my last name is Frelix. I prefer to be called Willow. I lived at 717 Rondo, and when I was ten we moved. That was because the freeway was coming through. That was because they were buying up all the houses on Rondo, and we had to leave. I remember my parents were very concerned. There was always the issue of money. My dad[2] owned property on that street, so he had to combine everything and move. We had to settle on one house, one piece of property. That seemed to be an issue to them. Because they were worried about it, that sort of had a trickle-down effect on us kids and naturally we picked up on that.

It was scary. There was the sense that something happened that was out of even the parents' control and that they just had to do the best they can to try to make it work for them. I remember my mom[3] trying to make things easier for us by telling us—I guess she was pregnant at the time—by telling us we were gonna get a new baby after we moved. And the house we lived in, to me, reminded me of a big old Victorian house and we rented the upstairs out. But we were never allowed to go into the basement, and so naturally that became a point of curiosity for the kids. So one of the promises that we got is that

●

The Carter Family
Back: Melvin, Jr., Teresina / Willow. Middle: Father Melvin Sr., Paris, Mother Billie, Mark.
Front: Larry, Matthew, c.1959

when we did move, my father would finally take that skeleton key and open that door so we could go see what the basement looked like.

There was that feeling of being afraid. I can remember some of the kids talking about the end of the world and what it was supposed to be like with the trumpets and the Bible and so forth. And so we sort of understood in a way that this was not just a move, but this was an event. This was a sort of a lifetime event, and we were all going though it. I think as kids, we were trying to figure out what the move meant and what our lives would be like once it was over, once we had left each other. Because all we knew was Rondo.

We had to honor the color barriers. We couldn't move past Lexington, and so there were certain confines that we had to move within, too. I think that was as scary as moving off of Rondo.

I was the oldest. I just listened to my mother and father talk. They never explained that to us. We just kind of knew that there was something going

Teresina at age 10 in her
Saint Peter Claver uniform

on that they didn't say. And of course, that had more power than what they did say.

I can remember, we looked at one house that was a block past Lexington and it was across the street from Central High School,[4] which they thought would be a good area for us to live in. Well, we went to that house and looked around, and we were sitting outside in our car, the kids and myself. My parents were talking like, "Well, if we get this, if we even get considered." To me it just felt funny. I wouldn't have known how to articulate it, but it just felt funny. We went in and the people were nice. They showed us the house and we liked it. We decided that we liked that house, but come to find out later on we couldn't move. We couldn't even move a block past Lexington because Lexington was the color boundary.

Well, they finally found a home for us on Aurora, 1026 Aurora, which is Aurora and Oxford. It was close to St. Peter Claver School,[5] and it would have been also close to Central High School, where I would go later on.

The community made me want to broaden my horizons, to peek around the corner, maybe take risks. I've found I enjoy being African American. I enjoy being part of the community, and I enjoy making friends and meeting new people.

◆ ◆ ◆

TERESINA "WILLOW" CARTER FRELIX has been married to Bill for thirty-five years, and they are the loving parents of Jamie Patrice, a chiropractic assistant, and William "Billy" Frank Jr., who is going to Inver Hills Community College and just purchased his first home. Willow graduated from St. Mary's with an A.A. degree in medical records and has worked for Saint Paul Children's Hospital for twenty-one years. She is never without a book and loves reading about history, family history in particular, which led her to do her own family genealogy. Believing in the power of play, Willow belongs to a doll club and enjoys her vinyl doll collection. She loves to work with colored pencils and create with stamp crafts.

◆ NOTES

1. Teresina "Willow" Carter Frelix was born January 17, 1947.

2. Father Melvin Whitfield Carter Sr. was born September 8, 1923.

3. Mother Billie Dove Harris Carter was born in 1927 and passed in 2000.

4. Central High School began in 1866 and consisted of two rooms in the Franklin Building in downtown Saint Paul. By 1872 it was known as Saint Paul High School and moved to Seventh and Jackson. In 1883, a twenty-seven-room building on Minnesota Street in downtown Saint Paul was completed and the school was named Saint Paul Central High. Because of space needs, a new school was built at 275 Lexington Avenue in 1912. In 1977, the building was reduced to its structural form, then rebuilt into the current building.

5. St. Peter Claver School, located at 1060 West Central, opened in 1950 grades K–8. The school closed in 1989 and reopened in 2001. Initially a bowling alley in the basement helped raise funds for the school and provided recreation. The school is affiliated with the Catholic Church of the same name that was built in 1957 at 375 Oxford. The school is named for Peter Claver (1580–1654), who was canonized by Pope Leo XIII in 1888 for his work with the African Negro of Spanish America.

WILLIAM "BILLY" L. COLLINS JUNIOR

We took care of each other.

Being raised in Rondo influenced my character and values. I AM BILLY COLLINS.[1] I am the executive director of the YWCA[2] Saint Paul, and a life-long resident of Saint Paul and the Summit-University area.[3]

I believe it was 1936 when my parents came up from Louisville, Kentucky. My father[4] was working on the railroad, and the railroad opportunity was greater up here than it was in the South. My dad was a waiter on the dining car for the Great Northern Railroad.[5] It was interesting and somewhat unfortunate because I really didn't get an opportunity to know my father until he got older. He was out of town six days and in town six days, and usually, the six days he was in town he was doing a lot of sleeping because he was working about twenty hours a day when he was out on the road. He was catching up on his rest.

When I was younger, I was into sports and I played sports the year round, and so a lot of times when he was awake, I wasn't home because I was either at football, baseball, hockey, basketball practice, or a game. As I got older, just in my pre-teens and in my early teens, was when I got an opportunity to experience him talking about his life. We had relatives in Chicago and also in Kentucky, and in my early years we would go down during the summer and visit relatives in Chicago and Kentucky. We got to ride the train for free. So we did get to sort of experience his working. When we were going to bed, he was still working.

I saw him working very hard providing service to the people on the train in the dining car, taking their orders and delivering their meals, and then, above and beyond that, sort of hustling pillows and pillowcases for people who did not have the berths to sleep in and were sleeping, basically, in the regular seats. And just a constant go, go, go, with picking up things for people beyond the dining times, breakfast, lunch, and dinner, and getting them coffee, tea, water, whatever the case may be. And basically working real hard to get those tips.

The compensation was all right, but the tips were really kind of what put you over the edge so that you could really survive. And we spent time down at the depot. Basically what would happen is that the typical run would be: my father would leave here and go to Chicago. He would spend the night in Chicago, and come back through here and then go out to Seattle, Washington. Leave Seattle, Washington, and then come back here. That would complete his six days out. Usually what would happen is that between here and Chicago and back again, we would meet him down at the depot and pick up the tips that he had earned because that was usually the largest tip run, right there with the businesspeople going back and forth between here and Chicago. And we would meet him there and get the tips and that would help put us over the edge financially until he returned with some other tips or until he got his paycheck.

My mother[6] used to work for the Armory[7] out at New Brighton and got laid off. She and many other Black females were laid off at the same time, and even though they had more seniority than some of the White females and some of the White males and some of the Black males that were out there, they just kind of came in and took a large number of Black females and laid them off. She had a very difficult time getting employment after that. She had a sixth-grade education, and she did some other odd jobs, but then just decided that it wasn't worth the hassle and she was going to spend time at home and help me and my sister[8] stay on the straight and narrow, as well as some other kids in the neighborhood. She was basically mother and father—being the primary caregiver most of our lives.

We had a very extremely diverse community. We didn't know it because we were all people! We had many Black families that lived in the community, Native Americans, Hispanics, a lot of Jewish people, Italians, White people. It was a very culturally diverse community. We had a lot of Black businesses, a lot of Jewish businesses, so on and so forth, that were reflective of the community. And we basically got along and basically interacted and socialized with each other as young people, and the adults basically socialized with each other.

We lived between Milton and Victoria, and there was a Red Owl[9] Supermarket over on Lexington. You could leave your door unlocked with nobody at home, and you could go to the store and come back and not worry about anything happening to your property or to your house. So it was a very close-knit neighborhood.

One of the big things was, up until a certain age, you could not ride your bicycle in the street. And naturally, when you get around the corner from your house, you thought you were safe, so you would go off the sidewalk and you would get on the street. We lived on St. Anthony and we would ride our bikes around the block. When we got on Victoria or on Milton, we pull right off the sidewalk and get in the street and go down Rondo in the middle of the street and look up and see somebody's mother staring at you, and you knew, "Uh, oh, when I get home I'm in trouble because they saw. They know." Everybody had the same rules.

Mother, Jeanne, and Billy, c. 1950

We all knew each other and all got along. We went to school together. We worshipped together, most of us. We did a lot of things in the neighborhood together. So it didn't make any difference. One of my best friends was Native American. A person that lived next door to us going west—not right next door, but two houses down, we were very close and he was White. The people next door to us, they were

Black. We all hung out and did things together, and everybody had a license to whip butt and correct.

My mother was the strong adult in my life. However, there were a few other males in the neighborhood who had an influence on me. Some of my friends, their fathers. If we were down in the yard playing or whatever the case may be, we would have an opportunity to talk and interact with people. As I got a little older and started going down to the old Oxford Playground[10] as I was growing up, we were fortunate to have a couple of good center directors down there. We were also fortunate enough to have some men from the community: Mr. John Pettiford, Johnny Cotton, Mr. Carter—they used to call him Big Six—and some others that used to come down and volunteer their time down at the old Oxford Playground when we were first developing it and creating it.

And then Bill Peterson came along about the early Sixties, and he sort of reinforced all the things we were getting and he was White. He was our center director, recreational director, and he was White. But he cared about people, the young people in the neighborhood, and he got along with the Black men in the community who had been working with us and supporting us for years. And those were the days when people, they worked jobs. They had a forty-hour-a-week job, and they pretty much worked anywhere from forty to forty-six hours a week and they came home, weren't stressed out or maxed too much and they were trying to do some things with their families and the children in the neighborhood. They took ownership of the kids.

Even through our sports, we were taught that if you play midget baseball, for example, you had to go to practice. You played your games, but you also had to spend time with the pee-wees, to help instruct them, to bring them along. And when you made it to juniors, you had to go back and help out with the midgets, and so on and so forth. And that was instilled in me and others at a early age.

And I think that helped build some character with us. I look at the approach, whatever I do. For example, here at the YWCA, when I was being interviewed for the executive director's position, and I'm involved in a lot of things in the community, and all through the process people said, "You do a lot of different things. When you're hired by the YWCA, if you are, as executive director, what would be your number one priority?" And I said the community, because without the community, you wouldn't need a YWCA or anything else. And that the YWCA would be my number two priority in terms of this is my job, my bread and butter, but it also has to fill a void or provide a service within the community. I learned that from my days growing up in the Summit-University area, around St. Anthony and through my activities at the old Oxford Playground.

Actually, in the smaller community where we lived, we really didn't see racism or discrimination. But then you'd wander too much outside of your neighborhood, if you went north of University, if you went west of Lexington. I'll give you an example. There was a restaurant up on University just east of Snelling on the north side of the street. But Bill Peterson, who's White, he took his baseball team up there and the majority of us were Black. We walked in there and they wouldn't serve us. Now this is a little less than a mile outside of the Summit-University area.

I think it was 1962 or 1963. He took us there because we'd won one of our baseball championships, so he took us out to treat us and get something to eat and we went up there and they wouldn't serve us. And we had to restrain Bill. He was more upset about it than we were. And then actually, he wound up filing the complaint with the NAACP,[11] and they did a boycott up there and put a lot of pressure on. This stuff went on for a couple of years, and ultimately they changed ownership up there. That was just right outside our neighborhood.

Around 1960, '61, something like that I can remember going downtown Saint Paul to the old W. T. Grant's[12] and they had a lunch bar in there. Blacks had to sit at the far end. You couldn't sit with everybody else, so it was segregated there. That was in the Fifties and the early Sixties. That was right downtown Saint Paul. I was kind of floored when I went with some friends. And actually, there was about a half a dozen of us. Two White, the rest were Black. The two Whites could sit in one spot, and we had to sit in the other spot. But they couldn't sit down at our end of the bar and we couldn't sit at their end. We went to sit in the middle of the snack bar, and they explained to us that it was okay for these two to sit there but the rest of us had to go down to the other end. And we kind of looked around, and we realized that White folks were kind of in the middle to the left and Blacks and everything else were from the far middle to the right. So we wound up leaving.

We were angry, but not external anger. You know, I didn't shout, I didn't cuss, I didn't stomp, I didn't beat on anything. It was frustrating that people were trying to drive a wedge between friends and that's how I looked at it. It wasn't so much that I gave a damn what they thought. It was that they were trying to separate friends that came in the store together. So they're trying to force us to realize there's some difference there, where we felt that there wasn't. We told our parents and basically my father said, "You just need to be careful and be aware of where you go." And he asked me, "How did you respond and how did you feel?" And I told him, "Well, I didn't do anything. I just looked at them and thought, 'Well, I'll take my money somewhere else.'" He was actually like, "Yeah. You can't show anger and you can't say anything and you really can't do anything. It's just not healthy."

We were taught to address the racism in the community, not necessarily a formal training, but they talked about things. They talked about being careful. They talked about if you felt threatened while you were in the community that you should make it to one of the neighbors' houses or businesses as the case may be. As we started getting older, and just before the freeway came through, they really started addressing some of those things and talking about some of those things and saying you need to be careful. They wanted us to extend the limit where we went, but not really limit where we went.

I'll give you an example. Halloween. One of the areas we weren't supposed to go was north of University, so we decided that we were going to wander north of University, a group of us, probably about a dozen. And we were knocking on doors and trick-or-treat and what have you, and then it was getting warm, so we were removing our masks. We still have the costumes on. And then people could see that we were Black. And there was an older gentleman—I'll never forget the big white house with a black screened-in porch, and he came to the door and he said, "You all aren't from this neighborhood. Go back on the other side of University where you belong. I don't want to catch you back over here again. Get off this block and I'm going to call all the people on the block to tell them don't give you anything and to chase you back to your own neighborhood." It was an older, White gentleman. Then we started realizing what our parents were telling us. But we were still young and kind of bull-headed, so we just continued on and finally the police came. People on the block had called the police because we weren't leaving, and the police suggested that we kind of move back over on the other side of University because there was some concern about some disturbances that were going

Parents Bill and Gene with Billy
and sister, Jeanne

on, so to speak. And it was real interesting because we had officers that had patrolled south of University, but that wasn't any of the officers that we ran into that night when we were on the other side of University.

We got back on the south side and we ran into Officer Skally[13] and talked to him about it. Actually, he explained to us that it was wrong. He was a White officer, and he said it was wrong, but also it was night and we needed to protect ourselves. And he said, "Do your parents know that you were over there?" And we said no, and he said well, he won't tell them, but that we should have followed their advice.

Well, basically, it has just made me a better person. I learned a lot in terms of values and the importance of things. I've been involved now in the human service field for thirty-seven years.

Basically I learned a lot about respect and respect of other people, respect of my elders. We took care of each other. Older youth took care of younger youth. If you did something wrong, and somebody's parent caught you, they would wear your behind out, send you home, get on the phone, call your mother or father, and by the time you got home, they had the whole story of what you did wrong, and you got it all over again, plus you got punished. In doing that, the conversations that went around were not you're a bad child or you're a bad kid. It was that you are disappointing the community. You are disappointing, you are not representing or reflecting things properly from your family, and you know you were raised better than that. There was a big lesson that went along with everything that would happen along those lines. It ultimately got to the point where you realized that by you doing things wrong, you were disappointing a whole lot of people and having an impact on a whole lot of people. It wasn't that I continued to be a perfect little angel, but it helped curb some of the activities that I might have done had that lesson not been taught to me.

◆ ◆ ◆

WILLIAM "BILLY" L. COLLINS and his wife of thirty years, Muriel, are the proud parents of Leigha, Dawn, and Brock. They have six grandchildren. Mr. Collins graduated from Central High School and attended the University of Minnesota. He has worked in public and private management positions throughout his career, including as the grants administrator for the Department of Public Safety Office of Drug Policy and Violence Prevention, Wilder Foundation, assistant executive director of the Inner City Youth League, and as a Model Cities coordinator. For the past ten years he has been the executive director of the YWCA of Saint Paul. The driving force behind all of his work is his commitment to making a difference in the community in which he was raised.

◆ NOTES

1. William L. Collins Jr. was born October 28, 1948.

2. The Saint Paul YWCA opened in 1906. Its first building was constructed in 1911 at 425 West Fifth Street. In 1961, a new facility opened at 65 East Kellogg Boulevard, with a final move in the 1990s to 375 Selby, four blocks south of the Rondo corridor. A Colored YWCA/YMCA opened in 1923 with a limited "Colored" program at 598 West Central Avenue. It closed in 1928.

3. Summit-University is a term used to refer to the area in Saint Paul that is enclosed by Summit Avenue in the south, University Avenue on the north, Summit Avenue on the east, and Lexington Avenue on the west.

4. Father William L. "Bill" Collins Sr.

5. The Great Northern Railroad's home offices were in Saint Paul. Saint Paul's early empire builder J.J. Hill built the Great Northern. In 1980, he acquired the Northern Pacific line and legally merged theses two lines and others to become the Burlington Northern.

6. Mother Eugenia "Gene" Hayden Collins.

7. Twin Cities Army Ammunition Plant of the Federal Cartridge Corporation covered a four-square-mile area in New Brighton. In 1942, it began production of four billion rounds of ammunition for war efforts. It was placed on inactive and standby status from 1950 to 1965, and again began production of ammunition during the Vietnam War. The facility was placed on shutdown status in 1971. In 2002, some land was transferred to Ramsey County Parks. The Ordinance Plant, as it was known, hired Blacks at all levels according to their skills, education, and training. At one point it employed twenty percent of the state's adult Black population.

8. Sister Jeanne Collins Givens Everette.

9. Red Owl Stores Incorporated was located at 415 North Lexington Parkway.

10. Oxford Playground and Pool is located at 1079 Iglehart at Lexington.

11. The National Association for the Advancement of Colored People (NAACP) was founded in New York City in 1909 by a multiracial group of activists. The NAACP believes that all men and women are created equal. Attorney Fredrick McGhee of the Rondo corridor was invited by W. E. B. Du Bois to attend the second meeting of the Niagara Movement. When he returned to Saint Paul, he organized the Twin City Protection League, which become the Twin Cities Branch of the NAACP in 1912.

12. W. T. Grant was located at Seventh and Cedar in downtown Saint Paul.

13. Bill Skally served as a Saint Paul Police patrolman from 1941 to 1973. During his assignment as a beat officer on Rondo, he had a reputation of taking youth to their parents before arresting them. He was well respected for his knowledge of the community and its members.

WILBERT JOHN DUGAS JUNIOR

We were tough kids.

I AM WILBERT JOHN DUGAS JR.[1] I lived at 551 Carroll Avenue, where the King Center is now. The Ober Boys Club[2] inspired me in the community. There was always mentors, always. I don't care if they were White or Indian or Black, they were mentors and these people cared. Like nowadays you get the care, but the kids aren't even listening. We had mentors that would gear us into positive things. It was like going to camp, learning how to row a boat, learning how to live out in the wilderness. Also learning sports and then our coaches were also good, I mean, they would know the family. Everyone in the community knew each other. There was Oxford[3] and there was Hallie Q. Brown.[4] And there was also the Ober Boys Club. There was Short Hill,[5] where we played baseball.

Ober Boys Club was affiliated with the Union Gospel Mission

Ober Boys Club

and that was Woody Harrison or Harold Moore. These were the sponsors of these community centers, and when you went to these community centers you were safe. There were so many activities, and it was so good. You wouldn't have to worry about nothing. The parents wouldn't have to worry about nothing.

Football was my favorite thing. I won a couple most valuable player awards. Two years in a row I was most valuable player for the pee-wee football team. I started when I was like eight, and then up until I was fifteen I was one of the outstanding players. They said I was inspiring 'cause when we had a losing team I was in the back saying we can beat these guys and I would be crying tears 'cause I had all my heart into it. So I was known as a heart player, and that is what they told me anyway. I didn't know what a heart was. All I knew was I'm not quitting. So I wasn't a quitter.

This picture was in the *Saint Paul Dispatch* with the following caption:

"MINNESOTA VIKING quarterback Fran Tarkenton is shown as he presented trophies to Ober Boys club football champions at the club Tuesday night. Accepting trophies from Tarkenton (left) are left to right Hiram Douglas Jr.; Percy Benjamin and Wilbert Dugas. Douglas is the team captain and Benjamin and Dugas are the most valuable players. Tarkenton was the guest speaker at the award program. Ober club won the Pee Wee baseball league title and was runner up in football." –Staff Photo

Two years in a row, I received most valuable player awards. That means a big ole letter, a jacket, a trophy, your name in the paper. And then there was a guy named Fran Tarkenton.[6] He was the quarterback for the Minnesota Vikings back in the day, and Bud Grant. And they used to come in and award us kids with these trophies. And we didn't play it up like grown-ups did, like this was a big honor. We just knew we did the job. But these people were coming in to be role models for us and for them to take that time out, even what we did know was inspiring to us. And to have somebody like Fran Tarkenton shake my hand. And we would wrestle and play, and I would remember that all my life. I've got pictures of myself in the papers holding up my trophy. Things like that.

At fifteen I was still playing football and I still had role models in football. I wanted to be like the Ransoms. I was known as one of the hardest little hitters in Junior League, or whatever we had, and I cracked my hip playing so hard. At Ober they would put the little guys up against the big guys, and I would tackle these big guys. I tackled the wrong one and my hip got damaged. And I didn't know it was damaged and I played football for years and it was a cracked hip. And it went into a leg bone disease, a childhood bone disease called Perthes disease.[7] And that kept me from going into the service, which I wanted to go very bad when I got eighteen, and it kept me from being in the Elks.[8]

So at Ober Boys Club I wrestled, I boxed there, I loved craft nights, and I liked to build things. They taught me how to do things and do them with care. You know, 'cause some people sluff over stuff. I took care in everything I did 'cause I was always trying to please my role models and mentors. Who were Willie, Willie Turner, he was our coach. At sixteen, seventeen BoBo Walker was our counselor. He was fair and gentle with us kids.

There was Clyde Siccarelli. He was our counselor at Ober Boys Camp. He was an ex-Marine. He was White, wore a little butch haircut with sort of red hair. He was everybody's idol. He had muscles. He could beat anyone one of us brothers down, and he didn't take no mess.

We were considered the low end of Rondo. We were the tough kids. We were the *Our Gangs*,[9] so when we had to respect him, you know he had it coming 'cause he was the one of the people that all of us looked up to. If we had a beef we'd take it to him. If he seen us out there fighting, he'd make us go put on boxing gloves and box. You know. Father Flanagan,[10] but he was no saint.

Certificate of Award
This Certifies That
Wilbert John Dugas Jr.
of the
Ober Boys Club
has been awarded this certificate for participation in
Football - Most Valuable Player
Season of 61-62
Stephen E. Burghdi
Anthony Pennant Co.- Mpls., Minn.

WILBERT JOHN DUGAS JR. loves God, his family, and the gift God gave him. His father, Wilbert John Dugas Sr., put him through school winning golf tournaments. His mother, Flo, played the bugle in the Gopher Elks and was one of those good souls everyone in the neighborhood knew. He is proud of teaching and watching his students take on the task of being artists. He teaches drum at Walker West Music Academy and appreciates the opportunity to make a musical contribution at Pilgrim Baptist Church. He owes his life and his music to God. Wilbert is the proud husband of Kathleen and father of Nikkia (eight) and Gabriella (six), who are praise dancers for Pilgrim Baptist Church.

◆ NOTES

1. Wilbert John Dugas Jr. was born December 5, 1949.

2. Ober Boys Club, at 375 St. Anthony at Western, was founded during World War II by the Union Gospel Mission. It was named for Edgar Ober of 3M and provided recreational activities and taught Christian values. Boys who participated also attended Snail Lake Children's Camp. There was a Girls Club located at Welcome Hall. Sometime after 1960, the club became part of The Boys and Girls Clubs of America, but the building is still owned by Union Gospel Mission.

3. Oxford Pool and Playground is located at 1079 Iglehart at Lexington and Oxford. In 1969 a recreation center was built that took over the management of the playground. Jimmy Lee Recreation Center was named for the first Black sports official at the University of Minnesota and the Minnesota High School League.

4. Hallie Q. Brown Community Center, Inc., was opened in the Union Hall at Aurora and Kent Streets in 1929 as a community center specifically to serve the Black community when the Black YWCA closed in 1928. Hallie Q., as it is affectionately known, has served all ages through child care, youth and senior clubs, athletics, music, and social events. In 1972, Hallie relocated in the Martin Luther King Building at 270 Kent Street at Iglehart in Saint Paul. The center's namesake was an educator who pioneered the movement of Black women's clubs in the late 1800s.

5. Short Hill at Marshall and John Ireland Boulevard was a baseball field built by neighborhood boys and a father.

6. Fran Tarkenton was quarterback of the Minnesota Vikings, 1961–1966 and 1972–1978.

7. Legg-Perthes disease is a hip disorder that primarily affects young boys. The condition carries the names of the physicians who first described it in the early 1900s.

8. Gopher Elks Lodge was the Elks Lodge and restaurant located at 559 Carroll sponsored the youth Drum and Bugle Corps. In 1955, the Lodge moved to 803 St. Anthony between St. Albans and Grotto. The Improved Benevolent Protective Order or the Elks of the World (IBPOEW), the Black Elks fraternal organization, was formed in 1898 when two Pullman Porters were denied membership in the all-White order in Cincinnati, Ohio. IBPOEW followed the same commitments to youth as the BPOE (White Elks) through artistic endeavors, athletics, scholarship, and camps.

9. *Our Gang,* also known as the Little Rascals, was a long-lived series of comedy short films about a troupe of poor neighborhood children and the adventures they had together. The Our Gang series is notable for being one of the first times in movie history that Blacks and Whites were portrayed as equals, though some historians do not look favorably upon the characters of the Black children today. The series began in 1922 as a silent short subject series by comedy producer Hal Roach. It went to sound in 1929. In 1938, Roach sold the series to MGM, who continued producing it until 1944. A total of 220 shorts and one feature film were produced.

10. Father Flanagan was the founder of Boys Town in Nebraska.

WILLIAM KELSO "CORKY" FINNEY

It's been an honor.

I'M BILL FINNEY,[1] SAINT PAUL POLICE CHIEF, and I grew up at 437 Rondo. My home would have been between Western Avenue and Arundel on Rondo, north side of the street. This is Cornmeal Valley,[2] a wonderful, diverse community. It was a community of people who knew each other, every house. People lived in those houses for generations. Doors were left unlocked and open. Everybody on the block was an adjunct parent of yours. There were some people that were the old characters on the block that the parents would just as soon you not associate with, and so you didn't. They were adults, and adults didn't interact with kids, especially adults that knew the parents wouldn't want you talking to their child, so they stayed their distance. They weren't bad people, but people that had maybe bad habits. Maybe they were alcoholic or they were the night-lifers who, you know, lived a little bit on the wild side, and so you didn't expose children in the neighborhood to that.

My dog was an old female Springer spaniel. Lady Pontess. And Lady Pontess was guardian for the kids in about a square-block radius. She would pull kids out of the street. She would step in between children and adults she didn't know. She just mothered everyone and so that was that.

Rondo had a streetcar that went down the middle of Rondo. I rode on a streetcar, you know, the trolley, and I think they took them out of business in about 1954. I was born in 1948, so I would have been a kindergartener riding on the thing, my recollection. But I mean it was a wonderful experience, you know, because it was a train. And trains were the big thing. My dad[3] was a railroad man, and so a lot of the Black middle-class were professionals, railroad men. And there were more railmen than probably the other professionals. When I say professionals—doctors, lawyers, teachers and other civil servants, postmen, and then the railroad guys. You either worked at the railroad, on the trains, or you worked as a Redcap[4] or in one of the little concessions at the depot. And then

TOT PLUS FAVORITE PET

FIFTEEN MONTH OLD William Kelso Finney is shown here introducing his favorite pet, Lady Fontoss, to the many readers of this paper. William Kelso is the son of Mr. and Mrs. Macco Finney, 437 Rondo Ave. Mr. Finney is an employee of the Northern Pacific railroad. William Kelso is the Finney's only child.—Buzz Brown photo.

there were the guys that worked for the packinghouse[5] in South Saint Paul, and so that was a little bit on the lower social economic scale, although those people were hardworking and made good livings.

The rough cut would be people from Cornmeal Valley and Oatmeal Hill,[6] and Oatmeal Hill is generally considered those that are middle class, the professionals. And generally, most of that attitude eroded in my generation, the baby boomers, but the pre-baby boomers were really familiar with it. And I'm just cursorily familiar with it through my family. But basically it was like this: people that live west of Dale Street were considered Oatmeal, okay, because it was on the hill and it was the back and that was the newer part. People below, east of Dale Street on Rondo, would have been considered Cornmeal Valley, although you had many Oatmeal people living in Cornmeal Valley.

We lived in Cornmeal Valley because of our geographical location. But my dad was definitely and my mother was definitely Oatmeal. Our house was also a business. My mother[7] ran Finney's Beauty Parlor[8] out of the house, and so that was why we stayed there. But we owned several properties, you know, including a house way, way, way, way out Rice Street—it's near North Oaks now—that we rented to a White family. We had a lake cabin in Wisconsin. So we were clearly considered—they have a derogatory term. The term then, and it sounds so vulgar now, but I think many people considered us nigger rich.

Lola Vassar at sixteen years of age, c. 1933

My mother ran Finney's Beauty Parlor out of the house, so I grew up seeing many people from the neighborhood. The beauty parlor was separate. You came in the side door of our house. I remember that the side door had a porch off of it, and then inside it was a one-room beauty shop. It had a couple chairs.

My mother graduated from high school at sixteen. She was very, very bright. If she would have been a White child, she would have gotten a scholarship to go to school. They didn't give them to Black kids then. So she went to Chicago to a school of cosmetology for Black hair. She got her degree there and came back and did hair. Now, prior to my mother having a salon, my dad's first wife had it. My dad was married to Mrs. Finney, and my mother, Lola Vassar, worked for her. Mrs. Finney then died, and my father asked my mother if she would run the salon with her degree from a school of cosmetology. She really took the business to the next level at the house. And it was about two or three years later that she married the boss! But it was Finney's Beauty Parlor before my mother was Mrs. Finney.

I remember the wonderful relationships that were made, the respect that people in the community had for my mother because she did their hair. And hairdressers are very, very important to the fabric of the Black community, very important. It's a social experience.

One of the processes for Black women back then—they didn't use cold perms, it was the hot comb. My mother was really good at hot combing and curling, so on Saturday she'd have just lines of customers because they wanted to look nice for church on Sunday. We call it fryin', hair–fryin'. So I remember the smells. I remember the women that came there. You know, when you're a boy of eight, nine, ten years old, they all look old to you because they might be in their twenties, they might be in their thirties, but they look old and you're young. And then I can remember some of the teenage girls, which you kinda looked at, and used to like, or the girls our age that had to get their hair done because of African American hair.

And girls were like the boys. They were rough and tough and they played with it and their hair would get full of stuff. So their mothers would have to comb that hair out, and it was thick and tangled. What Black women would do at that time is hold the girl between their legs. They're sitting on the floor. They sit in the chair and they hold them between their legs and they pull their hair out. So we'd be teasing the girls, laughing at them, "Ha, ha, ha, ha!" It was painful. I mean, even with technique it was still kinda painful, and so we'd tease the girls and they'd whine and tell us to get out of there. So my mother would give me one of those dirty looks and we had to leave. But it was kinda fun.

Mother wouldn't let me stay very long because too much gossip goes on there and you know too many things about people you shouldn't know about. The belief back then is kids don't listen to adult conversations. So they didn't bring their kids to the beauty salon because things were discussed there that kids shouldn't hear. Who was doing who, and those kinda things. And so she wouldn't let me stay around and I didn't want to. There was nothing but girls there anyway.

Sometimes you couldn't help but hear it. I mean playing in the other room. Like some of the mothers would bring their kid. You play with them in the house, and you'd hear the women talking about something and then you'd hear one of the other women shush them, you know, because they're afraid that maybe we overheard it. And we did! Little sponges sitting there, listening as much as we could. Things that were scandalous then, now would just be normal open conversation. The kids would be involved now, but things that were scandalous then, like somebody going out with somebody's husband, that was scandalous stuff back then.

My mom didn't cut hair. It was against the law for beauticians, hairdressers to cut hair. You had to have a barber's license to cut hair, and they used to check that. She could style, straighten, she could trim. Couldn't cut hair. You had to have a barber's license and you had to go to the Barber Academy to get that.

Boys didn't sit in women's beauty salons to get their hair cut, no, no, no, no. But my aunt Kitty[9] was one that cut boys' hair. Not for pay, she was just a mom that cut hair. I went to Clarence's barbershop,[10] down there where my dad got his hair cut. That was on the corner of Mackubin next to Millers' grocery store.[11] Mackubin and Rondo. Clarence cut my hair. As a real little boy, I went in with my dad, so I wasn't really paying attention to adult conversation. When you got to be ten, eleven, twelve, thirteen, that's when you listen to the old boys talkin'. And it was kind of funny. It would make you giggle. "You boys quit listening." Okay, you'd listen harder then. You wouldn't say nothing, you wouldn't show any expression on your face, 'cause they'd put you out. "I'm gonna send you home, young Finney." It was funny.

I was the only child in my household, and I grew up with my mother, my father, and my aunt, who's like my sister—my mother's baby sister, Petey Vassar,[12] who was sixteen years older than me, but my big sister.

I was an asthmatic kid growing up, very sickly. And I was always big. I was strong and I was determined. I didn't have any stamina. I couldn't run. I couldn't do the athletic things. I could wrestle, but I never was good at sports. Not because of my physical limitations, except for my asthmatic limitations. My mother always kept me close to the house.

I was never indulged in the victim posture for being sick. No, no. Sometimes kids who don't want to do things make themselves sick, and asthmatics will do that. They'll give themselves asthma attacks looking for sympathy. I would say with my mother it worked for about three times out of ten. I mean, she could tell when I was really having an asthma attack. She said, "You can bring 'em on." And I said, "I know that." And so I got to the point where I would stop doing that, and I wanted to do some of the things the other kids could do.

There's one real vivid recollection. There was one year I started taking the allergy shots. And first you get sicker. But one summer the doctor gave me cortisone, and for the first time in my life I felt like a normal kid. I didn't wheeze. I took the cortisone and that's when I found out I was stronger than most kids and could run faster than a lot of them. It gave me a great boost, and I would have done anything to keep that drug. And you know, they can't keep you on cortisone long and so they cut back on doses. It was only for about two weeks. As they cut back on it, I could feel some of those symptoms return.

But I had gotten that confidence or understanding that "Hey, I can run with these guys! I can catch 'em!" And so you get older and sometimes you outgrow a lot of the asthmatic effects, or sometimes you will it to go away. And then the allergy shots over the years took their effect, too. It made me immune to a lot of the allergens, the dust and the mold and ragweed, and so

I got stronger, and by the time I got to the police department I was good to go. My first year on the job, though, I did have an asthma attack on the job one time. I worked with a partner by the name of Craig Frye,[13] who had a child that had asthma, and he took care of me that whole shift. He's special to me. He's retired now, but he's still special.

When the freeway came through, a lot of Black people that lived in and around that area moved out to Wheelock Parkway and out to Maplewood. My mother wanted me to be raised in a community where they had Black people. There was racism in Minnesota. There still is. And not the overt type—"We're gonna hang you Black folks like they did down South." But there's racism, the racism of neglect, the racism of benign —how do you say it?—a benign indifference to your presence. You can be standing there and people ignore you.

I had mentioned that we had a house that was out on Rice Street near North Oaks. My father's first deal was to tell the family that was renting the house from us that we were going to move out there, and it was almost like a farmhouse because they had animals on the property. And my mother says, "We're not moving out there. I'm not moving my child to that." So she put her foot down and he said, "Well, why?" And she says, "Well, there won't be any African American kids out there." We said Colored back then. "Won't be any Colored kids out there. I don't want my kid to grow up in a totally White community." And the next thing she says, "I don't want him to drive too early either." But the real reason was that she wanted me to be in a mixed community and to fully be conscious of who I was and where I came from as a Black person. And Lola wasn't moving on that, and Dad didn't really fight it very hard.

Well, you know, at that time Black people knew we were Black, and White people knew they were White, and White folks treated you this way and Black people responded this way. It was just what you were taught. And so part of the teasing, part of the things that young Black kids do with each other—the teasing, the jokes—we call "playing the dozens." Yeah, the playing the dozens is to toughen you up to verbal abuse, so that when we do encounter those White folks that call you names, that you don't overreact because you were going to be wrong and the White person was going to be right. The system was set up that way, and so this helped you keep your cool.

I had my first gun when I was seven years old. Not a BB gun, a live gun, a 410 single-shot shotgun, which I still have. And my dad always taught me about weapons and the proper use of them. I always wanted a .22 rifle. And he said, "No, I won't give you a .22," he says, "because people think .22s are toys. They're a very, very deadly gun. Very dangerous. And because people think it's a minor firearm they use them recklessly, and I won't allow you to have one." So I had big-caliber guns. I didn't get a .22 until I was sixteen. And we had places to shoot them because of our lake cabin. We had forty acres at Big Round Lake, Wisconsin. We had that property from 1952 until 1977. We sold it after my father had passed. And so I always was familiar with guns. I always shot them, knew them and shot them well. My dad taught me. He was a crack shot. Not a hand-gunner, but a rifleman and shotgun. I had to learn hand gunning a different way, although we had four handguns and he could shoot them, but he didn't like handguns much.

I can remember we were victims of the Ku Klux Klan in Wisconsin in 1952 or '54. I've got the *Jet* magazine that has that in it. We were up at our lake cabin. We had bought a property from a guy named Schilling, German guy. Bought his old farm, my dad and another guy by the name of Emmett

Cabin at Big Round Lake, Wisconsin: unknown, Maceo Finney, Corky Finney, Leroy Lewis Coleman Jr.

Searles. Forty acres on the lake. Anyway, we were up there and they had bought one of these old World War II Quonset huts.[14] So our family is on the one side, their family is on the other side. We left for the winter. We always closed up for the winter. They burned us out. They burned all the Black families out of there. And it was right next to a reservation. They blamed it on Indians. It wasn't Indians. They had the FBI investigating that one. Never caught the guy or charged anybody, but the guy burned his own place down and left the state. He owned a tavern down the road.

This is what they did. It was the Ku Klux Klan deal. And you know Wisconsin has a fair amount of Ku Klux Klanners, especially during that time. It was the McCarthy era, stuff like that. And so this is where I get my dedication, commitment, and tenacity from. My parents said, "We're rebuilding. Instead of having one building, we're gonna have two. Searles is gonna build over here. We're gonna build this one." They got three other Black families, Alex Perry, Pearl Buckner, and Willie—oh, I can't think of his last name. They all built. My dad sold them property and they built. "So now we're here. Sheriff, you protect our property." Never had any more trouble after that. But that's also why they taught me to shoot young. I told you I got my first gun at seven. Dad taught me to shoot early.

Shooting a gun was not as a statement for protection. They never talked that stuff. "These are skills you may need to know." Never shot anything that even looked like a human target, never. Shot at cans, shot at a board on the edge, a board with a round bull's-eye target on it. But I never shot at a civilian until I became a police officer. My parents were not militants. My parents were conservative African Americans who believed that "we're doin' it by the American way, and by God we'll protect it the American way."

"Corky" is a nickname that has been with me ever since I was a child, when I was just beginning to speak. My name is William Kelso Finney. Black mothers like to nickname their children. And so my mother wanted to nickname me Kelly. And I never could pronounce the "L." So I would say, "Corky." So after a while they said, "You want to be called Corky? That is your nickname."

I was Corky until I made chief and people decided that they shouldn't call me Corky. The news media asked me how would I like to be known as. Will, I never liked Will, William. William's my name. I said, "No, you're not going to call me Willy." And so I said, "Bill Finney." "So you don't want

Chief Finney 1992

to be called Corky anymore?" I said, "People that know me as Corky can call me Corky. It is part of me. It is my name and I certainly will answer to it. But if you ask me how I want to be referred to in the press, Bill Finney." When I ran for school board I ran as Bill Corky Finney, on the ticket for school board. A lot of people from the old community, that's how they know me, as Corky. Now people know me in all areas as Bill Finney. Fewer people call me Corky now.

And so chief is what I do. I love it. I love being your chief, your police officer. Did I ever just seek the title? No. I sought the job. The title went with it. My nickname seems to be Chief. It is one of those things that come with certain jobs. It is like once you become senator or you become governor or the mayor—if you're the mayor you're always, "Your Honor." Or a judge, it always, "Judge." It just goes with your name. Once you've been a chief, especially if it's a successful chiefdom, people will always forever call you Chief. I've been a cop most of my life. I've been a cop since I was twenty years old, so it's hard to separate. Corky is a rich life outside of it, but it is very much a part of my personality. I had it when I became a police officer, "Corky," "Corky the Cop." So now it's Chief, and it's been an honor to be Police Chief of Saint Paul.

◆ ◆ ◆

WILLIAM KELSO "CORKY" FINNEY, the son of Maceo Alexander Finney and Lola Mae Vassar Finney, and nephew to his Vassar aunts, is proud of his family and of serving Saint Paul for so many years. He served on the Saint Paul School Board from 1989 to 1992 and in 2005. He was an officer with the Saint Paul Police Department beginning in 1971, and chief of police 1992–2004, retiring after this interview. Very important to him are his wife, Linda, who is the superintendent of the Minnesota Bureau of Criminal Apprehension, and his sons Jon, a Saint Paul police sergeant, Todd, who is in the United States Army, and Curtis, who is a businessman. He and Linda take great pride in having the opportunity to coparent their nephews Kasey, Kelley, and his niece Koryn. He shares a special love and joy with his nephew Leroy L. Coleman IV and grandchildren Kasie, Khasidhe, Wesley, Jillian, and Dominique. Corky has had a lifelong appreciation of vintage cars and Harley-Davidson motorcycles, and he is an Old West history buff.

♦ **NOTES**

1. William Kelso "Corky" Finney was born November 28, 1948.

2. Cornmeal Valley, also known as Lower Rondo or Deep Rondo, was east of Dale Street. This was a lower-middle-class residential neighborhood predominantly with single-family homes. From the 1930s, this area struggled with growing poverty.

3. Father Maceo Alexander Finney was born November 13, 1898, and passed April 30, 1972.

4. Redcap Porters worked at the Saint Paul Union Depot. The uniform included a red cap, so as to be easily identified by passengers. Redcaps' salaries were minimal, and they supported their families mostly through tips. Responsibilities included carrying baggage for travelers, mopping floors, polishing brass, parking cars, and cleaning offices.

5. The Armour Packing Plant was located on Armour Avenue two blocks east of Concord Avenue in South Saint Paul. The plant was open from 1919 to 1979, and covered about forty acres. Because this was one of the few industries that hired Blacks, many from Rondo took jobs at Armour and rode the streetcar to South Saint Paul daily.

6. Oatmeal Hill was a term referring to Rondo west of Dale Street toward Lexington, sometimes known as Upper Rondo. More affluent residents tended to move into this area, giving the impression the residents had a higher social standing. This middle-class neighborhood consisted of predominantly single-family homes.

7. Mother Lola Vassar Finney was born September 15, 1917, and passed August 8, 1993.

8. Finney's Beauty Salon was located at 437 Rondo.

9. Aunt Kitty is Eula Vassar Taylor Washington Murphy, mother of cousins David and Clarence Taylor and Vant Washington.

10. Clarence Lewis's Barber Shop was located 497 Rondo at Mackubin.

11. Gladys Clemons Miller, her husband Jesse Miller and her brothers Thomas and Julius Clemons owned Lincoln Food Market at 350 Mackubin and Rondo.

12. Barbara "Petey" Vassar Gray was born September 2, 1932.

13. Craig E. Frye was hired as a patrolman with the Saint Paul Police Department March 2, 1964, and retired September 6, 1991.

14. Quonset huts were developed for the U.S. military at Quonset Navel Base in Rhode Island to serve as barracks. They are a semicircular metal shelter with end walls.

YUSEF MGENI

Born and raised in the Rondo community as
Charlie Anderson

It is because of the Rondo community that I am who I am.

MY NAME IS YUSEF MGENI,[1] AND I AM A LIFETIME RESIDENT OF THE SUMMIT-
University[2] community. My great-grandparents homesteaded on the area
that is now St. Albans and University. As I understand it, Saint Paul was the
end of one trunk of the Underground Railroad, and on my father's[3] side of
the family, the ancestors came from Alabama by way of North Dakota and
then to Minnesota. They homesteaded here, had a farm, and wanted to raise
a family.

My father was in the Negro baseball leagues, and he worked on the Great
Northern Railroad.[4] The train was leaving Sioux City, Iowa, and he was on
the platform on his knees, begging my mother[5] to marry him, and he said
he would not run and catch the train until she agreed. She was a student at
Briarcliff College in Sioux City, Iowa. She agreed, and my father had to run
up the tracks for a quarter mile and jump on the back of the train. She was
afraid that he would lose his job if she didn't say yes! My mother's family,
also, interestingly enough, came from Alabama to Iowa to Minnesota.

Saint Paul was a very progressive community. At the time the Civil War
broke out, there were only about 269 African Americans in the state of
Minnesota. More than half joined up to fight with the Union Army to go
back South and free the slaves. In the period between 1850 and 1900, a

higher percentage of African Americans in Saint Paul owned land and were literate than in any other part of the country. Blacks in the workforce earned a higher percentage of the pay of their White counterparts than anywhere else in the country. This was a great regional center because of all the railroads meeting here—the Great Northern, Northern Pacific,[6] Milwaukee,[7] Canadian Pacific.[8] All the railroads came through Saint Paul, so Saint Paul was a real hub of information and opportunity.

Of course, up until almost the second half of this century, the only places that Blacks in Saint Paul could work were the packinghouse, the post office, the railroad, some government agencies, and then large hotels or in domestic work. But there were many independent Black businesspersons, men and women, who offered jobs and housing. There was a Robert Banks Literary Society.[9] There was a Negro History Study Club, and there were so many mutual assistance associations, self-help organizations, churches, and other opportunities for African Americans. Saint Paul was a wonderful, welcoming, safe harbor for single African Americans and families who were looking for a better way of life for their children and the opportunity to practice some self-determination.

My great-uncle was the first African American admitted to practice law before the bar in the state of Minnesota, Fredrick L. McGhee.[10] My grandfather was the pro bono general council for the Saint Paul NAACP.[11] And W. E. B. DuBois[12] has credited him in a number of his written works with being the organizer of the original Niagara Movement in 1906, several years before the formation of the NAACP.

My grandmother[13] was one of the first children baptized at St. Peter Claver Church[14] around 1888. It was the first African American Catholic Church, and Father Steven Theobold was the first African American priest west of Chicago. He was the pastor of St. Peter Claver. My grandmother would become the first female and the youngest chairperson of the board of the Urban League.[15] Whitney Young, who became the national executive director of the Urban League, worked

Fredrick McGhee

here under the chair of the Urban League, Roy Wilkins.[16] Wilkins, who became the head of the national NAACP for several decades, was also the chair of the board of Hallie Q. Brown Community Center.[17] So all these people were in Saint Paul. As a small child I remember Joe Louis[18] used to come over to our house when he came to town at 519 Carroll to say hello to my grandmother. Our family was very involved in the civic and religious, and social community life, and belonged to the Robert Banks Literary Society, the Negro History Study Club and debate clubs, and would attend the union picnics and was very active in St. Peter Claver Church and Hallie Q. Brown.

Well, my grandfather, Evan Henry Anderson,[19] they called him Attorney Anderson. He died, and my grandmother, Constance Anderson, my grandma Connie, would dole me out my grandfather's books. I had read everything in the library at St. Peter Claver and a book report would be due, so she would give me a book by Richard Wright[20] or Carter G. Woodson,[21] who was the founder of Negro History Week and Black History Month. All of the great Black historians, social critics. Books by Du Bois, Richard Wright, Carter G. Woodson, J. A. Rogers,[22] John G. Jackson,[23] because my grandfather loved to read about Black history and contemporary political movements. And so I would be given these books by Richard Wright and these other great Black authors. I read Carter G. Woodson's *Mis-Education of the Negro,* which was written in 1916, when I was in the second grade. It's so funny because if you read it today, it's almost prophetic in terms of the description that he gave of the African American community and the challenges facing the Negro, particularly in public education, where I currently contribute.

So I went to St. Peter Claver School,[24] which was an African American Catholic school that was about ninety percent Baptist. All of our teachers were Black, the Oblate Sisters of Providence. And they would drill Black history and civics and values and poetry and literature into us every day. So it was part of my upbringing. In church they were always talking about the civil rights movement, or gains and advances that African Americans were making. We would get

St. Peter Claver Church,
322 Aurora Avenue

weekly reports from Birmingham or from Atlanta or from other hot spots in the civil rights movement.

So this was part of the fabric of growing up back in Saint Paul. You were expected to be knowledgeable and aware of issues that had an impact on African American people nationally and even internationally. Around my Sunday table they would discuss international affairs and things that were happening in Ghana and Ethiopia and different countries in Africa.

It was just part of the fabric of our being, because we were really isolated, a very small Black community. So whenever someone's aunt or cousin would visit, they would come in here by train. And all of the neighbors would go over and gather and they would say, "Tell us what's going on in Chicago and Indianapolis and Saint Louis and Kansas City." And that was one of the ways that people found out what other Black people were doing. "And do you know so-and-so, she's a relative of mine. How is she?" And the extended family, anytime that anyone Black would come to Saint Paul, you would recognize that they were new, first of all by language and culture. They were just welcomed with open arms and became a part of your extended family.

Frederick Douglass[25] came here. Du Bois, Paul Robeson,[26] Marian Anderson[27] would come here. Daniel Hale Williams[28] used to come here, and they would go to Fred McGhee's farm on the Apple River.[29] Fred McGhee had a cabin there, and Daniel Hale Williams, who performed the first successful open-heart surgery, dedicated one of his books to my grandmother and her sister. And these people would come here and would work on speeches and would discuss strategy for national organizations and actions and things of that nature. Fred McGhee was very involved in the National Black Catholic Congress.[30]

They burned a cross in our front yard on Central and Grotto because my mother worked in the public school district. It wasn't as visible as it was in Birmingham and Atlanta and places in the South, but it was here and we were very aware of it. We were in the living room praying, on our knees, saying the rosary. And my mother was a very proud, very strong Black woman. My father left when I was two years old, and she raised her children on her own.

And we were always cautioned, "Don't you leave the sound of my voice, so that if I call for you, you can come." Whether we were in a department store or a picnic or Como Park[31] or wherever we happened to be.

I can remember going with my mother to look for apartments and being told, "We don't take no niggers in here, no darkies. Don't even bother to apply." I can remember my mother being told that we couldn't try things on. We had to buy them and take them home and that was it. And she'd say then, "We'll take our trade somewhere else." She was so proud she refused to bend her back. A single mother raising kids without any support from our father, financially or otherwise. So our education, our church, our community life, our home family life was about not being willing to submit yourself to any form of dehumanization.

I can remember when I was in kindergarten, going to the Saint Paul public school, that my teacher's name was Mrs. Windgate. I'll never forget it. And every day she'd read *Little Black Sambo*,[32] and I would encourage Little Black Sambo to run the tigers in the butter. And she would tell us how when Little Black Sambo's mother would have a difficult pan to scrub, she'd use his head, because his hair was so defiant. And how he was the best one on his block at hide-and-seek because he was so Black. All he had to do was close his eyes and his mouth, and no one could see him.

And there would be one cookie that she would run under the water fountain and she gave that cookie to me. There was one carton of milk that wasn't put in the freezer, it was put on the radiator, and she gave that one to me.

I was handpicked to become a Catholic priest. And at Catholic Youth Camp, which was a camp for altar boys they were trying to encourage to become priests, one of the young White campers said, "Last one to the swimming hole is a greasy Black nigger," and I grabbed him and made him apologize. And the next thing I knew, someone had picked me up from the back of my neck and was kicking me in my backside and calling me "Black bastard" and "nigger" and "son of a bitch," and it was one of the young men who was a seminarian, because they were our camp counselors. And the other leaders of the church were holding their sides and laughing as he was kicking me physically and calling me all of these names. And then later that night they had an initiation, and I refused to be beaten with paddles by all of the camp counselors for my behavior. I threatened to run away and walk home if I had to before I'd allow them to punish me for demanding an apology for what this young man said.

There also was a lot of fear growing up Black in Saint Paul. There was a lot of pain. There was racism. And our parents, our grandparents,

Charlie as a freshman at Central High School

remembered the Duluth lynching.[33] My grandmother and my great-aunt used to talk about when they were small girls, eight or ten years old, they would walk all over the City of Saint Paul and could sometimes walk all day without seeing another Black face. But they felt safe because they were females.

When I was a kid and if you came south of Selby or north of University, you would probably have to fight your way back into the community. So there were very prescribed routes about safety. So you knew where you were welcome and where you didn't dare go. And kids laugh about having to be home when the streetlights are on, that meant be in your own neighborhood, be on your own streets. Don't be in a strange neighborhood after dark because horrible things happened to people. I mean, deforming physical things and vulgar things. They were happening when I was an adult. There were neighborhoods where grown Black men were afraid to go after dark, and you just did not go. You didn't have to post signs to tell you that you weren't welcomed there. If we went to McCarran[34] or Phalen[35] or Highland,[36] we'd go in a group because more often than not we'd be challenged, or we'd have to fight and make somebody else back off and leave us alone before we could enjoy ourselves and have a good time.

But race wasn't something that we dwelled on. As James Baldwin[37] said, "It was just a door that we had to go through every day of our lives." Sometimes multiple times during the day.

On Rondo the barbershops, the beauty shops, the shoe repair shops, the record shops were all cultural centers where, in addition to conducting trade and commerce, you also interacted with other people and there were social gatherings and people would ask, "How's your grandmother?" And tell you stories. "Your grandfather and my husband did this." And "I know you, and you need to know that." So there was a lot of oral history in the community.

You could go into the barbershop and there would be issues of Black magazines that went back for five years. They never got thrown away because someone would always be looking for an issue they missed, or pick something up and read another story in a particular issue. *Ebony* magazine and *Jet* magazine and the *Spokesman Recorder*[38] were publications that portrayed a positive image of African Americans, and I might say a more accurate image. They were treasured and passed around.

I can remember as a lad shining shoes in the Flamingo Bar,[39] which is where Western State Bank[40] is now located. Going into the Flamingo Club to shine shoes as a ten-, eleven-year-old kid, there was a hangman's noose that said, "No niggers, no dogs, no Indians allowed." And I would walk in underneath it, and tug on the pants leg of the White patrons and ask if I could shine their shoes for fifteen or twenty cents. I would go alone or with a buddy, usually in twos. We didn't understand all of the real implications of racism and so the names, the things people would say, we just figured people were drunk and when they had alcohol they became stupid. And you know, they'd give you a $5 bill and think it was a dollar, and we'd say thank you and walk out. There were a couple of people who lunged at me and other guys sort of grabbed them and pulled them back. And you know, as a kid, you don't know if they were playing or really wanted to hurt you. They were drunk and didn't want us in there and called us a lot of names. But we didn't scratch and itch, or laugh, or dance on sand or do shit like that. You know, we were shining shoes, and I was trying to raise some money to help my mom. I got a pocket full of change and left and went down the street to the next bar. You had to be cautious. There were a couple of White kids who shined shoes too, and we weren't going to let them beat us to all the customers and make all the money.

And we used to make $30, $40 shoveling snow. I mean, you'd go around and knock on people's doors, and you'd shovel the snow and they'd give you a couple bucks. We used to pour water on the hill, on Mackubin, and the cars would turn the corner on Rondo and try to drive up and the water would freeze, and they'd be in the middle of the block. Five or six of us would run out and say, "Hey, can we give you a push?" We'd push them up to the top of the hill, then they'd reach down and take their parking change and throw it out in the street. And we'd make twelve, fifteen bucks a night pushing cars up a stuck hill. We were too poor to go window shopping, but we didn't know it!

And there was always a way to scrape up a buck, which could take three, four kids all day to spend and you'd go home with a tummy ache. You know, because you ate and drank so much, and you saw four movies, and went swimming and had a great time. We used to walk through this streetcar tunnel down on Selby and go down to Wilder pool[41] on Seven Corners. Wilder was a public bathing house, so mostly poor, mostly immigrant. All the winos, all the street people, all the hobos used to go down there and for a nickel you'd get a towel and a bar of soap and take a hot water shower. They had a swimming pool, a public pool. And we never could figure out why we had to swim butt naked. Now they told us that it had to do with cheap dye in bathing suits, or something like that. But White kids and the Black kids had to swim naked.

If you cashed in four or five pop bottles you'd have twenty-five cents. You could go swimming for five hours. And literally, you'd swim for forty-five minutes, and then you'd get a towel, and you'd dry off and put your clothes on, and go out the back door and go around to the front door and get in line and go back in. And you'd take all your clothes off and put them in a wire mesh basket and you'd swim for forty-five minutes, and then you'd go out and come back in line and do it all over again. So we'd go down there and swim four or five hours a day, and then we'd go in people's back yards and get plums and apples and things like that. Or reach over a fence and grab some rhubarb out of somebody's yard and eat it. There was always something you could do. Or we'd go over to somebody's house and fix Kool-Aid or make sandwiches.

The Rondo community was a multifaceted, complex array of social arrangements and relationships. It was an extended family, it was a mutual assistance association, it was where you fell in love, where you got your heart broke, where you skinned your knees, where somebody's grandmother would stick her head out the window between the curtains and put her hand on her hips and say, "Boy, if you don't quit throwing rocks at them bottles I'm coming out there and whooping your ass. And you're Connie Anderson's grandson, aren't you? I'm carrying you home and I'm having your grandmother whoop your

Wilder Public Baths, 319 Eagle Street, Saint Paul. Photographer: Charles P. Gibson; reprinted with permission of the Minnesota Historical Society

ass when I'm done with you." And you said, "Yes ma'am." And you swept up the glass and put it in the trash can and went on down the alley, got the hell out of there before you got in trouble.

It was a place where you knew who you were, you knew where you came from, and you knew where you were going. You knew that if you dared say anything disrespectful about anyone who was at least five years older than you, you had an ass whooping coming and they knew about it at home before you got there. And you could knock on any door and ask a Black person for help, and they would welcome you into their home. If somebody said anything disrespectful about your sister and you didn't come home with a broken arm and your clothes torn half off you, you got whooped when you got home for not defending the women in the family. Even if they were ten and you were twenty, you were still expected to lay down your life. You dropped out of college and parked cars if one of your sisters wanted to advance her education, because it was easier for Black men to get jobs than it was for Black women, and that was expected of you.

So the values, the character, the integrity, the close-knit connection, the extended family. I mean, we never locked our doors until I got into high school. And ninety-five percent of people on our block put the key under the doormat, because you were always playing football or baseball or bike riding or climbing trees or wrestling or doing something like that. Or the door was locked and the windows were open. So I miss that. It's romantic, it's nonchalant, it's in part naive to even wish that.

But it was part of our culture. You know, culture is anything that is learned and shared among a given group of people. And I was real proud of it. I was real proud to pass as much of it along to my kids, as painful as they thought it was.

My favorite memory is waking up, having a good breakfast, putting on my clothes, and walking out into the world. This was my world. I mean, when I walked out on to the sidewalk, this was my neighborhood. And people waved and they said, "Good morning, Charles. How are you today? How's your mother? How's your grandmother?" You could go in places and people welcomed you. They didn't follow you around and you weren't profiled. If you went into the local restaurant, the women who ran it would come out from behind the counter and give you a hug, and ask you, "How's your mom? Tell your grandmother I said hello. You won't forget now, will

1966: High school senior yearbook: "Charles Anderson, The Mellow Fellow"

you? And here, take a little piece of this pie here with you." It was that sense of belonging. It was that feeling of ownership of home. It was safety. And it was like you were connected to everything you were surrounded by.

The level of respect was tremendous because people respected you for who you were, who your parents and grandparents were, and they respected you as a member of the community. Disrespect was unheard of. I mean, we never heard of people molesting children, or abducting or beating them or anything like that. Now there were kids, when they got beat, would run out of the house naked and their grandmother would run out behind them with a strap or a switch, beating them for something they had done and we would laugh. And because she would say, "It hurts me more than it hurts you. And if I didn't love you I wouldn't beat you." You know that drill. But it was funny. I mean, it wasn't child brutality or anything like that.

And you could go to anybody and ask anything and they'd say, "Have you eaten? Come on in. Here's twenty-five cents. Don't spend it all in one place." Or "Would you like to make some change?" You know, "I got things I need to be carried out of the basement." Or, "Do you want to cut the grass?" I mean, the connection. That's my favorite memory. That it was a continuum, so you really felt like you were part of a larger entity than yourself. I mean, it was a microcosm of the human race, but it was your microcosm.

So the connectivity was part of your self-esteem, and when you left the community you really missed that. Because when you were out of your community, you were all alone. Your antennae were up, your eyes were open, you were on guard. I don't know if you've seen this television program called *The Gate*, where people go through this bubble and they're in another dimension or another world or something. There was a protective bubble around this community, and when you left the community you felt as though you had walked through a waterfall or through a bubble. You were in another dimension, and you really had to watch out, to be careful, to protect yourself. And when you went back into that community you were safe and you were warm and you were protected.

It was like a castle. It was a self-contained community. You knew everybody, everybody knew you. You couldn't get away with anything because of this extended family. And when somebody in the community hurt or lost a loved one, everybody shared that pain. That was part of the connection and the unity. And part of it was because—it was because of segregation. The other part was by choice, because we were comfortable with one another, we loved one another, and we felt good about being in close proximity with one another on an ongoing basis.

Yusef, 1976

It is because of the Rondo community that I am who I am. That's why I grew up. That's how I grew up. That's what I'm all about. That shaped who I am today, and I'm trying to pass it on to future generations.

◆ ◆ ◆

YUSEF MGENI, born and raised in the Rondo community as Charlie Anderson, an award-winning journalist and producer in radio, television, and print, is most proud of serving and giving back to the Rondo community. For forty years Mr. Mgeni worked in nonprofit organizations doing just that. He served as a volunteer in correctional institutions and on the boards of nonprofit organizations. He continues to live in the community and has been a mentor for many young Black men and women in the community. Married for thirty-six years to Iva Jean Brown Mgeni, he is the proud father of Victor Sean and Aisha Mgeni. Yusef is director of the Office of Educational Equity for the Saint Paul Public Schools.

◆ NOTES

1. Yusef Mgeni was born with the given name of Charles Anderson on July 26, 1948. In 1972 he changed his name in an African naming ceremony,

then in a court of law, to Yusef Mgeni. He changed his name because, he says, "Your name not only identifies who you are, but also points out your rightful place in history," and as part of his desire to project positive images of African Americans. *Yusef* is from the Yoruba language and means "a person seeking wisdom to benefit others." *Mgeni* is Kiswahili, a non-ethnic trading language, and means "outsider" or "visitor from a faraway place." It was derived from work by Malcolm X, Dr. W. E. B. DuBois, Richard Wright, and the then popular book and TV miniseries, *Roots*.

2. Summit-University is a term used to refer to the area in Saint Paul that is enclosed by Summit Avenue in the south and University Avenue in the north, Interstate 35E on the east, and Lexington Avenue on the west.

3. Charles Crane Anderson was born in 1922 and passed in 1999.

4. The Great Northern Railroad's home offices were located at 175 Fourth Street at the northeast corner of Jackson Street in Saint Paul. Saint Paul's early empire builder J. J. Hill built the Great Northern. In 1880, he acquired the Northern Pacific line and legally merged theses two lines and others to create the Burlington Northern. The Great Northern yard was located at Mississippi Street on the northwest corner at East Minnehaha.

5. Theresa Agness Baker Anderson was born June 20, 1920, in Sioux City, Iowa, and passed January 31, 2000.

6. The Northern Pacific Railroad's home offices were in Saint Paul. J. J. Hill, Saint Paul's early railroad empire builder, financially acquired this line in 1880. The Northern Pacific merged with the Great Northern and other railroads to become the Burlington Northern Railroad. A Northern Pacific office was located at 175 East Fifth Street.

7. The Milwaukee Railroad had offices at 362 St. Peter Street.

8. The Canadian Pacific Railroad had offices at 214 East Fourth.

9. The Robert Banks Literary Society formed in 1875. The society was composed of men and women who met to discuss philosophical and practical aspects of race issues. A local newspaper placed the membership at approximately forty persons in 1875.

10. Fredrick L. McGhee was Minnesota's first Black criminal lawyer and was influential in bringing other Black professionals to Minnesota. He worked with DuBois to form the Niagara Movement.

11. The National Association for the Advancement of Color People evolved from the Niagara Movement, and was founded in 1909 by a multiracial group

of activists that included Saint Paul's Fredrick McGhee and Dr. Valdo Turner. Saint Paul's early chapter was formed in September 1913.

12. W. E. B. Du Bois (1868–1963) was a nationally influential Black intellectual. He spoke and wrote on racial justice, and wrote many books, including *The Souls of Black Folk* and *Dusk of Dawn*. Du Bois was involved in the founding of the NAACP and wrote articles for their newspaper, *The Crisis*.

13. Grandmother Constance Henrietta Anderson-Wiley.

14. St. Peter Claver Catholic Church began in an unstructured way in 1889. A new building was erected for the segregated congregation at Aurora and Farrington Avenue in 1892. After the new school and convent were built, the new church building was completed at 375 Oxford at St. Anthony in 1957.

15. The Urban League has served the Black community since 1923 as a human service advocacy organization. The Urban League addresses issues of quality employment, housing, education, and health care. The Saint Paul and Minneapolis agencies were combined until 1938. Saint Paul offices were initially located in various buildings downtown until the late 1960s, when they moved into their own building at 401 Selby Avenue, four blocks south of the Rondo corridor.

16. Roy Wilkins (1901–1981) grew up in Saint Paul and graduated from the University of Minnesota in 1923. He became executive director of the NAACP in 1955. Saint Paul's River Centre complex at 175 Kellogg Boulevard includes the Roy Wilkins Auditorium.

17. Hallie Q. Brown Community Center, Inc., was opened in the Union Hall at Aurora and Kent Streets in 1929 as a community center specifically to serve the Black community when the Black YWCA closed in 1928. Hallie Q., as it is affectionately known, has served all ages through child care, youth and senior clubs, athletics, music, and social events. In 1972, Hallie relocated in the Martin Luther King Building at 270 Kent Street at Iglehart in Saint Paul. The center's namesake was an educator who pioneered the movement of Black women's clubs in the late 1800s.

18. Joe Louis (1914–1981), known as the "Brown Bomber," began his professional boxing career in 1934. In his climb to becoming the Heavyweight Champion of the World in 1937, he was defeated in Berlin by a German, Max Schmeling, in 1936. As Hitler was rising to power, Schmeling was seen as the "the great white hope." In a New York City rematch on June 22, 1938, Lewis knocked out Schmeling in two minutes, four seconds. Celebrations were held

that night throughout the nation in Black communities, and many Blacks were reportedly killed in retaliation. Schmeling's defeat was seen as a damaging blow to Hitler and his racist beliefs. Louis has the distinction of defending his title more times than any other heavyweight in history. He was eulogized as one of the greatest boxers of all times.

19. Evan Henry Anderson.

20. Richard Wright (1908–1960) was among the first Black Americans to achieve literary fame. His novel *Native Son* may be his best-known work.

21. Carter G. Woodson (1875–1950) was an American historian who popularized Black studies in Black colleges. He received a Ph.D. from Harvard in 1912 and was dean of the School of Liberal Arts at Howard University and West Virginia State College Institute.

22. J. A. (Joel Augustus) Rogers (1885–1965) was a notable historian, writer, and journalist who spent more than fifty years of his life doing corrective research, documenting how White historians have rewritten history to exclude, ignore, or recast Black achievement by ascribing achievements to Europeans.

23. Historian John G. Jackson, from the Chicago area, wrote *Man, God and Civilization, Christianity Before Christ,* and the foreword for Gerald Massey's two-volume work, *Egypt: Light of the World.*

24. St. Peter Claver School, located at 1060 West Central opened in 1950, grades K-8. The school closed in 1989 and reopened in 2001. Initially a bowling alley in the basement helped raise funds for the school and provided recreation. The school is affiliated with the Catholic church of the same name that was built in 1957 at 375 Oxford. The school is named for Peter Claver (1580–1654), who was canonized by Pope Leo XIII in 1888 for his work with the African Negro of Spanish America.

25. Frederick Douglass (1818–1885) is recognized as one of America's great Black speakers. He fought to end slavery before the Civil War, and was a powerful voice for human rights and against racial injustice. He served as an adviser to President Abraham Lincoln.

26. Paul Robeson (1898–1976) was a singer, actor, linguist, and political activist.

27. Marian Anderson (1897–1993) was a strong Black woman with a soul-filled contralto operatic voice who broke many racial barriers, including being the first Black to sing at the Metropolitan Opera. In 1939, when she was denied

a concert at Constitution Hall, Eleanor Roosevelt arranged for her to sing at the Lincoln Memorial for 75,000 people.

28. Daniel Hale Williams, M.D. (1856–1931) was a charter member of the American College of Surgeons. In 1913, he founded the Provident Hospital and Medical Center in Chicago, the oldest freestanding Black-owned hospital in the United States. In 1970 the U.S. Congress issued a commemorative stamp in his honor.

29. The Apple River runs past Somerset, Wisconsin.

30. The very first *National Black Catholic Congress* was called together by Daniel Rudd, in 1889 at St. Augustine Catholic Church in Washington, D.C. The purpose of the meeting was to address the needs of Black Catholics. Distinguished men of African descent came from all over the United States to participate in this historic event. President Grover Cleveland invited 200 delegates to the White House for a meeting. Additional congresses were held in 1890, 1892, 1893, 1894, 1987, 1992, 1997, and 2002.

31. Como Park surrounds Lake Como and is between Lexington, Hoyt, and Como Avenues. It was initially planned in 1872. In 1873, $100,000 was donated to purchase land for a park, and the city acquired the 300 acres around Lake Como. The lake was named in 1848 by Charles Perry, who farmed a tract of land on the shore of the lake. Today there are 1.67 miles of paths around the lake, picnic shelters, tennis courts, ball fields, swimming pools, fishing, paddleboats, a conservatory and gardens, a zoo, amusement rides, a golf course, and a historic streetcar station.

32. *Little Black Sambo* is a children's book published in 1899 by Helen Bannerman, a Scot living in India. The original book contained racist caricatures and stereotypes. The word *sambo*, partly as a result of the book, has a long history as a racial slur.

33. On June 15, 1920, a mob lynched three Black circus workers in Duluth after a White woman accused them of raping her. She later admitted she had lied. This event was well known through the oral tradition of the Black communities, but went largely unreported, never making it into history books until very recently. In October 2003, the City of Duluth had an atonement ceremony and dedicated a seven-foot-tall bronze statue of the three lynching victims: Elias Clayton, Elmer Jackson, and Isaac McGhie.

34. McCarron Lake is located in Roseville, Minnesota, with public access at

1795 Rice Street. The lake has 9,000 feet of shoreline (eighty-one surface acres) and a maximum depth of fifty-seven feet—small and deep by metro norms. The lake is surrounded by single-family homes, except for a fifteen-acre park located on the east shore that includes beachfront, recreational amenities, a picnic shelter, a play area, a fishing pier, and a beach building. McCarron Lake was named for John E. McCarron, a farmer who lived beside the lake. McCarron served in the Fourth Minnesota Regiment in the Civil War and died in Saint Paul in 1897.

35. Phalen Park is located between Frost Avenue, Maryland Avenue, Arcade, and East Shore Drive, and was first planned by the Saint Paul City Council in 1872. The city acquired the land in 1899 at a cost of $22,000, and it was opened to the public soon afterward. The park was named after early settler Edward Phalen, who staked one of the first claims to the land around Phalen Creek. Today there are 3.2 miles of trails around Lake Phalen, a playground, beach, golf course and clubhouse, and an amphitheater.

36. Highland Park, located between Snelling Avenue, Lexington Avenue, Highland Parkway and Edgcumbe, was acquired by the City of Saint Paul in 1925, largely due to the efforts of Commissioner of Parks Herman Wenzel. Undeveloped when it was purchased, within seven years Highland Park featured an eighteen-hole golf course, ten tennis courts, a picnic area, and football and baseball grounds. It also sported a stadium seating 2,700 people, an artificial "swimming hole," and a new clubhouse/reception facility proclaimed the best of its kind in the Northwest. Most of those facilities, either rebuilt or renovated, still stand today.

37. James Baldwin (1924–1987) was a fiction and nonfiction writer and a leading Black commentator on the condition of his people in the United States.

38. The *Minneapolis Spokesman* was founded in 1934 by Cecil F. Newman and is the longest-lived Black newspaper in Minnesota. The *Saint Paul Recorder* later began publication under Newman. The newspaper remains under the same family ownership and is now known as the *Minnesota Spokesman-Recorder*.

39. The Flamingo Bar was located at 663 University Avenue.

40. Western Bank is located at 663 University Avenue.

41. Wilder Pool and Wilder Public Baths were located at 319 Eagle Street.

David Vassar Taylor, Ph.D.

I remember my grandfather Joseph Vassar. His home was on Central Avenue, two doors west of Pilgrim Baptist Church. Back in the day, when we had family gatherings at one or another of his daughter's homes (he had seven), he seemed ill at ease with the level of activity generated by so many grandchildren. On occasion he would stare out of the window and utter in seeming exasperation, "Chillun, time marches on." I didn't understand his musings then; I think I do now. As the song suggests, "Everything must change, nothing stays the same . . . 'cause that's the way of time, nothing and no one goes unchanged."[1]

The Rondo community as it was known has changed and is changing. The physical area has become home to many racial and ethnic groups seeking affordable housing. Businesses along University Avenue reflect that diversity. New community centers and service agencies respond to the needs of a growing multicultural clientele. Selby Avenue has experienced a commercial rebirth with pronounced gentrification in the several blocks east of Lexington. After years of decline this urban neighborhood appears to be on the cusp of revitalization.

This pattern of urban migration, settlement, resettlement, decline, and revitalization is a characteristic history of many urban neighborhoods in cities across the country. Urban landscapes, commercial business, social service centers, and faith-based institutions change over time to meet the needs of residents. What remains remarkably constant are the needs, desires, and aspirations of people's lives.

What you have read are the remembrances and musings of a community's elders reflecting on aspects of their lives individually and collectively in the Rondo neighborhood as captured in oral interviews. Equally interesting might be the perspectives of children who, although they grew up in their parents' community, may see the "neighborhood" in a different light.

I recall that many of us, during the restless years of our youth, could not wait to leave provincial Saint Paul and this postage stamp community to explore uncharted destinies, wherever they might lead us. It is more than amusing to witness that a number of us, after having explored that larger world, have found ourselves drawn back to this community where we annually recount the moments in our memories at Rondo Days celebrations. These days at our celebrations some people delight in the crowd, while others seem ill at ease with the level of activity generated by so many grandchildren and great-grandchildren. For some, echoes of the past hang thick in the air, while for others the connection to days gone by is a grandfather's hand pointing to the store where he used to buy (or steal) sweets. Indeed, time marches on. No one and nothing goes unchanged. Still, I see my old friends laughing in the faces of their grandchildren, and when I listen carefully I can even hear their voices, the voices of Rondo.

♦ **NOTE**

1. "Everything Must Change" was made popular by Barbra Streisand. Words and music by Bernard Ighner.

THE HISTORY OF THE RONDO
ORAL HISTORY PROJECT

The Rondo Oral History Project was first conceived of by Summit-University resident Kate Cavett as she looked for more information about this historic community. In 2002, Cavett began talking with individuals in the community to see if there was interest in expanding the documented history then available about the Rondo neighborhood. Early in her exploration, Dr. David Taylor, preeminent Minnesota Black American historian, offered his support. Community members agreed to support the project through a community advisory committee. In 2003, Hamline University's Department of English offered its participation through a service-learning project.

Over the next two years, oral history interviews were conducted, transcribed, and edited for clarity; pictures were gathered, scanned, and placed in each document. Each of the primary documents is archived at the Minnesota Historical Society, Ramsey County Historical Society, and Saint Paul's Central and Rondo Outreach Libraries. From the full oral history documents, shortened versions were created for inclusion in this book. In addition, a video with some of the storytellers sharing parts of their stories was produced to compliment the book.

In telling a community's story each voice is important, and it must be acknowledged that we were unable to interview many families and individuals of Rondo. *Voices of Rondo* is a beginning in telling the stories, and we hope others will continue to preserve the history of ordinary people with extraordinary lives.

The Rondo Oral History Project is a project of HAND in HAND Productions, a 501(c)3 Minnesota Nonprofit Corporation. HAND in HAND Productions was created in 1996 by John Harrington and Kate Cavett to conduct a Minnesota gang oral history research project, in which oral history interviews were completed with 103 gang members from five ethnic groups. Qualitative analysis was conducted and a report submitted to the Minnesota Legislature. Based on the research, and using excerpts from the oral history interviews, Cavett and Harrington provided more than 100 educational presentations around the State of Minnesota and nationally.

As when it began, HAND in HAND remains committed to the oral tradition in supporting families, communities, and organizations in preserving their stories hand in hand.

HAND in HAND Productions
Saint Paul, Minnesota
651-227-5987
www.oralhistorian.org

ORAL HISTORIAN KATE CAVETT

KATE CAVETT grew up in Minnesota listening to her father's stories about his childhood in the Indian Territory of Oklahoma and the Italian campaign of World War II. She has collected oral histories from over 150 men, women, elders, youth, parents, community members, business owners, police officers, college professors, musicians, and gang members. She has had the opportunity to spend hundreds of hours listening to reflections on parenting, careers, neighborhoods, friends, sorrows, passions, racism, fears, and joys. Her initial interest was sparked for this project when she learned that many national civil rights leaders had spent time in the Rondo community, but then was unable to locate significant background about the culture of this neighborhood.

Ms. Cavett, who has a B.A. in counseling and an M.A. in human development, has presented to groups of five to 1,000 around the United States. She is an award-winning consulting producer of *Oh Freedom Over Me*, a radio documentary about the history of Mississippi Freedom Summer 1964 as a challenge to address racism today. When not listening to people's stories, Kate finds joy in her creative and intelligent son, theater, art shows, jazz, blues, friends, and walking her Yorkie.

THOSE WHO CONTRIBUTED AND INFLUENCED

THE RONDO ORAL HISTORY PROJECT IS ABOUT A DYNAMIC COMMUNITY AND the many individuals who shaped and nurtured it. This project must acknowledge those who gave it life. In the end they, too, have built a community.

The women and men whose voices you will read in this book have shared of themselves in telling their stories of Rondo. They and their family members gave their time for interviews, reviewing transcriptions, and providing pictures. This book exists because of their generosity.

Others who have participated on so many levels have become part of the Rondo Oral History Project community. Without them, *Voices of Rondo* would not have been possible.

CONSULTANT
David Vassar Taylor, Ph.D.

TRANSCRIPTION
Thubten Mindrol
Mary Jo Seidl
Kim Zielinski
Buelah Baines Swan
Hamline University Students

COPYEDITING AND ADMINISTRATIVE SUPPORT
Thubten Mindrol
Amy Gavel

DEVELOPMENT OF CURRICULUMS
Carol Dawson
Jennifer Eisele
Amy Gavel

GUIDANCE AND EXCEPTIONAL FRIENDSHIP TO THE PROJECT
Dr. Mary K. Murray Boyd

EDITORIAL COMMITTEE
Mary K. Murray Boyd
Carol Dawson
Melvin Henderson
Yusef Mgeni

VIDEO PRODUCTION
Benjamin Mchie

HAND IN HAND PRODUCTIONS
  BOARD OF DIRECTORS
John Harrington
Kateleen Cavett
Chris Crutchfield
Terri Thao
Nieeta Presley
Shelley Jacobson
Kent Shifferd
Kevin Reinke
William Finney
Barb Rose
Lisa Tabor

COMMUNITY ADVISORY COMMITTEE
Russ Balenger
Mary K. Murray Boyd
Melvin Carter, Jr.
Billy Collins, Jr.

Chris Crutchfield
Pat Wilson Crutchfield
William "Corky" Finney
Estelle Hartshorn Jones
Nathaniel "Nick" Khaliq
Yusef Mgeni
Debbie Gilbreath Montgomery
Phillip Minor
Nieeta Laurene Neal Presley
DeVelma "Dee Dee" Lewis Ray
Mychael Wright
Lori New-Roberson
Buelah Vivian Baines Swan
Debbie Jackson Walton

SERVICE-LEARNING

With Bush Foundation support
Hamline University's Department of English provided a service-learning project with students in David Hudson's 2003 class "Special Topics in Journalism: Reporting Oral History"
Intern
Kim Zielinski productively contributed to several oral histories and provided the David Taylor oral history
Faculty support from:
Dr. Veena Deo
Dr. David Hudson
Dr. Alice Moorhead

FINANCIAL SUPPORT FOR THE RONDO ORAL HISTORY PROJECT THROUGH JUNE 2005
Grotto Foundation
Saint Paul Travelers
Saint Paul Travelers Arts & Diversity committee and COMPAS
American Composers Forum
Saint Paul Foundation
Elmer L. and Eleanor J. Andersen Foundation

3M
Boss Foundation
Archie D. & Bertha H. Walker Foundation
Western Bank
Star Tribune
TCF National Bank
Thompson West Group
St. Paul-Reformation Lutheran Church
Dayton Avenue Presbyterian Church
St. Philip's Episcopal Church
Cathedral of Saint Paul
Target Foundation
Greater Twin Cities United Way—CIF
Leonard, Street and Deinard Foundation
Saint Paul Cultural STAR Grant
Minnesota Humanities Commission
University Bank

SYREN BOOK COMPANY'S TALENTED STAFF

GUIDE FOR GRANDPARENTS, PARENTS, AND TEACHERS IN USING THIS BOOK WITH YOUTH

By Amy Gavel
With Contributions by Carol Dawson

In this book the sounds of wagon wheels, club meetings, and band practice echo across time. *Voices of Rondo* speaks directly to the experiences of a specific Black community in Saint Paul, Minnesota. Yet the tales these voices tell portray all of the pain and agony of racism, and the triumph of survival; they convey the tenacity of maintaining family and community despite pressures that would pull them apart; and they represent the struggles and the hope of a people realizing their potential. These oral histories relate a piece of the broader narratives of Black, American, and human history. They provide opportunities for us to be inspired to learn and to become more than we have been.

Voices of Rondo will enhance existing curriculum from social studies to math, become the central text of a broader and deeper study of Black history, and be an invitation to a family to encourage children to question and learn. This guide is intended to assist parents, grandparents, extended family, and educators in creating learning plans of a variety of depths and lengths. Suggested themes, enduring understandings, activities, assessments, and resources are offered to trigger ideas and assist in shaping your engagement with the stories.

SUGGESTED THEMES
Community and Family: Hallie Q. Brown and other community centers; faith; contributions of churches; social clubs (youth and adult); geographic stratification (Oatmeal Hill and Cornmeal Valley); community "schooling"; close-knit and extended families; migration, mobility, and the creation of community.

Education and Employment: Values of family and employment, school life, and experiences; college-educated and underemployed; entrepreneurship; postal workers; railroad workers: Redcap Porters, Pullman Porters; unions: the Brotherhood of Sleeping Car Porters and Local 516—Brotherhood of Railroad Waiters; service industry jobs; women's employment; working several jobs to keep families comfortable; Black sororities and fraternal organizations.

Racism and Civil Rights: In employment; in schools; lack of safety outside of community; stereotyping, prejudice, discrimination, segregation, and de facto segregation; methods for working for change; changes in the Rondo community; participation of members of the Rondo community in the civil rights movement.

THEME: COMMUNITY AND FAMILY
Recommended for pre-K through K; adaptable for any age.

Enduring understanding: Community is important.

Lessons:
- An introduction to Rondo and Black history in Saint Paul;
- An introduction to oral history;
- An introduction to recording history;
- Learning about community and the importance of each person in a community;
- Geography affects community;
- Black history is everywhere; Black history is American history.

The teacher or adult should read several of the oral histories and become familiar with the Rondo community.

Begin a discussion with the students, asking:
1. What is a community? (People playing together, people who know each other, people who live near each other, people who worship

together, people who take care of each other, people who know each other's names, etc.)

2. What makes our class a community? (We learn together, play together, care about each other, know each other's names, etc.)
3. How do we get to know the people in our community? (We play, talk, ask questions, etc.)

Show the students the book *Voices of Rondo*. Turn the pages and show them some of the pictures of the storytellers. Talk to the students about Rondo. Tell them that, like their class or school, the Rondo community was made up of a lot of people. Those people were interviewed about their community (someone asked them a lot of questions and recorded their answers), and from all the stories a book was made.

Read or tell the students some of the stories from the book. For example: Melvin Carter's story of the St. Peter Claver Band, David Taylor's story of starting a newspaper, Kathryn Coram Gagnon's story of being in a play, or Wilbert Dugas's story of the Ober Boys Club.

Assessment of Understanding and Adding Depth to the Experience
Give each student paper and art supplies—as basic or as complex as you want: markers, paint, crayons, etc. Ask the students to draw or paint something they like about their class, school, or neighborhood; or have them make a picture map of their school or neighborhood. If you have enough adult hands to help, also write down what they tell you the picture is about. Create a wall mural of their pictures or a book titled *Voices of*_____ (the name of your school or the name of your class).

List some places mentioned in the stories that were in the Rondo community area and plot them on a map. ***Community centers:*** Hallie Q. Brown, Welcome Hall, Ober Boys Club. ***Churches:*** Pilgrim Baptist, St. Peter Claver, St. Philip's Episcopal, St. James A.M.E. ***Schools:*** Elementary—Gorman, J. J. Hill, McKinley, Maxfield, St. Peter Claver; Junior/senior high—Central High School, Marshall, Mechanic Arts High School.

Follow-up: Invite one or two members of the Rondo community or a Black community in your area to your class to tell their stories. Work with students ahead of time to prepare a list of questions to ask the guests. Remind the students about *Voices of Rondo* before the guests arrive, and have your students tell your guests about their class or school community and share the pictures or recordings they made.

Teach a piece of Black history as American history today?

More Learning Opportunities
Visit the Southern Poverty Law Center's Web site. It offers games, activities, and resources for parents and teachers to support youth ages four and beyond around multiculturalism, nurturing tolerance and understanding in building communities (www.tolerance.org).

Everyone Makes a Difference: A Story about Community, by Cindy Leaney; illustrated by Peter Wilks (Rourke Publishing, 2004). Matt and José help welcome a new young boy from India by introducing him to the activities of the community center. Ages 4 to 8.

SOCIAL STUDIES
THEME: COMMUNITY AND FAMILY
Recommended for Grades 1–3; adaptable for any age.

Enduring understanding: Learning stories from the past helps us know where we come from.

Lessons:
- An introduction to Rondo and Black history in Saint Paul;
- An introduction to oral history;
- An introduction to being a history detective;
- Black history is everywhere; Black history is American history.

Begin class by showing the children a map of where the Rondo community was. Tell them about the freeway cutting through the neighborhood, causing homes to be torn down, people to be displaced, businesses to be closed, and community life to be disrupted in so many respects. Direct a discussion about what a historian could do to learn about a place that is no longer there. Teresina "Willow" Carter Frelix and Nathaniel Abdul Khaliq's stories share their pain for the freeway destroying the neighborhood.

Ideas: Archaeologists dig for evidence of the past and catalog what they find. Historians read letters and diaries, legal documents, and other primary sources from the past. What other source do we have to learn about the past? People!

Show the children *Voices of Rondo* and explain to them how the book was made by interviewing people who had lived or worked in the Rondo neighborhood. These interviews became oral history primary documents when they were transcribed verbatim, edited only for clarity, and published as oral history.

Select two to four age-appropriate and reading-level-appropriate sections of the book for your child or students to read. You know best where they are developmentally and what concepts they will be able to understand. If you have enough strong readers, have students read aloud. Otherwise, read the sections to the class. Select stories you enjoy, but also stories that will be meaningful to your students. Select stories of men and women, one from the earliest days and one more recent.

After reading the stories, have the students write down two questions they have about Rondo or about the people who lived in Rondo. Invite members of the Rondo or another Black community to class, invite a Black historian who knows about Rondo, northern urban Black communities, or the era, or use some other creative way for the students to be history detectives and get answers to their questions. Talk about how the Rondo community in the book became a community because people migrated there from other parts of the country. Older children might be history detectives at the library and research the topics or time periods.

Assessment of Understanding and Adding Depth to the Experience
Have the students write letters to members of the Rondo community about
what they learned about Rondo and the people who lived there. While they
are writing, play music relevant to the *Voices of Rondo*. For example: classical as in Ora Lee O'Neal Patterson's story, jazz or band music as in Melvin
Carter Sr.'s story, piano music as in Mary K. Murray Boyd's story, classical
church music as in Kathryn Coram Gagnon's story, or gospel music, which
Wilbert John Dugas Jr. still plays.

Ask them to address the following questions in their letters:
1. Who did you read about?
2. What questions did you have after you read the histories?
3. How did you find the answers to those questions?
4. What did you learn about Rondo?
5. How are you like the people you read about who lived in Rondo?
   How are you different?
6. What will you remember about Rondo?

Make a list of historical sites the children have visited. What questions do
they now have about who lived and worked there? Encourage them to talk
about ways to find out the "ordinary" stories of the past. Encourage them to
find Black history in American history.

Recommended for Junior and Senior High School Students
Oral history is the spoken word in print. Oral histories are personal memories shared from the perspective of the narrator, recorded verbatim, and
minimally edited for readability. Oral histories do not follow traditional
writing standards. Rather, they capture the flavor, tenor, and tempo of the
storyteller's speech patterns.

Have students conduct an oral history project. The process would involve:
- Choosing someone to interview;
- Researching topics or areas of the person's life;
- Developing a list of questions appropriate to the person;
- Acquiring a good-quality audiotape recorder and microphone to
  conduct the interview;

- Scheduling and audiotaping the interview;
- Transcribing the interview verbatim;
- Editing as lightly as possible for clarity;
- Having the storyteller review for accuracy and correct spelling of names;
- Scanning pictures and placing them in the document;
- Printing/publishing the document; and
- Sharing it with friends and family.

Conducting interviews and producing oral histories will create primary history documents that can stand on their own or become part of a larger history research project.

Help the students assess what they learned from collecting personal histories and how that history fits into their city's history, state's history, or the nation's history. Help your students find Black history in their city's history, state's history, or the nation's history.

More Learning Opportunities
The Great Migration: An American Story, by Walter Dean Myers; illustrated by Jacob Lawrence (HarperCollins, 1993). A series of paintings chronicles the journey of Blacks who, like the artist's family, left the rural South in the early twentieth century to find a better life in the North.

Color Me Dark: The Diary of Nellie Lee Love—the Great Migration North, Chicago, Illinois, 1919, by Patricia C. McKissack (Scholastic, 2000). Beginning on January 1, 1919, Nellie chronicles the trials and tribulations of her family's life in Bradford Corners, Tennessee, and later in Chicago, where the family became involved in the suffrage and anti-lynching movements.

BLACK HISTORY IS EVERYWHERE (EVEN IN MATH CLASS)
THEME: COMMUNITY
Recommended for grades 3–5; adaptable for any age.

Enduring understanding: Math and Black history are both part of everyday life.

Lessons:
- An introduction to Rondo and Black history in Saint Paul;
- Applying math concepts to reading maps;
- Exploring how learning about maps is one way to learn about a community;
- Learning about measuring distance.

Prior to class, the teacher should read through the oral histories and become familiar with the stories. Use the addresses in the endnotes, or have the students find the addresses in the endnotes, to make a list of locations for students to plot on a map. For example, locate beauty shops, grocery stores, community centers, and churches.

Come to Saint Paul and drive around the neighborhood.

Begin by looking at a current large map of Saint Paul. Find the area where the Rondo neighborhood used to be. (It may be referred to as Summit-University. This area is between Lexington Parkway and Rice Street, University Avenue, and Marshall Avenue.) Enlarge this part of the city map on a copier at an appropriate scale so that students can make better estimates of distance. What is there now? (The I-94 freeway, Concordia College, new buildings like the Martin Luther King Center, the new Hallie Q. Brown.)

Show the students the map of Rondo in the front of the book.

Read sections of the oral history that name places and their locations for students. (Yes, this is still math class!) When students hear a place-name and location, write it on the board and find it on the map.

Teach students how scale on a map works. Using that knowledge, work with them to calculate the distances between the places in the oral history.

Assessment of Understanding and Adding Depth to the Experience
Give each student a map of the neighborhood where your school is located, or a map of your school. Have the students plot out landmarks, figure out the scale, and calculate the actual distances between those landmarks.

Follow-up discussion:
1. How do we use math to read maps?
2. What did we learn about the Rondo community by looking at a map of Rondo?
3. What did we learn about the people who lived in Rondo by looking at a map of Rondo?
4. What are opportunities to use math to learn about people's lives besides when we read maps?

ENGLISH/READING/WRITING
THEMES: FAMILY AND COMMUNITY, EDUCATION AND EMPLOYMENT, RACISM AND CIVIL RIGHTS
Recommended for grades 5–6; adaptable for any age.

Enduring understanding: Personal stories are a good way to learn about perspective.

Lessons:
- An introduction to Rondo and Black history in Saint Paul;
- An introduction to oral history;
- An introduction to storytelling as a way to learn about people and perspective;
- An introduction to the distinctions between personal and oral history;
- Black history is everywhere; Black history is American history.

Select four oral histories; ensure a balance by choosing a man's story, a woman's, a story that covers more recent times, and one from the past. Each class period for the first four days, begin class with the students in groups of three to four, taking turns reading aloud.

Make a chart to hang on the wall. After the reading time, write the name of the subject of the oral history on the chart. During a directed discussion about what students have read, record what they learned about the person telling the story and about Rondo. On the second day, record what was the same and what was different about this person and about the person or people from the first day. On the third and fourth days, ask questions such as the following:

1. What are the differences in the perspectives of the people telling the stories?
2. What are the clues in the stories that tell you about the four people?
3. What makes the stories interesting? Does anything make them not interesting?
4. What kinds of details make a good story?

Prepare age-appropriate and experience-appropriate interview questions about an event class members would have in common; for example: questions about a field trip, an all-school program, a class project, or something in the community in which all of the students would certainly have participated.

Tell the students how the book *Voices of Rondo* was created. Describe the process of conducting oral history interviews and then editing them to create the story of a community. Talk about the elements of a good story, and what makes a story interesting.

Pair the students and have them interview each other.

After the interviews, ask the group if any questions were left out that should have been asked.

Explain that in the process of conducting personal histories or oral histories, sometimes it is not until after the first draft of the story is written or transcribed that the interviewer realizes there are more questions he or she needs to ask. Have the students suggest two to four additional questions. Write them on the board. Have students get back into their pairs and ask each other these questions.

Either as a project in class, or as homework, have students write the other person's personal story using that person's words. Remind students that oral history is recorded in the words of the other person, not in the words of the person who is writing down the story.

Follow-up discussion:
1. What were the challenges of writing someone else's story?
2. Did they tell the story differently than you would have?
3. If you wrote the story after you recorded it, how did you write it differently than they told it?
4. When people talk about the same experience or place in different ways, it's because they have different perspectives. What have you learned from the different perspectives and different storytelling styles of the people who lived in Rondo?
5. Oral history involves the word-for-word transcription of a person's story. Go to the definition of oral history in the introductory pages of *Voices of Rondo*. Oral history creates primary documents. Personal history is a second-person account of a personal experience. What are the differences between oral history and personal history in both process and outcome?

Assessment of Understanding and Adding Depth to the Experience
The stories we read really happened. Imagine you lived in Rondo in [choose a year that the students have read about]. Write your fictional story, from your own perspective. What was your family like? If you were in a club, what was the club's focus? Why did you want to join it? If you were a Pullman Porter, what was your job like?

Imagine you traveled back in time to the Rondo of one of the oral histories we read. Write about what it is like to be there from your perspective. Include the names of the person you are visiting. Are you a guest in his or her home? Do you go to Hallie with him or her? What do you do there? What do things look like? What is the same and what is different from your neighborhood?

Think of a family member of your own who lived at the time of one of the Oral Histories. Imagine that family member in this place. What would his or her life have been like? What role might he or she have had in the community? Would he or she have lived in Rondo? Why or why not?

Homework activity. Create a Diversity Scavenger Hunt for your students. Send students into the community to be detectives of uniqueness and differences in people. Some examples of the differences may include: different heights; different genders; hair that is different in color, texture, curl density; different eyes; different clothes; how many different color skin tones can they find; speaking English with different accents; speaking different languages; having different faith or religious practices and beliefs; being from different ethnic backgrounds. Besides seeing visual differences, help the children explore other differences, such as beliefs and values. Expand this list for your students' ages, creativity, and the community. After several detective experiences, discuss with students what they observed, learned, and felt about recognizing difference. Have students expand the list of differences to observe in ongoing detective experiences. Continue sending students out to be detectives for diversity and other differences, and continue to discuss with them their observations, lessons, and feelings, as well as how their perspective changes as they recognize individual differences.

More Learning Opportunities

Remember: The Journey to School Integration, by Toni Morrison (Houghton Mifflin, 2004). On May 17, 1954, the U.S. Supreme Court declared segregated schools unconstitutional in *Brown v. Board of Education.* Toni Morrison recalls this tumultuous time by combining archival photographs along with a fictional account of the dialogue and emotions of students who lived during the era of upheaval in supposedly separate-but-equal schooling.

The Children's March: A Teaching Kit for Middle and Upper Grades (produced by Teaching Tolerance in association with Home Box Office). In 1963, the young people of Birmingham, Alabama, braved fire hoses and police dogs and brought segregation to its knees. The kit includes a forty-minute documentary film, available in VHS or DVD format, and a teacher's guide with nine standards-based lesson plans for social studies, language arts, and music classrooms (http://www.tolerance.org/teach/resources/childrens_march.jsp).

Eye on History. The Civil Rights Movement (Social Studies School Service, 10200 Jefferson Blvd., Box 802, Culver City, CA 90232). *Eye on History* is a set of economical books with activities that flow from fictionalized letters, journals, and other writings created by "eyewitnesses" to history, in addition to background readings and reproducible worksheets. Grades 6–12. Answer keys (800-421-4246; e-mail: access@socialstudies.com; www.socialstudies.com).

Warriors Don't Cry: A Searing Memoir of the Battle to Integrate Little Rock's Central High (Washington Square Press, 1995). *Warriors Don't Cry* is Melba Pattillo Beals's story about the Little Rock Nine and the integration of Arkansas schools.

ENGLISH/SOCIAL STUDIES/THEATER
THEMES: COMMUNITY AND FAMILY, EDUCATION AND EMPLOYMENT, RACISM AND CIVIL RIGHTS
Recommended for grade 5 through junior high; adaptable for any age.

Enduring understanding: Knowing who we are helps us get where we are going.

- An introduction to Rondo and Black history in Saint Paul;
- An introduction to oral history;
- An introduction to storytelling as a way to learn about people and perspective;
- An introduction to performing history;
- Black history is everywhere; Black history is American history.

Have the younger girls get into groups and read the Alumni of the Three Fours Girls Club story aloud by assigning parts and taking turns.

For younger boys, choose one of the stories by the men of Rondo: Wilbert Dugas; Melvin Carter's discussion of the St. Peter Claver Boys Band and about his father. Have the boys get into groups and read the story aloud by taking turns.

Have older girls take turns reading aloud the story of Kathryn Coram Gagnon, Dr. Constance Jones Price, Barbara "Petey" Vassar Gray, Mary K. Murray Boyd, or Deborah Gilbreath Montgomery.

For older boys, have them read aloud the story of James Griffin, Willie Frelix, Marvin Roger Anderson, Floyd Smaller, Melvin Henderson, or Yusef Mgeni.

Discuss *Voices of Rondo*:
1. Who are these people?
2. How was this book created?
3. What do we learn about people by hearing their stories?
4. From reading the stories aloud, what differences in speech patterns did you recognize?
5. How is hearing the stories read aloud different from reading silently?
6. What differences do you hear in inflection? Accent? Tempo? How do those differences affect your interest in the story?

Assessment of Understanding and Adding Depth to the Experience
Create performance pieces by assigning different sections of the stories to different groups of students. Have them do more research on the time period, clothing, music, and other aspects of "their" story. Learn about story as a way to tell history, and about performance as a way to share that history with others. Have students perform the pieces either as "readers' theater," in which they can read from the scripts of the oral histories, or by memorizing the sections of the oral histories they are performing.

Discussion:
1. What did you learn about the people of Rondo by performing their stories?
2. What did you learn about yourself?
3. What is similar and different between you and the people of Rondo?
4. What are some of the things that affect who you are? Community? Peers? Clubs? What you learn?
5. How did you find Black history in American history in this activity?
6. What impact did education have on the lives of the people in these stories?

7. What effect did racism have on the lives of the people in these stories?

Invite members of the Rondo community or another Black community to come and watch students perform, and then answer students' questions about Rondo and other Black communities.

More Learning Opportunities

Alpha Kappa Alpha Sorority. The headquarters for this sorority is in Chicago, Illinois. The Web site (http://www.aka1908.com/) is a rich source of ideas for further research into Black women's history and culture. Mary K. Murray Boyd, Kathryn Coram Gagnon, Linda Griffin Garrett, Paula Thomson Mitchell, Dr. Constance Jones Price, Barbara "Petey" Vassar Gray, founding member of the Minnesota chapter Mrs. James (Edna) Griffin, and other women of Rondo are members of Alpha Kappa Alpha.

Jimmy Griffin, a Son of Rondo: A Memoir, with Kwame JC McDonald (Ramsey County Historical Society, 2001).

The Days of Rondo: A Warm Reminiscence of St. Paul's Thriving Black Community in the 1930s and 1940s, by Evelyn Fairbanks (Minnesota Historical Society Press, 1990). This is one woman's memoir about growing up in Rondo.

Cap Wigington: An Architectural Legacy in Ice and Stone, by David Vassar Taylor, Ph.D., and Paul Clifford Lawson (Minnesota Historical Society Press, 2002). Taylor and Larson painstakingly pieced together the body of Wigington's professional work as a leading Saint Paul municipal architect and his leadership role in Saint Paul's Black community. The book won a Minnesota Book Award in 2003.

HISTORY
THEMES: RACISM AND CIVIL RIGHTS, EDUCATION AND EMPLOYMENT, COMMUNITY AND FAMILY
Recommended for high school; adaptable for any age.

Enduring understanding: Learning about the past affects how we understand the present.

Lessons:
- Learning the history of Rondo and Black history in Saint Paul;
- An introduction to oral history as a historical method;
- Learning about community is one way to build community;
- Racism has been as apparent as a hurricane and as imperceptible as a breeze stirred up by a hummingbird, and it affected the Rondo community and our shared histories;
- Black history is everywhere; Black history is American history.

Assign a selection of the oral histories to the students to read. Discuss them in class. Ask: Where is racism obvious? Where is racism masked and yet painful?

Assessment of Understanding and Adding Depth to the Experience
Have students choose one of the histories to research further. Have them develop history projects based on the stories. Such projects could be research papers about a specific theme or an event referred to in the oral histories. For example:

The Tuskegee Airmen
Jim Crow laws
The great migration north
Pullman Porters
Black females' work as matrons or domestics
Black union organizing
Traditional Black sororities and fraternities
Traditional Black colleges
Black gospel music
Black music's role and influence in American music
Racism
The civil rights movement
Women of the civil rights movement
National Black Catholic Congress

Cripus Attucks

The Niagara Movement

The Duluth lynchings in June 1920

Fredrick L. McGhee

Judge Stephen Maxwell

W. E. B. Du Bois

Roy Wilkins

St. Peter Claver

Hallie Q. Brown

Carter G. Woodson

Paul Robeson

J. A. (Joel Augustus) Rogers

John G. Jackson

Frederick Douglass

Maria Stewart

Marian Anderson

Daniel Hale Williams, M.D.

James Baldwin

Medgar Evers

James Meredith

George Washington Carver

Thurgood Marshall

A. Philip Randolph

William Hastie

Coretta Scott King

Toni Stone

Lena O. Smith

Charles Scrutchin

J. Frank Wheaton

Dred Scott case

Whitney Young

Carl Rowan

"Uncle Tom"

Bobby Marshall

Cap Wingington

Stephen Theobald

The Appeal Newspaper

Denzel Carty

Nellie Stone Johnson

William T. Francis

William F. Williams

Frederick M. Jones

(Please note: Dr. Martin Luther King Jr. has not been overlooked. He is a central and essential figure in Black history, and his life and work affected the Rondo community. The goal of these additional projects is to assess understanding and add depth to the experience of learning Black history as American. There are abundant opportunities to learn about Dr. King. It is hoped that *Voices of Rondo* will inspire learning about other Black men and women who made a difference in American history, other aspects of Black History, and other stories from the Black experience.)

Have students explore the African American Registry (aaregistry.com) to see how Black history is American history. The registry provides information in twelve broad categories: Education, Activists, Film and TV, Music, Theater and the Arts, Literature, Politics and Law, Business and Medicine, Abolitionists, Sports and the Outdoors, Religion, and Episodes (events in the Black American experience that include people, places, items, and timelines).

More Learning Opportunities

Eyes on the Prize. According to PBS's Web site, "*Eyes on the Prize* is the most comprehensive television documentary ever produced on the American civil rights movement. It focuses on the events, issues, triumphs and tragedies of ordinary people as they tested their power to effect change in America during a period termed 'the Second American Revolution.' " The resources on this Web site are intended "to help teachers and their students engage in the issues of the civil rights movement in America between 1954 and 1965." The video series is available through most libraries (http://pbsvideodb.pbs.org/resources/eyes/index.html).

PBS Kids *Inequity!* A challenging and engaging online game that exercises students' intellects as well as their sense of fairness (http://pbskids.org/wayback/fair/quiz/quiz_textonly.html).

The Rise and Fall of Jim Crow. PBS's award-winning four-part series tells the story of the African American struggle for freedom during the era of segregation. In addition to the comprehensive public television Web site describing the video series (http://www.pbs.org/wnet/jimcrow/), a companion Web site provides a gallery of images, including primary documents and political cartoons, as well as in-depth , episode-by-episode lesson plans (http://www.jimcrowhistory.org/series/overview.htm).

African Americans in Minnesota, by David Vassar Taylor, Ph.D. (Minnesota Historical Society Press, 2002). African Americans have had a profound influence on the history and culture of Minnesota from its earliest days to the present. David V. Taylor tells this story through first-person accounts, newspaper articles, and careful analysis of census records.

BLACK HISTORY IS AMERICAN HISTORY: THERE IS ALWAYS MORE TO LEARN.

Thank you for bringing *Voices of Rondo* to life in your homes and classrooms. The world is the place it is because of the people who have come and gone. The stories of their lives echo across time. We can learn the past from barbershop chairs, fishing poles, sorority crests, lake cabins, rose bushes, renamed buildings, and the tales people tell. We will never know the whole story, but voice by voice we will know more. Their voices are their legacy to us, and our promise to them is that we will continue to learn.

INDEX

Italicized numbers refer to pages on which photographs can be found; endnotes are indicated by *n*.

To order additional copies of *Voices of Rondo*

Web: www.itascabooks.com

Phone: 1-800-901-3480

Fax: Copy and fill out the form below with credit card information. Fax to 763-398-0198.

Mail: Copy and fill out the form below. Mail with check or credit card information to:

Syren Book Company
5120 Cedar Lake Road
Minneapolis, MN 55416

Order Form

Copies	Title / Author	Price	Totals
	***Voices of Rondo* / Kateleen Cavett and HAND in HAND Productions**	$17.95	$
	Subtotal		$
	7% sales tax (MN only)		$
	Shipping and handling, first copy		$ 4.00
	Shipping and handling, ___ add'l copies @$1.00 ea.		$
	TOTAL TO REMIT		$

Payment Information:

__ Check Enclosed __ Visa/MasterCard	
Card number:	Expiration date:
Name on card:	
Billing address:	
City:	State: Zip:
Signature :	Date:

Shipping Information:

__ Same as billing address __ Other (enter below)	
Name:	
Address:	
City:	State: Zip: